A History of Crime in Australia

This book provides a lively and accessible account of Australia's most prominent crimes and criminals of the nineteenth and twentieth century and offers an informative background for those seeking to understand crimes committed today.

A History of Crime in Australia examines the imposition of English law on this ancient continent, and how its operation affected both transported offenders from Great Britain and Ireland, and the Aboriginal and Torres Strait Islander peoples whose own systems of Law were overlaid. Drawing upon cutting-edge research in the field, original work by the author, and essays from leading crime history researchers, it addresses the question of whether there was an Australian underworld. In doing so, it provides background for well-known offenders including bushranger Ned Kelly and the razor gangs of the 1920s and for sensational crimes like the Mount Rennie Outrage, the Pyjama Girl Mystery and the Shark Arm Murder and the miscarriage of justice following the disappearance of Azaria Chamberlain at Uluru in 1980. Through these case studies, the book draws out points of tension and cohesion within Australian society, exposing the enduring anxiety around those who were considered to be outsiders, and how the criminal justice system was used to manage these concerns. This book includes a guide to conducting research in the field of Australian crime history and sources for further study.

Designed as an introductory text for students, this book will be of interest to those studying criminology and crime history, and anyone who would like to deepen their understanding of crime's place in Australia's social and cultural history.

Nancy Cushing is Associate Professor of History at the University of Newcastle, Australia. She is an environmental historian interested in human-other animal relations, most recently co-editing *Animals Count* (Routledge 2018) with Jodi Frawley. This book is based on her undergraduate course Australian Underworlds which she has taught as an on-campus and massive open online course to over two thousand students since 2017.

A History of Crime in Australia

Australian Underworlds

Nancy Cushing

Routledge
Taylor & Francis Group
LONDON AND NEW YORK

Designed cover image: © Getty Images

First published 2023
by Routledge
4 Park Square, Milton Park, Abingdon, Oxon OX14 4RN

and by Routledge
605 Third Avenue, New York, NY 10158

Routledge is an imprint of the Taylor & Francis Group, an informa business

British Library Cataloguing-in-Publication Data
A catalogue record for this book is available from the British Library

Library of Congress Cataloging-in-Publication Data
Names: Cushing, Nancy, author.
Title: A history of crime in Australia : Australian underworlds / Nancy Cushing.
Description: 1 Edition. | New York, NY : Routledge, 2023. | Includes bibliographical references and index. | Identifiers: LCCN 2022034295 (print) | LCCN 2022034296 (ebook) | ISBN 9781032226538 (hardback) | ISBN 9781032226521 (paperback) | ISBN 9781003273561 (ebook)
Subjects: LCSH: Crime--Australia--History. | Criminal law--Australia--History.
Classification: LCC HV7173.5 .C87 2023 (print) | LCC HV7173.5 (ebook) | DDC 364.40994--dc23/eng/20220718
LC record available at https://lccn.loc.gov/2022034295
LC ebook record available at https://lccn.loc.gov/2022034296

ISBN: 978-1-032-22653-8 (hbk)
ISBN: 978-1-032-22652-1 (pbk)
ISBN: 978-1-003-27356-1 (ebk)

DOI: 10.4324/9781003273561

Typeset in Bembo
by KnowledgeWorks Global Ltd.

Contents

Contributors

Laurie Allen is an early career researcher in the field of Indigenous history in Australia. His PhD thesis at the University of Newcastle was entitled "A History of the Aboriginal People of the Central Coast of New South Wales to 1874."

Michelle Arrow is Professor of History at Macquarie University. She specialises in cultural history and histories of popular culture and the women's movement. Books include *Friday on Our Minds: Popular Culture in Australia Since 1945* (2009) and *The Seventies: The Personal, The Political and the Making of Modern Australia* (2019), which won the 2020 Ernest Scott Prize for Australian History.

Melissa Bellanta is Associate Professor of Modern History in the Australian Catholic University's National School of Arts. She is a social, cultural and gender historian with interests in historical material culture, fashion, the history of emotions and masculinities. Her book *Larrikins: A History* was published in 2012.

Michael Bryden is a Research Associate at the Jumbunna Institute for Indigenous Education and Research, University of Technology Sydney, and a PhD candidate at the Cambridge Institute of Criminology, University of Cambridge. A palawa man of Tasmanian Indigenous descent, his research focuses on police legitimacy, Indigenous self-determination, and public policy. Bryden's doctoral study examines police self-legitimacy in the United Kingdom. He is also the host of the Rethinking Deviance podcast.

Catharine Coleborne is Professor and the Head of the School of Humanities, Cultural Industries and Social Sciences at the University of Newcastle. She publishes in the histories of mental health, families, colonial worlds and medical institutions, with a particular interest in vagrancy. Her books include *Why Talk About Madness?* (2020), *Insanity, Identity and Empire* (2015) and with Professor Katie Pickles, *New Zealand's Empire* (2016).

Nancy Cushing is Associate Professor of History at the University of Newcastle. She is an environmental historian interested in human-other animal relations, most recently co-editing *Animals Count* (Routledge 2018) with Jodi Frawley. This book is based on her undergraduate course Australian Underworlds which she has taught as an on campus and massive open online course since 2017.

Meg Foster is Mary Bateson Research Fellow at Newnham College, Cambridge, where she is researching the connections between British highway robbery and the origins of Australian bushranging. She is an intersectional historian working across race, class and gender histories as well as imperial, colonial, ethnographic and public histories. Her first book, *Boundary Crossers: The hidden history of Australia's other bushrangers*, was published by NewSouth in 2022.

Rachel Franks is the Coordinator for Scholarship at the State Library of New South Wales and Honorary Associate Lecturer at the University of Newcastle. Holding doctorates from both the University of Sydney and Central Queensland University, her research spans crime fiction, true crime, popular culture and information science. Her biography of Sydney hangman "Nosey Bob" Howard, *An Uncommon Hangman*, was published by NewSouth in 2022.

Andy Kaladelfos (they/them) is Senior Lecturer in Criminology at the University of New South Wales. Kaladelfos' research specialities are sexual and gender-based violence, queer criminology, immigration regulation, and homophobic and transphobic violence. Their research is interdisciplinary, examining the nature of the criminal justice system, and the shifting relationship between law and society. Kaladelfos is the author with Lisa Featherstone of *Sex Crimes in the 1950s* (2016) and a co-creator of "The Prosecution Project."

Michael Kilmister is an Instructional Designer at the University of Reading, United Kingdom. He holds a PhD in political history from the University of Newcastle (2011) and has published on Anzac mythology and authentic assessment in history. In parallel, he has developed expertise in learning design. Kilmister has been awarded for his work in supporting excellence in university teaching, including in the course upon which this book is based.

Hamish Maxwell Stewart is Professor of History and Project Lead in Heritage Studies and Digital Humanities at the University of New England, Australia. He has made a major contribution to the reinvigoration of studies of convicts transported to Australia through the application of digital methods, in particular in the form of life course studies. Maxwell Stewart has over 100 scholarly publications in this field and has led numerous large-scale projects including Founders and Survivors (https://foundersandsurvivors.com/) and the Digital Panopticon (https://blog.digitalpanopticon.org/).

Victoria Nagy is a Lecturer in Criminology at the University of Tasmania. Her research areas are focused on female offending, historical criminology, as well as sexual violence, digital sexual harassment, feminist criminology practices, and criminological teaching and learning practices. Her book *Nineteenth-Century Female Poisoners: Three Women Who Used Arsenic to Kill* was published by Palgrave Macmillan in 2015.

Yorick Smaal is Senior Lecturer in History at Griffith University. His research investigates histories of sexuality and sexual violence and the institutions including law and criminal justice, the armed forces, war and society, medicine, subcultures and selfhoods that shape these experiences. His first book was *Sex, Soldiers and the South Pacific, 1939–45: Queer identities in Australia in the Second World War* (2015) and *Boys, Sex and Crime: Prosecution and protection in England and Australia, 1870–1930* will be published with Routledge in 2022.

Tyson Yunkaporta is Senior Research Fellow in Indigenous Knowledges at Deakin University. He is a member of the Apalech Clan of far north Queensland, a carver of traditional tools and weapons and an arts critic. Yunkaporta writes on story, Law and pedagogy and the interface between Indigenous Knowledges and AI, data analysis and memorisation. His first book, *Sand Talk: How Indigenous thinking can save the world*, was published by Text in 2019.

Acknowledgements

This book would not have been written without the great generosity of the history of crime community in Australia. When I began developing the course on which it is based, Professor Mark Finnane and Dr Alana Piper of the Prosecution Project at Griffith University and Dr Rachel Franks of the State Library of New South Wales became great supporters and advisors. As the course grew in popularity, I was assisted by Dr Michael Kilmister, Adam Khamis and others to reframe and film it as an online course on the FutureLearn platform, with guest appearances from two contributors to his book, Alana Piper and Professor Catharine Coleborne. The almost two thousand students who have now completed the open version of the course posed questions and raised issues which sent me back to the literature and have helped to refine the contents of the book, as did the students who completed the whole course at the University of Newcastle. When I sought essays to enrich the text from leading scholars in this field, all were quick to agree. Their contributions have greatly enhanced the book's currency and rigour. Funding from the University of Newcastle's College of Human and Social Futures allowed me to bring in Dr Robyn Dunlop as research assistant to begin the process of wrangling the logistics of manuscript production, while also providing quiet encouragement when it was greatly needed. For all of this support, and that of my colleagues in the School of Humanities, Creative Industries and Social Sciences at the University of Newcastle, Australia, especially the Wednesday and Friday Shut Up and Write groups, I am very grateful. This scholarly community, sustained through a pandemic, has led to a book with many parents, although any shortcomings are entirely my own.

Introduction

Modern Australia is founded on crime. This took place at two scales. The first is monumental: the theft of almost eight million square kilometres of Country from its Aboriginal and Torres Strait Islander custodians, a crime which has still not been properly accounted for and which leaves scars on the nation to this day.

The second scale of crime is personal, individual, in many cases slight. These offences were committed in Great Britain, Ireland and other places colonised by the British, and those convicted of them were sentenced to transportation beyond the seas. The passage of time has made some of the crimes seem curious: feloniously stealing three wooden ink stands, eight dog skins or nine live tame rabbits. They reflect a lost world of work done by hand and a level of desperation not often encountered in today's Britain or in Australia, with their relatively generous provisions of social support. But many of the crimes are humble, tawdry, repetitive and familiar: assault near the King's Highway, breaking and entering a dwelling house and stealing therein. These small crimes and the system of convict transportation have been endlessly fascinating to historians and to the general public, while the larger crime of dispossession was so long denied that many still do not recognise it for what it was, and what it meant. The focus of this book is on the small crimes and the many like them that followed but the impacts of the large crime are the background against which this action took place.

Interest in Crime in Australia

Some argue that the large leavening of convicted criminals in the settler colonial family tree has made crime of particular interest to Australians. Evidence seems to exist in the high level of attention to crime news, the popularity of crime fiction and the flourishing of true crime in written, video, web based multi-media and podcast forms. However, reading, watching and listening to accounts of crime are also popular pursuits in other countries, in particular the United States and Great Britain, from which many of the accounts of crime consumed in Australia originate.

DOI: 10.4324/9781003273561-1

Indeed, it is not so long ago that Australians tended to be firmly anti-crime, or at least anti-convict. From the 1830s, there were movements to stop transportation. Opponents argued that the Australian colonies deserved an opportunity to thrive and that this would not happen as long as Britain was bringing out shiploads of its ne'er do wells who would set themselves up as an underworld downunder. The labour of convicts and the British government's investment in public infrastructure which had given the eastern colonies of New South Wales (established in 1788), Van Diemen's Land (1825, renamed Tasmania in 1855), Victoria (1851) and Queensland (1859) their start were overlooked, even as Western Australia (1829) agreed to accept convicts in 1850 to gain access to the same benefits See Figure 0.1.[1] Instead, those in the eastern colonies complained about having to pay for police forces and jails which they claimed were largely occupied with managing former convicts, and about having wages held down by the presence of unpaid convict labourers in the workforce. Campaigns were conducted to blacken the reputation of convicts and the convict system in Britain and Australia, culminating in a British Select Committee on Transportation chaired by William Molesworth in 1837. Just a few years after the abolition of slavery in the British Empire, the Select Committee found that elements of slavery were continued within the convict system; that it was corrupt and corrupting; and that it should end.[2] In 1840, NSW was removed from the list of places to which offenders could be transported; and transportation to Van Diemen's Land was stopped in 1853, after the Victorian goldrush made a free trip to Australia seem like more of a reward than a punishment.

In the following decades, the memory of convictism became something to be suppressed and convict ancestry, a feature to be denied.[3] Those who offended were scrutinised to see if they had convict forbears. If they had the convict stain, beliefs about the legacy of convictism were confirmed. Some people changed their names to escape their background and convict records, buildings and relics were destroyed. When the NSW Colonial Secretary's Office directed magistrates to send remaining convict records back to Sydney for destruction in 1869, one of the reasons was that they were sometimes being referred to "from curious or improper motives".[4] James Bonwick transcribed early colonial records from the originals in London to create the *Historical Records of New South Wales* (7 vols, 1892–1901), but he omitted the names of convicts to avoid creating embarrassment for descendants. The 1870 Marcus Clarke novel *For the Term of his Natural Life* put on display the worst aspects of the convict system and this perspective was kept in the public eye through films based on the book made in 1908, 1911 and 1927. Convicts were all but absent from the 1938 sesquicentennial of colonisation with the focus of re-enactments being on Governor Arthur Phillip, his officials and the marines. While Aboriginal men were brought in from Barkindji Country at Menindee and the land of the Ngemba, Ualarai, Murrawarri and Wailwan people around Brewarrina to perform a stylised version of the Dharug people's resistance, convicts were not welcome at the celebration of "plant[ing] a fresh sprig of Empire in this new and vast land."[5]

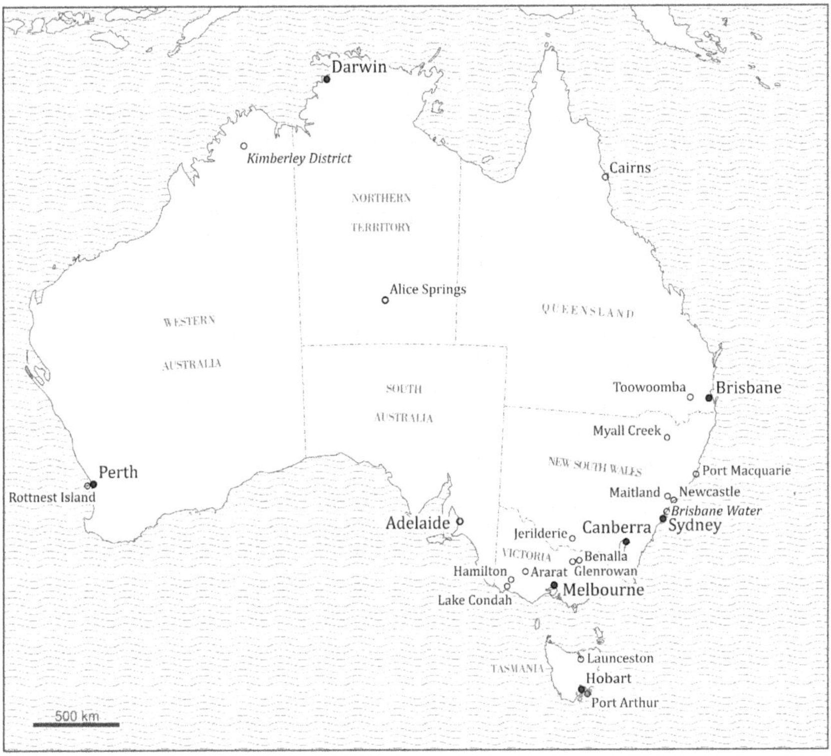

Figure 0.1 A map of Australia showing current state and territory boundaries and places named in the text.

Source: Cartographer: Olivier Rey Lescure.

It took another anniversary, the bicentenary of Lieutenant James Cook's claiming of Australia in 1770, to bring cachet to convict heritage. The Fellowship of First Fleeters was established in 1968, in parallel with other associations of descendants of those present at foundational moments, like the Daughters of the American Revolution. The Fellowship included prominent and respectable members of society and both reflected softening views towards the convicts and advanced them, in demonstrating that the convicts' descendants had not been held back by their DNA. Academic research normalising convicts as typical members of the British working class and the rise of family history have effected a reversal in attitudes to convict ancestry, which is now counted as a point of pride amongst Australians.

It is possible that the aversion to reminders of Australia's convict past could ironically have spurred contemporary interest in crime. Certainly, all of the family historians searching through the National Library of Australia's wonderful Trove online newspaper database will have found that crime was well covered in the press and was put before their wide readership on almost a daily basis. Court proceedings for even very minor offences were reported in local newspapers and more serious crimes received long treatments which were reprinted or adapted for other newspapers around the continent. Particularly notorious cases were allocated many column inches in which almost verbatim accounts of the courtroom proceedings were embellished with additional background on the accused, the victims and the circumstances, and from the 1870s, with woodcuts and later photographs of the accused. Celebrated cases were presented as soap operas with regular instalments leading up to sentencing and detailed coverage of an execution, or, in the case of not guilty verdicts or prison sentences, later follow-up stories with any slight additional news of the offender. Attendance at court was a pastime for some, whether just to see who ended up facing charges, or to witness justice being served and perhaps make a small contribution to the courtroom drama.

There are many reasons why people were interested in crime in the past, and why that interest continues, leading you, the present reader, to pick up this book. Keeping informed about crime happening in your own time and place is only sensible. If there are regular muggings in your local park or telephone scams being run in your city, finding out about them means prudent steps can be taken to avoid becoming a victim. Caution suggests that one should keep informed about whether reported crimes are continuing or have been resolved. As Neighbourhood Watch reminds us, taking an interest in crime can increase preparedness and the capacity to avoid becoming a victim, making people feel safer in their homes and communities.[6]

This direct, personal interest in crime can then extend out to more distant crime, in time and space. People want to know about crimes beyond their own area, and beyond their own experience. For the law abiding, crime can be intriguing and many seek to understand why it was that an offender violated legal and social norms. There is enjoyment in accounts that expose what is hidden about crime: the plotting and subterfuge that went into committing it, and the logic and deduction that led to prosecution. When a crime is constructed as a puzzle, there is vicarious satisfaction in seeing it solved. Further, as presented in the media, fiction and true crime accounts, crime can be perceived as glamorous. The criminal becomes a celebrity with their name on everyone's lips and the subject of speculation and admiration for their cunning and their audacity. Motives like these have made crime stories a product with a vast set of eager consumers.

Historians and Crime

Historians no doubt share some of these motivations, but we also have additional reasons for our interest in crime. The first is in the crime itself. Knowing what acts were outlawed in a society in a time period is revealing about what those in authority had as their priorities, and what and who they were worried about. That laws were broken allows us to unpack more about the society. Either these values were not shared, or some people disregarded them, through choice or compulsion. Crime provides a window onto ordinary life in contrast with other records, both public and private, which tend to focus on elites. Records created to document criminal proceedings inadvertently provide a way into past worlds, revealing details of occupations, relationships and daily life which are often not otherwise written down. These rich opportunities have attracted a large number of scholars to study the history of crime in Australia, most prominently within the Prosecution Project at Griffith University and the Founders and Survivors group at the University of Tasmania, but also in other smaller clusters and as individual scholars around the country and beyond. Their work forms the foundation of this book.

Those who are used to reading crime fiction and true crime will notice some differences in the approach taken here. Crime fiction, while often informed by research into actual cases, is not held accountable to objective reality. The author can cause any events to occur, in any order. Beyond this, they can go inside the mind of their criminal characters and tell us their motivations and thought processes. This is something to which non-fiction writers rarely have access. True crime writing retains some of the qualities of fiction in setting out the crimes they are treating as "heightened, narrativized versions of historical criminal events," with a strong focus on making those involved into character types.[7] True crime writing fills gaps in stories with a level of speculation not permissible for historians and offers moralistic or darkly humorous asides. It is also often based on painstaking research into primary sources and so can be useful for historians as they piece together accounts of crime.

In comparison to these more creative approaches to telling crime stories, historians are more strictly confined to writing about what they can support with evidence from the past. This tends to mean more emphasis on what has been officially documented, in court proceedings and newspaper accounts, for example. However, historical researchers are very resourceful and make effective use other types of sources, from photographs, to artefacts, to private letters. For historians, it is not enough to provide a detailed narrative of the commission, investigation and prosecution of a crime. We also seek to make an argument about our topic, using it to contribute to the development of deeper understandings of the past. An essential question is: so what? Why does this crime matter and what does it reveal about the individuals involved, their community or the whole of society?

The Structure of the Book

I have used the subtitle "Australian Underworlds" to set up an underlying question which will be returned to in some way in each chapter. That is, was there an Australian underworld – or underworlds – populated by large numbers of people living outside of the law? Were there networks of like-minded repeat offenders supporting themselves through systematic crime and using their wits and nerve to stay beyond the reach of the criminal justice system? When they were caught did they use their time in jail to make further plans and connections before returning to their lives of crime on release? Could most of the crime in Australia be attributed to these irredeemable repeat offenders? There have been many reported sightings of an underworld: amongst the convicts, in Ned Kelly's wild northeast of Victoria in the 1870s, in the streets of inner suburban Sydney and Melbourne in the 1920s. But were these positive IDs or cases of mistaken identity? Was the underworld an objective reality or a projection of social anxieties and aspirations? Keep your mind open as you read and draw your own conclusions about an Australian underworld.

This book is intended to be an introduction to crime in Australia rather than a comprehensive account of it and could be called a history of crime in Australia in seventeen stories. In focusing on specific crimes and criminals, I have followed Australian historian of crime David Philips, himself inspired by British legal historian FW Maitland.[8] Maitland wrote that a trial for murder gives "many hints as to a multitude of matters of the first importance" to a society in a historical period. This also applies to the wider range of crimes examined here: kidnapping, sexual assault, robbery and lesser crimes from vagrancy to public drunkenness. By adopting this approach, each chapter becomes not a chronological treatment of the most common crimes, who was committing them and how they were punished, but a set of stories about specific, interrelated crimes or criminals which were considered important enough at the time to attract considerable attention. Extended treatment allows me to share fine details of life in the past as it was touched by these crimes, with descriptions of daily routines, clothing, transport and personal relationships. The intention is to help to develop empathy with both victims and perpetrators, moving beyond a ghoulish or sensationalist interest which sometimes forgets the real people affected by crime.

Of course, these specific cases need to be viewed in context and for this I draw upon both the wider field of Australian history and the rich literature on the history of crime on this continent. I am aided in this by the essays accompanying each chapter. These essays were commissioned from leading historians of crime with a view to extending upon the treatment provided in the main chapter by providing an alternative perspective drawing upon original research. The tension between the chapters and the essays is intended as a reminder that history is not fixed or settled but is an ongoing conversation between the past and present in which many different points of view can and should co-exist, challenging one another as we strive for deeper understanding.

The third element of each section is a primary source relevant to the themes being treated. As an image or document from the period under consideration, it puts you, the reader, in direct communication with the past and offers an opportunity to make your own analysis and draw your own conclusions. The three components are best read as they are presented: chapter, essay and then primary source so the relevant background and context is known first, allowing for an informed reading of the primary source.

Students of criminology will notice that there is limited discussion of the causes of crime here, and few attempts to match particular crimes with relevant explanatory theories. Many years ago, Stephen Garton took his fellow historians to task for not making use of criminological theory, arguing that they missed an opportunity to enrich their work.[9] And yet here I stand, guilty as charged. While historians are conscious of theory, we tend not place it at the centre of our work in the way that criminologists do. This relates to the overall aims of the respective disciplines. Social scientists seek explanations for social phenomena; criminologists aim to understand crime with the intention of reducing it in the future and improving the experience of those involved with the criminal justice system or who are victims of crime. Historians are more focused on the past than the future and insist on the particularity of events. We remain sceptical of expecting the same outcomes from distinctive series of events and painfully conscious that history does *not* repeat. For me in this book, changing theories of the causation of crime are of most interest for the way they affected how offenders were regarded by their own societies: neighbours, police officers, court officials and the media. *Criminologist Victoria Nagy addresses the value of crime history for criminologists in the essay which accompanies this Introduction.*

The final restriction to mention is that I have not tried to bring the treatment up to the present, but made the Azaria Chamberlain disappearance in 1980, which was treated as a crime, the final subject. This means that many of the attention-grabbing crimes of recent decades are left for future historians to consider, after they also recede into the past and can become the subjects of informed reflection.

A Note on Emotionally Difficult Topics and on Respectful Language

This book offers a history of crime in Australia and therefore necessarily treats illegal behaviour including murder, massacre, sexual assault, other violence, police brutality and judicial punishments, including flogging and execution. While I have made every attempt to provide only the details that are necessary for historical understanding, these are emotionally difficult topics and potentially upsetting, especially for readers who have themselves experienced trauma. The chapter headings and introductions are descriptive of their content. If you believe that a particular topic will be traumatising for you, then you may choose not to read the related chapter and essay.

This book begins with the Law of the original inhabitants of Australia, revealed through the Dreaming and never displaced, despite concerted efforts by settler colonists for close to 250 years. Aboriginal and Torres Strait

Islander people, the original and continuing custodians of the unceded lands and waters of Australia, feature throughout this book as upholders of the Law, as offenders, as unjustly accused persons and as victims of crime. In writing about them, I have been conscious of how words and labels have been used as instruments of colonisation and I have sought not to add to that harm. I am guided by current advice regarding respectful practice and specific language from the Australian Institute for Aboriginal and Torres Strait Islander Studies.[10]

Generalisations which obscure the diversity within Aboriginal and Torres Strait Islander groups are a concern. For this reason, I have avoided the term "Indigenous" and sweeping statements suggesting that all Aboriginal and Torres Strait Islander people held a single view or had the same set of experiences. Where known, I have used the names of specific language groups and the Country of which individuals were part, and when referring to the original inhabitants more generally, have used "Aboriginal people" reflecting my focus on southern Australia, unless explicitly including Torres Strait Islander people as well. I have preferred the term "settler colonist" for those who entered Australia from 1788 in preference for the more benign "settler" or the race-based term "white." I have followed conventions of capitalising the key terms including Country and Law; and the palawa kani practice of not using capital letters for place names in lutruwita (Tasmania). When directly quoting words written in the past, I have repeated the original language to capture the attitudes of the period, although these words may no longer be acceptable in the present. Similarly, I realise that language will continue to evolve, rendering some of my choices unwelcome. I apologise for any offence my words cause and ask readers to accept them as having been used with reflection and care at the time of writing.

In the Beginning Was the Law

Any history of crime in Australia must begin with the original Law of the land and with the words of Aboriginal and Torres Strait Islander people. In Chapter 1, I stand aside and allow the voices of contemporary Aboriginal scholars and storytellers to be heard.

ESSAY: CRIME HISTORY FOR CRIMINOLOGISTS

Victoria Nagy

This essay is a contribution to a book about the *history* of Australian crime. As a criminologist, I would like to explain why I think crime history is relevant for students and scholars of the discipline.

Criminology as a discipline has been accused of "presentism." That is, of focusing on the present with a disregard for the past. As Jones put it, in some criminological texts, "it is almost as if criminal justice has no past, and current policies and developments have no historical precedents."[11] The result of this has been the development of criminology as a discipline that understands the social harms and inequality we are seeing today as new, worsening or different from the problems of the past.[12]

This disregard for history is in part theoretical. The main purpose of criminology has been to examine the present state of criminal behaviour and victimisation in the hope of changing the future whether through research, policy or activism. History has concentrated on the past with the goal of being able to understand it for its own sake, without direct reference to the present. Also, while there are many schools of thought with many theories about why crime occurs and how it affects various populations (whether by policing, policy, the responses by courts or victimisation rates), historians have been reluctant to engage with these theories. The two disciplines also diverge methodologically, or in how research is undertaken. Historical research has to work around missing or incomplete primary sources, with those who are focusing on more recent history also having to contend with restrictions to public access to archival sources. Criminologists have a multitude of ways to access their data. Not only do they draw upon government-generated records and reports at the time they are created, with ethics approvals in place, but they can also generate data by surveying or interviewing the people who are impacted by crime.

Of course, some criminologists do draw upon history for their research. As Churchill, Yeomans and Channing so succinctly point out, there have been many criminologists who have used history or their own historical research to make important points about crime, justice, offending and victimisation occurring in their own times.[13] Much of this work has taken place in the UK, Ireland, the US and Canada, but there has been work in Australia as well.

Australian criminologists have tackled a range of contemporary crime and justice topics using history. Braithwaite's work questioned why many criminologists consider leaders and lay-people of the past to have been misguided on issues of punishment.[14] The historical record shows that rehabilitation, reform and community reintegration were much more likely during the nineteenth century for convicts transported to Australia than any prisoner has a hope of achieving today. Sexual violence (both against women and children) and family violence in Australian society and criminal justice responses have been explored at this intersection between history and criminology.[15] Other topics have included colonial policing and police memorialisation.[16] My own work has pointed out that both medical staff and guards in prisons in Victoria in the late colonial period were aware of the fact that rising social inequality was the reason why so many older women were ending up in jail and that the solution to this issue lay in the community, not in the criminal justice system.[17]

So, should all criminologists shift their attention from the present to the past? Not quite. Historical research is time intensive. Only for the recent past is it possible to ask questions of the people directly involved with crime. The records can be difficult to access, are often incomplete and gaps must be filled in with alternate sources. There are also ethical questions raised in historical research when attention is drawn to past crimes, with no opportunity for those involved to demand privacy or put their own point of view.[18]

What value then does crime history have to criminologists? If there are such differences in theory and methodology, limitations on sources and the possibility of drawing conclusions, then what is the point? For me, historical research has relevance to criminology that cannot be overstated. Churchill et al have noted there is a power in historical data to explain the criminal justice policies we live with today as well as to shape these practices and inspire the hope for better future policy development.[19] There is also value in engaging with historical research in order to bend and expand the "criminological imagination," an idea first proposed by C. Wright Mills in 1959 in his work *The Sociological Imagination*.[20] Mills argued "no social study that does not come back to the problems of biography, of history and of their intersections within a society has completed its intellectual journey."[21] In other words, our individual experiences and attitudes (in this case regarding crime and justice whether as researchers or the people who are the focus of our research) need to be placed in a broader context of the relevant social structure inhabited, social structures which belong within an historical context.

This latter point that Yeoman's argues is underdeveloped in criminological research.[22] That is not to say that criminologists should become historians, or that we should even expect criminologists to have the same grasp and depth of knowledge about history as an historian, but that historical contextualisation is important to criminological understanding. Any examination of current criminal justice issues, whether asylum seekers, border controls, policing, or prisons and rehabilitation, benefits from consideration of its historical context, to avoid proposed solutions which unknowingly rehash debates from decades or centuries earlier.

Notes

1 For those not familiar with Australian history, a good overview is provided in Mark Peel and Christina Twomey's *A History of Australia*, 2nd ed., London: Palgrave, 2018.
2 Philip Harling, "The Trouble with Convicts: From Transportation to Penal Servitude, 1840–67," *Journal of British Studies*, 53, no. 1 (2014): 83–4.
3 Anna Clark explores this in her chapter on convicts in *Making Australian History*, Melbourne: Vintage Books, 2022, 64–6.
4 Christine Shergold, "NSW Convict Records: Lost and Saved", NSW State Archives and Records, https://www.records.nsw.gov.au/archives/collections-and-research/guides-and-indexes/stories/new-south-wales-convict-records-lost (accessed 16 September 2022).
5 "The Landing Is Re-Lived," *Labor Daily*, 27 January, 1938, 8.
6 Neighbourhood Watch Australasia, https://www.nhwa.com.au/ (accessed 4 June 2022).
7 Melissa Gregg and Jason Wilson, "Underbelly, True Crime and the Cultural Economy of Infamy," *Continuum: Journal of Media & Cultural Studies* 24, No. 3 (2010): 414–15.
8 David Philips, "Anatomy of a Rape Case, 1888: Sex, Race, Violence and Criminal Law in Victoria," David Philips and Susanne Davies, eds. *A Nation of Rogues?: Crime, Law and Punishment in Colonial Australia*, Melbourne: Penguin, 1994, 98–9.
9 Stephen Garton, "The Convict Origins Debate: Historians and the Problem of the 'Criminal Class,'" *Australian and New Zealand Journal of Criminology* 24, no. 2 (1991): 66–82.
10 "Australia's First Peoples," Australian Institute for Aboriginal and Torres Strait Islander Studies, https://aiatsis.gov.au/explore/australias-first-peoples (accessed 20 May 2022). For further discussion of the issues around words and naming, see Luke Pearson, "Appropriate terminology for Aboriginal and Torres Strait Islander people – it's complicated," Indigenous X, 16 June 2021, https://indigenousx.com.au/appropriate-terminology-for-aboriginal-and-torres-strait-islander-people-its-complicated/ (accessed 20 May 2022).
11 M. Jones, "Reflections on Historical Study in Criminal Justice Curricula," *Journal of Criminal Justice Education* 5, no. 2 (1994): 167.
12 P. Rock, "Chronocentrism and British Criminology," *British Journal of Sociology* 56, no. 3 (2005): 473–91.
13 D. Churchill, H. Yeomans, and I. Channing, *Historical Criminology*, London: Routledge, 2021.
14 J. Braithwaite, "Crime in a Convict Republic," *Modern Law Review* 64, no. 1 (2001): 11–51.
15 R. Zajac, N. Westera, and A. Kaladelfos, "The 'Good Old Days' of Courtroom Questioning: Changes in the Format of Child Cross-Examination Questions over 60 years," *Child Maltreatment* 23 no. 2 (2018): 186–95; S. Zydervelt, R. Zajac, A. Kaladelfos, and N. Westera, "Lawyers' Strategies for Cross-Examining Rape Complainants: Have We Moved Beyond the 1950s?" *British Journal of Criminology* 57, no. 3 (2017): 551–69.
16 D. Palmer, "The Making of the Victorian Colonial Police: From Colonisation to the New Police" (Doctoral diss., La Trobe University, 1990); C.R. Linke, "Victoria Police Memorialisation: Commemoration and Remembrance" (Doctoral diss., Deakin University, 2018).
17 V. Nagy, "Women, Old Age, and Imprisonment in Victoria, Australia 1860–1920," *Women and Criminal Justice* 30, no. 3 (2020): 155–71; V. Nagy and A. Piper, "The Health and Medical Needs of Victoria's Older Female Prisoners, 1860–1920," *Health and History* 22, no. 1 (2020): 67–85.

18 M. Bosworth, "The Past as a Foreign Country? Some Methodological Implications of Doing Historical Criminology," *British Journal of Criminology* 41, no. 3 (2001): 431–42.
19 Churchill, Yeomans and Channing, *Historical Criminology.*
20 H. Yeomans, "Historical Context and the Criminological Imagination: Towards a Three-Dimensional Criminology," *Criminology and Criminal Justice* 19, no. 4 (2019): 456–77.
21 C.W. Mills, *The Sociological Imagination,* Oxford: Oxford University Press, 1959.
22 Yeomans, "Historical Context."

1 Law in Aboriginal Societies

I am writing this book on the land of the Darramurragal people in what is now northern Sydney. I am conscious that like the rest of the lands and waters of Australia, this is the unceded territory of the Aboriginal and Torres Strait Islander people. The original people of Australia know that they are of this place, having been created from its soil and inhabiting every environment across the continent and its islands, from tropical rainforests, to deserts, to coastlines swept by Antarctic winds. Aboriginal and Torres Strait Islander people are diverse, being made up of at least 250 language groups with their own beliefs, ways of life and world views. Over some 65,000 years, 1 billion people have lived and died on this continent.[1]

One important thing that all of these groups share is a practice of using story to keep cultural knowledge alive. These stories embed events of the deep past, from sea level rise to volcanic eruptions, but their principal purpose is to pass on knowledge of each group's Law. No account of the history of crime in Australia would be complete without acknowledgement of this Indigenous Law, but as an immigrant from another corner of the former British Empire and a university-based historian, I am conscious that this is not my story to tell. Despite my good intentions, as Bidjara and Birri Gubba Juru historian Jackie Huggins wrote, non-Aboriginal people who have not immersed themselves in culture and community can become intruders rather than accomplices when we try to interpret Aboriginal history and do damage to Aboriginal people and their struggles.[2] Instead, I will offer a brief introduction to the Law and then provide space for Aboriginal voices.

The concept of the Law is broader than that of western law. One explanation provided by descendant of the Iman people of central and southwestern Queensland anthropologist Professor Marcia Langton is:

> What our people mean when they talk about their Law is a cosmology, a worldview which is a religious, philosophic, poetic and normative explanation of how the natural, human and supernatural domains work. Aboriginal Law ties each individual to kin, to "country" – particular estates of land – and to Dreamings.

DOI: 10.4324/9781003273561-2

> One is born with the responsibilities and obligations which these inheritances carry. There are many onerous duties and they are not considered to be optional. One is seen to be lazy and neglectful if these duties are ignored and the respect, authority and advantages, such as arrangements for good marriages and opportunities for one's children, are not awarded. As many of our people observe, Aboriginal Law is hard work.[3]

In the Yolngu language of Arnhem Land, this concept of Law is encompassed by the term *rom*. *Rom* links clans, provides an identity and guides interpersonal relations as well as relations with Country.[4] It combines religion, kinship, intellectual knowledge, art and science and is learned by the Yolngu by listening to elders and acting according to their guidance until the sufficient knowledge and experience of the Law has been acquired to allow a young person to take their own place as a full member of the community. In the Walpiri language of what is now the Northern Territory, and for the Pitjantjatjara/Yankunytjatjara of South Australia, the term used for living well is *tjukaruru*, meaning living in a straight or true way in conformity with the Law.[5] For people in their own Country, all of the features of the environment, including soil, rock, hills, sky, plants and animals, "pulse with the life force of the *Tjukurpa* (the Dreaming)" and bring to mind the stories which convey its meaning.[6]

One of these stories is included as the primary source for this chapter: *Wundanyuka kulu Jujuju: The Sea Turtle and Osprey*. It belongs to the Yanyuwa and Marra people of Borroloola/Burrulula in the Northern Territory, and I am grateful for their generosity in sharing it. The retelling of stories reinforces both the rights of each person under the Law and their responsibilities to do what is necessary to uphold it. Listeners hear what happens when rules about gender roles, avoidances, marriage or other behaviours are not respected. *Tyson Yunkaporta and Michael Bryden show in their essay that having been subjected to appropriate punishments through the operation of the Law, offenders are readmitted to full status in Aboriginal communities, and order is restored, with no lasting stigma borne by the person who broke the Law.*

Despite the long-established systems of Law which had maintained societies where people's roles were clear, transgressions were relatively few, and effective corrections were quickly dispensed; settler colonists assumed that there was no Aboriginal system of laws. This was in keeping with their general underestimation of the Indigenous societies they encountered as they sought new lands to occupy and exploit. For the British, not having a system of laws was one of the absences which justified their occupation of Australia as *terra nullius*, a land claimed by no one.[7] However, those who took time to learn from Aboriginal people soon realised this was not the case. By the 1830s, Lancelot Threlkeld, a missionary at Lake Macquarie, NSW was able to confirm from his work with Awabakal and Darkinjung people that there was a system of law and punishment guided by elders, as others were also observing.[8] This made little impression on the colonial legal system. Giving a judgement in 1836 on a case of murder of one Aboriginal man by another, Judge William Burton in the Supreme Court of NSW said Aboriginal people did not have a legal system but only the "most indiscriminatory notions of revenge" which the colonial legal system should not recognise, and which he compared with the laws of another people colonised by the British, the "wild Irish."[9] Burton's opinion that colonial law was the only law in NSW and that Aboriginal people were subject to it guided future decisions.

But there *was* a strong and enduring traditional Law, and it persisted despite ongoing attempts to ignore, invalidate and disrupt it. It had some begrudging recognition in the reluctance of the colonial legal systems to interfere in matters between Aboriginal people, what are known in colonial references as *inter se* offences. In Western Australia in the 1930s, this recognition became more formal. Courts of Native Affairs were set up to try offences by and against Aboriginal people. These courts acknowledged that traditional Law was the reason behind some offences, and that Aboriginal people were not receiving justice in the state's existing courts. However, the effect was not greater autonomy but to establish a cheaper, separate system where the usual protections offered to those accused of crimes, including juries and appeals, were not in place and power of the state government's Native Affairs department over criminal matters involving Aboriginal people was increased.[10]

With the rise of assimilationism in the mid-twentieth century, when Aboriginal people were supposed to be absorbed invisibly into the general population, separate courts were abolished. As Aboriginal people began to demand more legal rights and recognition, including land rights in the 1970s, attention again turned to the idea of acknowledging Law. The Australian Law Reform Commission reported on this in 1986, noting that what was then referred to as customary law was a real force in the lives of Aboriginal people in many parts of the country and that it should be formally recognised, especially with regard to aspects of civil rather than criminal law including marriage, legitimacy of children, inheritance, adoption, sentencing and evidence.[11] In submissions in 1981 on what elements of traditional Law they would like to see enforced by the state legal system, people of the Lajamanu community in the central west of the Northern Territory talked about the Law guiding the sharing of goods, acceptable marriages according to skin group, the duties of relatives to initiate and correct children and ceremonial obligations.

Law in Australia's Aboriginal societies is a comprehensive web of rules and expectations which keeps the groups who share that Law in balance and harmony. The Law is not a separate entity created and able to be changed by distant legislators and administered by unknown judges. It is a legacy from the Dreaming, kept alive and vibrant by being handed on from person to person. The general tendency of Law and punishment in Aboriginal societies is to quickly resolve serious breaches of the Law while discouraging further disruption. The Law functions effectively, achieving balance and inclusion, privileging tradition and continuity while also being able to incorporate and respond to new challenges. For millennia, it has been effective at maintaining harmonious relations within Indigenous communities. This stability and commitment to caring for Country, including the human and non-human species with whom it was shared, created and sustained through the Law, enabled Aboriginal societies to thrive in Australia for tens of thousands of years, dealing with climate fluctuations, drought, floods, sea level rise and ancient soils, and to survive the onslaught of colonisation.

Understanding this original system of Law in Australia, which has coexisted with the introduced English-derived legal system from 1788, is important as we go on with our study of Australian Underworlds.

Suggested Readings

Bourke, Colin and Helen Cox. "Two Laws: One Land." Colin Bourke, Eleanor Bourke and Bill Edwards, eds. *Aboriginal Australia: An Introductory Reader in Aboriginal Studies.* Brisbane: University of Queensland Press, 1994.

Ginibi, Ruby. "Aboriginal Traditional and Customary Law." *Law, Text, Culture* 1 (1994): 8–12.

Griffiths, Billy. *Deep Time Dreaming: Uncovering Ancient Australia.* Melbourne: Black Inc., 2018.

Watson, Irene. *Aboriginal Peoples, Colonialism and International Law: Raw Law.* Abington: Routledge, 2014.

Yunkaporta, Tyson. *Sand Talk: How Indigenous Thinking Can Save the World.* Melbourne: Text, 2019.

ESSAY: INDIGENOUS LAW AND THE INTRUSION OF THE WEST

Tyson Yunkaporta and Michael Bryden

The first reality to acknowledge when thinking about Indigenous crime and punishment is that things have changed and will always be changed. Indigenous land and therefore Law still exist, but we are forced to live in colonial spaces, and this will continue to be the case for at least a few more decades.[12] This colonial space, which is ultimately policed by a punitive criminal justice system, has a criminogenic effect on Indigenous peoples; that is, what is understood as our "criminality" is partially the result of economic, social and cultural disconnection caused by imperial activity.[13]

For Indigenous and conquered peoples worldwide, many of us remain under our own Law, and although that way of life is very disrupted, it is the Law of the land and there is still that strong, permanent, immutable foundation in every place where you might stand on the planet.[14] This necessarily places you outside of the lower case "l" law of the empire that you must inhabit: the law that may imprison you, the law that may kill you if you happen to deviate from its constantly shifting jurisprudence inscribed in ink and digital codes. The rules of the bosses, seldom represent real Law – they merely facilitate extraction and then protect the illegitimate property of oligarchs. This is not justice from our perspective.

Nobody from outside our continent ever observed our old Law in its original state, which we know today only through our surviving Lore – our oral texts and Ceremony.[15] Even before any of those who arrived on the First Fleet set foot in the interior, the diseases that came with them swept across the entire continent. As with COVID-19, the people who died first were the elders, the ones who kept the Law and held the authority of knowledge. But authority is different from power under our Law.

Traditionally our justice system and ways of doing punishment have aimed to bring people back into good relation again, but more importantly, they also aim to transform a person who has begun to separate, someone who is at risk of coming into bad relation. It is not an individual responsibility, but a clan accountability that is still present in Indigenous communities today.[16]

Traditional punishment is about reconnecting, but paradoxically it is often quite violent. Violence is something that has been highly ritualised and regulated as a way of administering punishment, settling disputes, and expelling toxic emotion.[17] In our Law, it is not the unique domain of an exclusive group to administer – it must be evenly distributed throughout the community.[18] Everyone must have access to the affordances of physical conflict and every instance of violence must be public and transparent. It must be witnessed by the entire community, and it must be governed by rules to minimise the damage that it can do.[19] Ultimately, it transforms the participants and maintains dignity and social cohesion without excluding anybody. Unfortunately, this has not translated well into large permanent townships in remote communities today and can often result in harmful behaviours in places that are over-policed or where elder authority is precarious.[20]

Another key feature of Aboriginal Law is the matter of intent. In WEIRD (Western Educated Industrialised Rich Democratic) law, intent is an important thing to establish in the criminal justice processes.[21] So, if a person can show that they unintentionally transgressed, that they have remorse and good intentions, then it's a lesser sentence. Traditional Aboriginal Law is very unforgiving about intent. If you transgress, it doesn't matter whether you meant to do harm, you must be held to account. You're still going to have to get that punishment cut, or you're going to have to have your shoulder broken, or you're going to have to spend the next six months supporting all of the nutritional and shelter needs of the person you injured. Worst of all, you will feel "shame," and this will also be experienced by your family. Shaming is the one traditional punishment that is still practised today in every Aboriginal community, remote or urban, regardless of cultural disruption.

Yet, in the old ways and today, there is no permanent criminal record. If you've committed a crime and you are punished for that, it is forgotten. We say, "Finish." The crime doesn't define the transgressor forever or limit their access to social goods. In our old Lore, there are stories of great ancestor beings who committed heinous transgressions, who were turned into stone or other forms for their crimes; even they came through their punishment and were transformed. They became entities who carry the cautionary tales of the kind of damage that criminality can do. They keep and uphold the Law and are respected for it. Our Law is about returning people to dignity, agency and connectedness.

In Western societies, however, punishment often creates and maintains a permanent "criminal" underclass. This phenomenon is not unknown in the discipline of criminology. For example, a conviction may lead to social exclusion that is brought about by the "collateral consequences" of a criminal record, such as disenfranchisement or unemployment.[22] Often criminal justice institutions focus on lower-level crimes: homelessness, begging, theft and drug use, rather than the ubiquitous white-collar crimes and state crimes that inflict social harm on a global scale.

The legal system of the occupying culture today echoes its earlier iterations, which played a key role in the colonisation of the continent and its islands, suppressing and killing Indigenous people who resisted the seizure of their lands and the establishment of a new order, often conscripting defeated Aboriginal people as Native Police to assist with this task.[23] It was not only through kinetic violence, but through community self-administration and self-policing, that settler-colonialists succeeded in displacing Aboriginal and Torres Strait Islander Law with Commonwealth law. Arguably, this pattern of coercive compliance with our own annexation has shaped the formation of both Native Title and criminal justice law in the settler colony currently known as Australia.

PRIMARY SOURCE: *WUNDANYUKA KULU JUJUJU*

This story belongs to the Wurdaliya Clan of the Yanyuwa and Marra People of Borroloola/Burrulula in the Northern Territory. Their Country is the coastal plain where several rivers meet the Gulf of Carpentaria, some 1000 km southeast of Darwin. *Wundanyuka kulu Jujuju* explains the origins of the names and features of what are also known as West Island, Watson Island and North Island where the McArthur River flows into the Gulf. The Yanyuwa Families generously shared their story through the *Wunungu Awara: Animating Indigenous Knowledges* project as a way of passing on their knowledge in their own way. They gave permission for the story to be shared with outsiders as long as their ownership is fully acknowledged.[24] The story explains how the islands became a meaningful Country, a moral landscape, through naming and the creation of features by the actions of the Sea Turtles and the Osprey, as well as offering a lesson about adult sister (Sea Turtle) and brother (Osprey) avoidance.[25] The text presented here is the English translation of the Yanyuwa families' words prepared for an animation of the story which can be viewed on Monash University's Wunungu Awara site, along with other Law stories from elsewhere in the Northern Territory, the Torres Strait, Victoria and New South Wales.[26]

Wundanyuka kulu Jujuju: The Sea Turtle and Osprey, 2011

The Osprey flew over an open sandy beach and landed in a tree. He saw people in paddling canoes offshore. "What's this?" he asked himself. "Hey, you. Dugong Hunters! You who have come from the east. Do not come here! I have come a long way from the west. From Nawungkunya. This Country, Rrawali, is mine! It is Wurdaliya Country alone. Do not come here. Go away!!" The people paddled on.

"Ah," said the Osprey. "There in the east is another Country that is mine. It is a big Country. I will go there. I will name the Country Mindarra. Yes, Mindarra. That is the name of that Country." He flew east and landed on a high rock outcrop. In the sea, he saw Sea Turtles swimming.

"Hey, you! Sea Turtles! That Country there in the west, Babalungku and Aburri. That is my Country. It is not yours. No, never!"

A Sea Turtle spoke up. "Hey you! Osprey! There you are in the east! You are our kinsman. Don't pretend to not know us. We are Wurdaliya just like you. We are travelling east to Rrawali to lay our eggs on the sand." The Sea Turtles came out of the water and laid their round, white eggs while the Osprey looked on. "Look," one said, "there he is. The Osprey is there. He is so jealous for this Country."

The Osprey dived down amongst the Sea Turtles, sending them cartwheeling down the beach. He kicked at their eggs and smashed them. He shouted, "Go away!"

"Let us travel southwards," said the Sea Turtles. "There is good Country for us there." As they swam away, one noticed that the Osprey was chasing other Sea Turtles eastwards. "The poor things," she said.

"We are naming this Country Arlan," said a Sea Turtle in the main group. "Yes, Arlan will be the name of the Country. Come on, let's get going. It is into the south we are travelling." They left the water and walked inland across the sand. One put an eye on the ground, saying "We are placing our eyes at this place. It is spring water, the water will flow. It is good Country. And its name is Luldarra. Alright. We will travel to the south. To the point of land that is called Mamadathamburru. And from there we will continue southwards to Mathandurla and Liwintha. That is the way we are naming those places. They are large reefs. We will place ourselves there as a Dreaming. Because it is good Country." The Sea Turtles swam south.

A lone Sea Turtle moved with difficulty over the sand. Others watching from the sea said, "Oh, no, the poor thing! Our Kinsman has been left behind at Maabayn. She is all alone. Oh, she is going southwards to Mungkuwarubiliyirarra. It is a Country of plains and salt pans. Oh, the poor thing, she has lost her way there." Just then, the Osprey flew down and attacked the exhausted Sea Turtle, killing her.

Flying over the remaining turtles as they swam in the sea, the Osprey called out, "Are you breathless and panting for rest? I will follow you all the way. You are in the sea and I am above you. I am driving you all the way. Through the Country of Ngarrawulamba, and from there, Libaladala and from there Mungkuraminya. All the way I will pursue you! I will follow you westwards. I will drive you into the depths of the wide-open sea."

The Osprey dove into the sea and picked up one of the turtles, carrying her over the water. "Here we are at Liwayidbulungu. That is the name of the Country. Here you will stay, right here at this place. Forever!" He dropped the Sea Turtle onto rocks from a height, declaring "Your body will become a stone on the beach." Opening the Sea Turtle's shell, he said "I take your intestines. I am dragging them into the northeast. Your blood is flowing on the rocks. I am calling this Country Wunukakalijulakinda. That is the name of the Country." As he flew carrying the intestines, blood spattered on the ground.

Two other Sea Turtles on the beach saw what the Osprey had done. "Hey look. Look back! The Osprey. He has killed our kinsman. Oh, the poor thing. Quickly, quickly. We must be going along the west side of this island into the north to Wiyibi, then Wunjurr and from there to Ruwawalurr. That Osprey is completely evil." The Sea Turtles hurried as quickly as they could back to the water.

"There you two are!" said the Osprey, flying over them. "I can see you two there in the north at Wirimbilingaya! I am going to get you two there at Aralwiji. I am going to kill you two there at that place! At Aralwiji you two will remain forever!" The Osprey dove down and picked up one of the remaining Sea Turtles and carried her over the sea to an area of exposed rock, dropping her to her death. He prised open her breastplate and distributed her body parts: intestines to the west; stomach to the east; flippers to the north; lungs; to the north, the head; the shell. At last, he said, "That's all of the parts of the Sea Turtle."

"Oh poor me! I am the only one left alive," cried the last Sea Turtle, looking out to sea. "Here I am, the only one. I am alone. The Osprey has killed all of my kin. Here I am alone at Limalurrbala. That is the name of the Country. I am alone. I am frightened. And waiting for him to come." The Osprey dropped down from the sky and picked up the last Sea Turtle.

Later, the Osprey flew over land and sea, carrying an empty turtle shell. He said, "Here I am at Limalurrbala. To the west is Aralwiji. To the east is Langadanga. I have killed all of the Sea Turtles. This shell I carry northwards. It will become a small island called Murrungka. I will place a hollow log coffin on top of it. Yes, I am naming this place Murrungka. Yes, here I am alone at Langadanga. I am feeling full from all of this Sea Turtle meat. Later I will travel northwards to Jalma. That is my true home. Yes, Jalma. That is the name of that place."

Bawuji – The End

Notes

1 Estimate by archaeologist John Mulvaney, in Billy Griffiths, *Deep Time Dreaming: Uncovering Ancient Australia*, Melbourne: Black Inc., 2018, 1.
2 J. Huggins, R. Huggins and J. Jacobs, "Kooramindanjie," R. White and P. Russell, eds. *Memories and Dreams, Reflections on Twentieth Century Australia*, Sydney: Allen and Unwin, 1997, 230.
3 Marcia Langton and the Aboriginal Issues Unit of the Northern Territory, "'Too Much Sorry Business': The Report of the Aboriginal Issues Unit of the Northern Territory," *Royal Commission into Aboriginal Deaths in Custody* 1991: Appendix D (I), par. 2.3.1, http://www.austlii.edu.au/au/other/IndigLRes/rciadic/national/vol5/11.html (accessed 18 January 2022).
4 Arafura Swamp, Rangers Aboriginal Corporation, *Arafura Swamp Rangers Healthy Country Plan 2017–2027*. Ramingining, Arnhem Land: ASRAC, 2017, 6.
5 Daniele M. Klapproth, *Narrative as Social Practice: Anglo-Western and Australian Aboriginal Oral Traditions*, Berlin: Mouton de Gruyter, 2004, 263–64.
6 Griffiths, *Deep Time Dreaming*, 92.
7 Irene Watson, *Aboriginal Peoples, Colonialism and International Law: Raw Law*, Abington: Routledge, 2014, 19.
8 Henry Reynolds, *Aboriginal Sovereignty: Reflections on Race, State and Nation*, Sydney: Allen and Unwin, 1996.
9 Bruce Kercher, "Recognition of Indigenous Legal Autonomy in Nineteenth Century New South Wales," *Indigenous Law Bulletin* 4, no. 13 (1998): 7–9.
10 Kate Auty, "Western Australian Courts of Native Affairs 1936–1954: One of 'our' little secrets in the administration of 'justice' for Aboriginal People," *University of New South Wales Law Journal* 23, no. 1 (2000): 148–72.
11 Australian Law Reform Commission, Aboriginal Customary Laws, https://www.alrc.gov.au/inquiry/aboriginal-customary-laws/ (accessed 5 June 2022).
12 Out of respect for the inalienable and sacred nature of the Law of the land, Aboriginal Law is capitalised when written here. Throughout this essay, we are speaking from our own knowledge and experience of Indigenous Law and culture. We recognise that there are other rich and diverse Indigenous perspectives across Australia and beyond.

C.F. Black, *The Land is the Source of the Law: A Dialogic Encounter with Indigenous Jurisprudence*, London: Routledge, 2011.
13 C. Cunneen and J. Tauri, *Indigenous Criminology*, Bristol: Policy Press, 2016, 57.
14 T. Yunkaporta, *Sand Talk: How Indigenous Thinking Can Save the World*, Melbourne: Text, 2019.
15 Yunkaporta, *Sand Talk*, 2019.
16 L. Behrendt, *Aboriginal Dispute Resolution: A Step Towards Self-determination and Community Autonomy*, Sydney: Federation Press, 1995.
17 V.K. Burbank, *Fighting Women: Anger and Aggression in Aboriginal Australia*, Berkley: University of California Press, 1994.
18 G. Macdonald, "A Wiradjuri Fight Story," I. Keen, ed. *Being Black: Aboriginal Cultures in "Settled" Australia*. Canberra: Aboriginal Studies Press, 1988, 179–99.
19 E. Rennie, T. Yunkaporta, I. Holcombe-James, *Cyber Safety in Remote Aboriginal Communities: Final Report*, Melbourne: Digital Ethnography Research Centre, 2018.
20 G. Cowlishaw, *Blackfellas, Whitefellas, and the Hidden Injuries of Race*, Malden, MA: Blackwell, 2004.
21 J. Henrich, *The Weirdest People in the World: How the West Became Psychologically Peculiar and Particularly Prosperous*. New York: Farrar, Strauss and Giroux, 2020.
22 V.S. Burton, F.T. Cullen and L.F. Travis, "Collateral Consequences of a Felony Conviction: A National Study of State Statutes," *Federal Probation* 51, no. 3 (1987): 52–60.

23 H. Reynolds, *Forgotten War*, Sydney: University of New South Wales Press, 2014.

24 Wununga Awara, *Animating Indigenous Knowledges*. Monash Indigenous Studies Centre, Monash University, https://www.monash.edu/arts/monash-indigenous-studies/wunungu-awara (accessed 4 June 2022).

25 John Bradley, Team Leader Wunungu Awara, personal communication, 30 May 2022.

26 *Wundanyuka kulu Jujuju*, https://www.monash.edu/arts/monash-indigenous-studies/wunungu-awara/animations/the-sea-turtle-and-the-osprey-2011 (accessed 4 June 2022).

2 Australian Criminal Justice Systems

A new legal system was introduced to Australia as part of the British invasion and colonisation of the continent from 1788.[1] While Aboriginal Law was unitary and could not be broken into component parts, the English law was segmented into many divisions including canon, equity, commercial, land and criminal law. Still, it did not extend to many of the aspects of life and behaviour governed by Aboriginal Law. This book takes an even more narrow focus, being concerned with crime and, therefore, only with English criminal law. What it defined as criminal were offences like theft, assault and murder which are understood not only as harming the individual victim, but the society as a whole, as represented by the state. Therefore, it is the state which has the responsibility of proving the guilt of the accused person, and if they are found guilty, of imposing a penalty on them. This chapter introduces this criminal law and how it operated in Australia as a foundation for our explorations of the experiences of individuals caught up in its net.

Transplanting English Law

Establishing a system of law is important for any society but was particularly central in the British colonisation of Australia. In contrast with Aboriginal societies, colonies elsewhere and Britain itself, where it could be assumed that most people would be law abiding, the colonisation of Australia was started using people who had already been found guilty of a criminal offence. These convicted men, women and some children, the vast majority of them found guilty of theft, provide the focus of Chapter 3. Along with those offenders came a smaller number of officials to manage them, military personnel to contain and defend them and, increasingly over time, free settlers seeking better lives in Australia. This unusual social structure had implications for the system of criminal law which was established, as did the long-denied reality that the colonisers were not peacefully filling an empty land but forcefully displacing sovereign societies with their own complex Law.

While the nation that colonised Australia was Great Britain, the law which was imported and imposed was the English law. Great Britain was a union

DOI: 10.4324/9781003273561-3

of previously independent states: England, Wales which had been politically merged with England in the 1500s, and Scotland which agreed to an Act of Union in 1707. In 1800, Ireland, which had been colonised by England from the 1500s, was added to what then became the United Kingdom of Great Britain and Ireland (UK). With England as the most populous and politically powerful element of the British union, it was the English law which was transplanted to the Australian colonies.

This law had two sources. One was the common law. Like Aboriginal Law, common law was based in custom and the precedent of previous decisions by judges which had been built up in England since "time immemorial," not The Dreaming in this case, but 1189, when the first King Richard came to the English throne. The other source of law was the London-based government, the British Parliament, made up of a hereditary House of Lords and an elected House of Commons. The statute law they enacted was more responsive to current priorities than common law. Acts of Parliament could create new crimes or decriminalise what had been an offence. Penalties for particular crimes could also be changed by statute.

The English system of common and statute law was officially put in place in NSW on 7 February 1788 when the colony was formally proclaimed by Judge Advocate David Collins. In theory, from that time, the elements of this law that were deemed necessary or convenient in the emerging colonies were in place and everyone in the eastern half of the continent of Australia was subject to them.[2] This was extended to the separate colony of Western Australia when it was established in 1829 and to South Australia in 1836. At the top of the local hierarchy in each colony was the governor who was appointed by the British Parliament through the Colonial Office. Governors held delegated authority to rule their colonies guided by written instructions and the need to be accountable to the Secretary of State in London. On a day-to-day basis, the governors had a great deal of authority to make and enforce regulations to fill gaps where English law was silent or did not fit with the "circumstances and situation" of their colony.

These local regulations were put in place as proclamations or Government and General Orders. From 1803, they were printed in the continent's first newspaper, the *Sydney Gazette and NSW Advertiser,* to ensure that they were clearly communicated to residents. In 1804, for example, it was ordered that no serving convict was to be hired by a private employer unless that convict had permission from the government in the form of a Certificate of Leave. Anyone suspected of employing a convict without this official arrangement would have to appear before two magistrates, and if found guilty, to pay a fine.[3] A specific order was needed because the situation of employers wanting to hire those under criminal sentences did not arise in Britain. Notices were also published to inform the public about changes made to English laws which affected their colony. In NSW, criminal matters were heard in the Court of Criminal Judicature between 1788 and 1824. In this court, the Judge Advocate played a large role, both running the trial and helping to decide the verdict, alongside jury members. They could sentence an offender to corporal punishments, including execution.[4]

This practice of having some laws which were carried over directly from Britain and others which were specific to the colonies continued until the British parliament passed the *Australian Courts Act* in 1828. This Act stated that all the laws and statutes in force in England in July of 1828 were formally received as laws of the two colonies then in Australia, NSW and Van Diemen's Land (later Tasmania). However, from that year forward, any new legislation passed in England did not automatically apply in the Australian colonies. With appointed and later elected legislative councils and assemblies being put in place, this Act allowed the colonies to respond to local issues with their own laws. Often they simply passed their own versions of British legislation but sometimes they put something of their own in place. They could not range too far from English law, however, as approving colonial laws was one of the powers retained by the British-appointed governors. In official language, the laws had to be judged not to be repugnant to the laws of England, meaning that they could not be contradictory to or to go against the spirit of English law. This test remained in place for all colonial laws even after Tasmania, NSW, Victoria, Queensland and South Australia were granted responsible government in the 1850s, enduring until the 1865 Colonial Laws Validity Act (UK).[5]

Multiple Jurisdictions

As the colonies matured, each developed their own laws and courts, on separate but related timelines and responding to local conditions. At no time was there a single, unified Australian criminal law. When the colonies later federated as the Commonwealth of Australia in 1901, responsibility for criminal law remained with the states except for offences against the federation, its institutions and property, such as corruption, fraud and drug importation. The Commonwealth's criminal jurisdiction was extended by the 1914 Crimes Act to include treason and divulging official secrets, and additional crimes were added over time. Outside of these restricted areas, the states and the two self-governing territories retained control over criminal matters.[6]

The way criminal law was managed also varied amongst the states and territories. NSW, Victoria and South Australia continue to have a mix of common law originally inherited from Britain and the statutes passed by their parliaments, while other jurisdictions made a change to a unified Criminal Code: Queensland (1899), Western Australia (1902), Tasmania (1922), the Northern Territory (1983) and the Australian Capital Territory (2002). The advantage of having a criminal code is that courts only need to refer to this single source for directions about criminal matters, rather than having to consider hundreds of changing statutes.

These differences in the criminal law matter for crime historians because they mean that we cannot generalise across Australia. Although politicians and legal practitioners looked to what was occurring across the borders, and police forces assisted one another, each colony and then state had its own criminal laws, court system and sanctions for breaking the law and operated independently. While we may see parallels within the crime histories of different states, each jurisdiction must be considered as a separate case. They did, however, share elements including police, court systems and means of inflicting punishment and these will now be explored, with examples from the various jurisdictions.

Encounters with the Criminal Justice System

The Police

The first contact most offenders (and suspected offenders) had with the criminal justice system was with their colony or state's police force. In the first 50 years of colonisation, policing shifted from just a few convict constables keeping watch in Sydney's streets at night to specialist mounted, water, border and native police active across whole colonies, to centralised systems directed from the capital cities.[7] These changes were influenced by the emerging "new police" forces in Great Britain, the first of which was the Metropolitan Police force established for London in 1829.[8]

Given this timing, police were amongst the first institutions to be established in the later colonies. From 1829, Governor James Stirling in the new Swan River Colony in Western Australia quickly appointed magistrates, employed police, established a Court of Quarter Sessions and built a jail. Police Acts were passed in Van Diemen's Land in 1838 and South Australia in 1839, and in Victoria and Queensland after they were separated from NSW. At first these Acts provided police forces for the capital cities and constables directed by local magistrates in rural areas and country towns. However, by the early 1860s, facing the challenges of bushranging, the influx of goldrush immigrants and ongoing resistance from Aboriginal Australians, the preferred model in each colony other than Tasmania was a strong centralised force directed by a commissioner or inspector-general based in the capital city.[9]

Away from the cities, police were important representatives of the central government, filling a wide variety of roles, from registering births to enforcing restrictions on opening hours of pubs and shops to controlling the movement and employment of Aboriginal people.[10] These roles were in addition to their primary responsibilities of patrolling their districts, encouraging orderly behaviour through their presence and investigating reports of crime. Being a police officer was not a well-paid or highly coveted role and it was often taken up by recent arrivals, with little local knowledge, few connections and minimal training. Turnover was high, as police either left for better jobs or were dismissed. To try to make up for these shortcomings, the forces were run on an authoritarian basis, leaving local officers with limited capacity to adapt their practices to suit their communities.[11]

Police not only enforced law and order amongst the settler colonists but were deployed to suppress Aboriginal resistance. The Military Mounted Police first established in the 1820s in NSW were used to conduct actions against Aboriginal people in rural areas. Aboriginal men were drawn into these police forces as trackers, scouts and interpreters, often for the purpose of apprehending Aboriginal people or acting as negotiators.[12] In NSW, Port Phillip (from 1830) and Moreton Bay (from 1848), dedicated "Native Police" forces were formed to be deployed against other Aboriginal people. The Queensland Native Mounted Police was formed when Queensland was still part of NSW (in 1849), but it ran for over 50 years. It was active over the whole state and was "explicitly constituted to protect the lives, livelihoods and property of settlers and to prevent (and punish) any Aboriginal aggression or resistance."[13]

The Courts

If police decided there was sufficient cause to charge a person with a crime, they were taken before a court. At the core of the criminal trial was the presumption that the accused person was not guilty, making the prosecution responsible for demonstrating guilt beyond a reasonable doubt. Most of the colonies followed the model of having three tiers in their court system with Tasmania being the exception with just two. The least serious charges were heard in lower courts known variously as Courts of Petty Sessions, Police Courts, Magistrates Courts or Courts of Summary Jurisdiction.

Lower Courts

Lower level charges were heard by local magistrates, a practice carried from England where magistrates (also called Justice of the Peace) were appointed from the well-to-do, respectable men of a district to administer local justice. In the Australian colonies, this role was filled by senior civil servants, military officers and some clergymen until a landholding class was established. These untrained magistrates served as both judge and jury on lesser matters. They heard minor charges against convicts like insolence, drunkenness and neglect of work but several hearing a case together could also rule on matters involving free people and charges as serious as forgery and attempted rape.[14]

Magistrates presided over the lower courts, along with paid police magistrates, who were often civil servants or former police officers. Their roles became more professionalised across the twentieth century. In these lower courts, most cases were prosecuted by members of the police force rather than lawyers. After the charge against the defendant was read out, they were given the opportunity to plead guilty or not guilty. If they accepted that they had committed the crime, the matter would usually proceed to sentencing. If the plea was not guilty, the police prosecutor set out the case. Written submissions could be made in support and witnesses could be called by the prosecutor and the defendant.

Any evidence provided by a witness had to be given on oath, meaning the person undertook to tell the truth or face divine consequences. Christianity was intertwined with British governance, including having the monarch as the head of the Church of England, and the usual authority appealed to in court was the Christian god through the symbolism of swearing on the Bible. This practice created issues for those who were not Christian, as we will see in Chapter 4 on Aboriginal people's entanglements with the colonial law. Those who followed other religions were permitted to hold their own religious books – a Torah for Jewish witnesses and a Koran for Muslims – or adopt different practices, such as breaking a plate for Chinese witnesses.[15] By the second half of the nineteenth century, non-religious (secular) affirmations were also permitted, as under the 1867 Oaths Act in Queensland. After having heard these brief statements of the facts of the case, the magistrate gave his verdict and imposed a sentence.

For more serious charges, known as felonies, an accused person's first appearance was also in a lower court for a committal hearing to decide whether the case should go forward to a full trial. The defendant did not have to enter a plea but could make a statement on their own behalf and had the opportunity to cross-examine witnesses called by the prosecution. The magistrate had to determine whether there was a *prima facie* (on first glance or superficial) case to be answered: whether an injury had been committed and if there was evidence that the defendant was responsible. Possible outcomes of committal hearings were that the case should be heard in a higher court, and therefore the accused person had to remain in custody on remand until that time unless released on bail; or that there was not enough evidence that the crime had been committed by the accused and they should be released. Defendants could also enter a guilty plea at the committal and proceed directly to sentencing.

We might think of courts as orderly and quiet places but in the late nineteenth century, these lower courts, particularly those in the large cities, gained a reputation for raucous behaviour from both onlookers in the public gallery and the numerous accused who packed into the court to await their trial. The one person who did not say much in court was the defendant. Because they were assumed to be innocent, they did not have to say anything to prove that they were and not giving testimony was a way of protecting them from saying something which might help to convict them. They had the right to remain silent, and most people coming before the courts made use of this right, even if they longed to speak up to try to establish their innocence.

Intermediate and Higher Courts

Above the Petty Sessions Courts were intermediate courts referred to as District Courts, Quarter Sessions or General Sessions which heard felonies and indictable offences like robbery, arson and bigamy. These courts were modelled on the English Courts of Quarter Sessions and were established in the larger towns across the colonies. Residents agitated to have their own District Courts because they could generate an economic boost as people came to attend them, as well as giving some social cachet as a mark of the importance of a centre. Courthouses were substantial, usually stone buildings, located in a principal street and often accommodated several levels of court. Sessions were held regularly to ensure that cases were heard without extended delays.

Criminal cases in these courts were tried by judge and jury, with the judge usually a resident of the local community. The judge's role was to run the trial, to make decisions related to points of law that it raised, ensure correct procedures were followed and determine the appropriate sentence. Juries heard the evidence and decided whether the accused was guilty or not guilty. *The essay by Rachel Franks accompanying this chapter discusses the early use of military juries in NSW and how they were replaced by all male civilian juries, with just one exception.* There were serious issues around whether juries fulfilled the ideal of enabling a person's guilt to be judged by their peers. Taking the Western Australian criteria of 1832 as an example, jurors had to be men between the ages of 21 and 60 and to own £50 of real estate or have other assets to the value of £100. They could not work in the legal system, be civil servants, clergy or physicians and had to be British subjects.[16] Restrictions like these meant that there were limited pools of eligible people from which jurors could be selected and that they tended to share life experiences and assumptions which affected the decisions they made. The accused in most criminal trials did not see themselves reflected back in the faces of the jurors who sat in judgement on them.

The highest level of court were the Supreme Courts, where cases which could result in execution, known as capital cases, were heard by a judge and jury. Initially, Supreme Courts sat only in the capital cities. As the colonies' populations expanded outward, the logistics of attending Supreme Court hearings discouraged prosecutions in more distant settlements. To address this issue, from the mid-nineteenth century, Supreme Courts were convened in regional centres in what were called Circuit Courts. A judge would travel along a set route or circuit every few months to hear scheduled cases. These court sessions could often be rushed as the judge would only have a few days to hear all of the accumulated cases before being due in the next town. If time ran out, the remaining cases were rescheduled to the next session, leaving the accused waiting several months in custody.

The accused person could be represented by a lawyer in these higher courts, after the principles of the UK Prisoners Counsel Act of 1836 were adopted in each colony. Although it was widely thought that a correct verdict would naturally emerge through a trial, subsequent acts like the 1840 Defence on Trials for Felony Act (NSW) allowed that the individual's right to defend themselves could extend to having legal counsel undertake that defence.[17] If charged with a capital crime, defendants could apply for state aid to pay the lawyer's fees, while those on lesser charges had to find the money to pay for counsel themselves or go without. Those who ran their own defence against indictable offences could not give sworn testimony until laws were changed to permit it from the 1880s, but as in committal hearings, they could give an unsworn statement to challenge the prosecution's version of events, cross-examine prosecution witnesses and call upon witnesses and character references to help to make their case. Without legal expertise or experience of legal processes, it was difficult to mount a good self-defence, especially if the accused was in jail on remand.

A belief that lawyers used legal tricks and subterfuge to have guilty clients go free delayed the extension of free legal counsel for defendants. Again following the lead of Britain, Poor Persons Defence Acts began to be passed by the states in the early twentieth century. In Victoria, a Public Solicitor's Office was established to provide legal aid in 1928. While these measures increased the rate of legal representation in Victoria from below 60% in the nineteenth century to above 60% in the twentieth century, crime historians Alana Piper and Mark Finnane found up to a third of those being tried were still unrepresented by 1961. This mattered because legal representation could influence outcomes in the courts. There were clear benefits for the defendant in having a lawyer. Legal representation increased the likelihood of being acquitted, being convicted of lesser charges than the original and of being recommended to mercy if found guilty.[18]

In addition to the three levels of courts, there were also specialised courts within the justice system. One was the Coroners' Court which conducted inquests into sudden or suspicious deaths and from the 1850s into events such as fires. Inquests had been conducted by Police Magistrates until the 1840s and people in this role were made coroners, as were some police officers, physicians and barristers. Inquests, in the presence of the body of the deceased, were often conducted in a pub near the scene of the death but could also take place in the Court of Petty Sessions, police stations and hospitals. A jury was gathered and evidence heard from witnesses to identify who had died, in what circumstances, the cause of death and who (if anyone) had contributed to the death. If there were no suspicious circumstances, the death was officially registered. If there was found to be a sufficient case against a person or people as having caused the death, a verdict of wilful murder could be passed, and the accused would face trial in the Supreme Court. The sophistication of coronial investigations grew through the nineteenth century, with experts like the Government Analyst able to be called upon to test the body for the presence of poisons. A later innovation was the Children's Courts, established between 1895 and 1907.

In all of these criminal courts, the standard of proof was "beyond reasonable doubt." That means that those involved in making the decision – the magistrate in the lower courts and the jury in the higher courts – had to be certain that the accused committed the crime. If they found the accused person not guilty, the defendant was free to go. If guilty, the next step in the criminal justice system was sentencing.

Sentencing

When found guilty of a crime, offenders faced a variety of possible sentences. In some instances, judges had discretion in determining the form and duration of the punishment from a range set down in legislation; in others, there was a set punishment. In *Discipline and Punish*, French philosopher Michel Foucault drew a distinction between two types of punishment: punishments of the body and punishments of the mind or psyche, and argued that psychological punishments gained dominance in European legal systems in the nineteenth century.[19] Both psychological and physical punishments were part of Aboriginal Law. With the imposition of the English law, punishments of the body increased, to an extent which was distressing to the Eora people of the Sydney region. In May 1791, local people were gathered to witness the flogging of a convict who had stolen fishing implements from an Eora woman. Floggings were administered by tying the offender to wooden posts in the shape of an upright triangle and then applying a prescribed number of strokes to their back with a multi-strand lash.[20] According to Lieutenant Watkin Tench, "There was not one of [the group of Eora people] that did not testify strong abhorrence of the punishment and equal sympathy with the sufferer," with some crying and others threatening the executioner administering the punishment.[21] The pinioning of the convict and continual flogging even after drawing blood made this punishment seem extreme to these outside observers.

Some bodily punishments used in Britain, like branding and cutting off a hand or ear, were not implemented in the justice systems in Australia, but measures such as shaving women's hair, and for men, time operating a treadmill were used.[22] These punishments did not outlast the convict era, but flogging had a longer life, continuing to be added to some prison sentences through the nineteenth century.

The ultimate punishment of the body was execution, also known as capital punishment. Capital punishment was widely used in England in the 1700s. Under what was known as the "Bloody Code," over 200 offences including minor property offences such as pickpocketing, stealing a sheep and forgery carried a death sentence. While hangings of those convicted of murder or violent assault attracted large, unruly and approving crowds, means were found to avoid most executions for lesser crimes. Chief amongst the alternatives was transportation, introduced in 1718. The first execution in settler colonial Australia occurred within a month of the establishment of the colony, for the crime of stealing food. Executions for murder, housebreaking, stealing livestock, rape and other offences peaked in the decade from 1826 when there were 363 public executions in NSW and close to 200 in VDL.[23]

In keeping with Foucault's observation, Britain began to move away from the death penalty in the early nineteenth century. Its Judgement of Death Act of 1823 reserved execution for treason, murder, wounding, violent theft, arson and sodomy. After the 1861 Offences Against the Person Act, only two capital offences remained in the UK: murder and high treason (disloyalty to the state, such as selling defence secrets to a foreign power).

This was one of the areas in which the Australian colonies deviated from English law. In Australia, executions were moved out of the public eye behind prison walls from the 1850s but capital punishment was retained for attempted murder, robbery with wounding, some forms of sodomy and arson, and rape.[24]

Judges had some discretion in handing down a death sentence. The prescribed ceremony was that they put a black cloth over their bewigged heads and recited the words:

> The law is that thou shalt return from hence, to the Place whence thou camest, and from thence to the Place of Execution, where thou shalt hang by the Neck, till the body be dead! dead! dead! And the Lord have Mercy upon thy Soul.[25]

In cases in which the judge accepted the jury's guilty verdict but thought there were reasons the death sentence should not be carried out, they could dispense with the ceremony and simply "record" a sentence of death. Consideration of the case then moved to the Executive Council made up of the colonial or state governor and senior government ministers. They took into account the judge's and jury's recommendations and any petitions or letters from members of the public before making a decision on whether the sentence should be carried out or mercy extended. Rachel Franks described this capacity to show mercy as a "bridge between cultural expectations and legal requirements."[26] If spared, the offender was made to serve a long term in prison.

The rate of reprieves grew through the nineteenth century as lobbying for the abolition of capital punishment became widespread. Cases in which death sentences were actually carried out fell from one in three in the 1890s to just 6 in 100 in the first decade of the twentieth century.[27] In 1922, Queensland became the first state in Australia to abolish the death penalty and New South Wales was the last in 1985, although it had not performed an execution since 1939. The final execution in Australia occurred in Victoria in 1967, when convicted murderer Ronald Ryan was hanged. Overall, almost 1700 people had been executed as part of settler colonial criminal justice systems in Australia.

The alternative type of sentences were punishments targeting the offender's mind, their freedom and their economic well-being. While older punishments had assumed offenders, and witnesses of floggings or executions could best be deterred from future crime through fear of physical pain or disfigurement, the newer ones were intended to impose some financial penalty or restriction on personal freedom which it was hoped would change a person's perspective so they would choose not to break the law.[28] This reflected a shift from an assumption that offenders were simply bad and incapable of reform, to a sense that aspects of a person's life experience or biology might have led them to crime, offering a possibility of redemption.

Fines were imposed mainly for the less serious offences which were tried in the lower courts. They were felt much more severely by those with little access to money. Many of those who were convicted of offences against the public order could not pay even small fines and so instead had to serve time in jail. This meant that jails, especially those for women, filled up very quickly with people who had only committed minor crimes, making institutional conditions crowded and unhealthy.

Other financial punishments included the imposition of bonds or sureties. This required a person who was found guilty to post a set amount of money as a guarantee of good behaviour. There might be additional conditions as well, such as remaining in a certain area or avoiding particular companions or locations. If the person reoffended, they forfeited the bond and in some cases also had to serve time in jail. Similar to the bond was the suspended sentence in which a convicted person was given a term of imprisonment but it was not enforced unless they reoffended or broke other conditions set by the court. These non-custodial sentences began to be used much more from the 1940s, particularly for property offences, and are now the predominant form of sentence delivered by the courts.

Custodial sentences or imprisonment were commonly used in colonial Australia but had been infrequent in Britain when convict transportation began. The Australian colonies followed this trend, building only small jails to house convicts who reoffended in the colonies and preferring re-transportation to dedicated penal settlements like Newcastle in NSW and Macquarie Harbour in VDL, or sentences to chain gangs. Female factories were built to house women convicts, including on Queen Street, Brisbane; at Parramatta near Sydney; and at the Cascades, outside of Hobart.[29] These facilities were a combination of jail, workhouse and refuge, housing women who were pregnant or had young infants and those awaiting work assignments, as well as a "crime class" of those who had committed offences in the colony.

The female factories shared some characteristics with the newer form of penal institution, the penitentiary, which grew out of ideas about reforming offenders which were being developed in the UK and the United States. The penitentiary was designed to remould offenders into contributing citizens by creating a highly structured environment in which people had to conform to strict behavioural rules and set timetables for work, eating, and sleeping.[30] Combined with basic education and religious services, this regime was intended to bring about reflection, repentance and a commitment to living a better life on release. Anyone who did not obey faced immediate punishment, which could include being held in a dark or solitary cell, being made to perform hard labour or being put on a restricted diet of bread and water. The extreme development of the penitentiary was the separate prison built in 1850 at Port Arthur in Van Diemen's Land.[31] It was designed on the panopticon concept developed by English philosopher Jeremy Bentham which had been implemented just eight years earlier in Britain's Pentonville Prison. Inmates lived and worked alone in their separate prison cells, with food delivered through a slot in the door. They left their cells only for solitary exercise, chores and religious services and then were under constant surveillance and had to wear hoods to limit their capacity to see or be seen by other inmates. Penitentiaries were in effect a large-scale psychological experiment in how the imposition of an orderly environment would affect human behaviour.

More and larger prisons were built from the mid-nineteenth century as the incarcerated population shifted from British convicts to people born in the colonies and immigrants who committed their first crimes in Australia. These new prisons included Maitland Gaol in the NSW Hunter Valley (1848), Pentridge Prison in Melbourne (1851) and Fremantle Prison in Western Australia (1855), all of which remained in use until the 1990s and can now be visited as heritage sites.[32] These prisons were run on principles of instilling order into inmates and extracting work from them and they developed fearsome reputations for their strict regimes, rough living conditions and the violence of both prison guards and inmates. Separate women's prisons were established including in Sydney, the State Reformatory for Women opened at Long Bay in 1909.

Although intended to encourage reform, it came to be recognised that imprisonment could instead lead to more criminal associations and actions. Sarah Mattie, who gave evidence in 1887 to a Board of Inquiry established to investigate Queensland's prisons, felt that she left jail worse every time she served a sentence because other inmates encouraged younger women to continue to reoffend.[33] It was in the jails that many argued the Australian underworld thrived and reproduced itself. To address this, First Offenders Acts were passed in each colony and later state from the 1890s. These enabled judges to show leniency to those appearing before the courts for the first time for minor offences such as larceny or false pretences, especially if they were young, of good character or there were extenuating circumstances.[34] First offenders could have complaints dismissed, pay only damages or court costs (in instalments) or receive a suspended sentence or a period on probation, with or without lodging a sum of money as a guarantee of their good behaviour. They were spared time in jail and, it was hoped, would be better able to turn away from crime.

For those who still served custodial sentences, a number of innovations followed. Dedicated facilities for young offenders were one. The idea that time in incarceration could be used to gain skills for life outside encouraged a shift to a focus on training after the Second World War. In minimum security facilities, inmates were given opportunities for day release for work or recreation, and to complete vocational courses within the prison. Despite efforts to divert people from prisons, their populations have continued to grow and calls continue for more attention to early interventions, alternative sentencing options and mental health rather than punitive approaches, especially for those with drug and alcohol addictions.

Conclusion

The complexity of the criminal justice system, with its components of police, courts and jails, and its variations in each colony and state, the money invested in it and the large number of people who worked within it all reflect its importance in Australian settler colonial society. Court houses and jails were deliberately constructed to be visible reminders of the power of the law, and uniformed police carried it into the back streets of the cities and the backblocks of rural areas. The intention was that this system of law would protect the innocent and punish offenders, offering all who came before it equal treatment and a promise that they would be considered innocent until proven guilty. Armed with an understanding of these structures and principles, we can now go on to specific cases and see how the law worked in practice. We begin with the convicts whose experience of the British criminal justice system was what propelled them to Australia, where some went on to a close acquaintance with the colonial versions of police, courts and punishment regimes.

Suggested Readings

Cane, Peter, Lisa Ford and Mark McMillan, eds. *Cambridge Legal History of Australia.* Cambridge: Cambridge University Press, 2022.

Dunstall, Graeme and Barry S. Godfrey, eds. *Crime and Empire 1840–1940: Criminal Justice in Local and Global Context.* Cullompton: Willan Publishing, 2005.

Lincoln, Robyn and Shirleene Robinson, eds. *Crime Over Time: Temporal Perspectives on Crime and Punishment in Australia.* Newcastle upon Tyne: Cambridge Scholars, 2010.

Finnane, Mark. *Punishment in Australian Society.* Melbourne: Oxford University Press, 1997.

Kercher, Bruce. *An Unruly Child: A History of Law in Australia.* Sydney: Allen and Unwin, 1995.

Piper, Alana and Mark Finnane. "Defending the Accused: The Impact of Legal Representation on Criminal Trial Outcomes in Victoria, Australia, 1861–1961." *Journal of Legal History* 38, no. 1 (2017): 27–53.

ESSAY: FROM MILITARY TRIBUNALS TO TRIAL BY JURY

Rachel Franks

James Spigelman, a Chief Justice of New South Wales, noted the "fundamental importance" of the jury system is that: "The direct involvement as decision-makers of members of the public, in their capacity as such, does more to ensure the maintenance of a high level of trust and confidence in the administration of justice than, perhaps, any other single factor."[35] Trial by jury is entrenched in popular conceptions of how justice works. Indeed, it is often assumed that it is a long-held right available to all citizens; but access to trial by jury and the right to sit on juries, for all adult Australians, was only achieved after many decades of lobbying.

When NSW was first colonised in 1788, responsibility for law and order fell, largely, upon the shoulders of David Collins who was the colony's first Judge Advocate. A man with some military experience but no legal training, Collins had the "power to inquire of, hear, determine, and punish all treasons, misprisions of treasons, murders, felonies, forgeries, perjuries, trespasses, and other crimes whatsoever that may be committed in the colony."[36]

In a place with more crooks than men of good character, the first criminal proceedings in Sydney Town were heard by the "Judge Advocate and a panel of six military officers."[37] This approach to justice – and perceptions these men would follow the orders of their superiors or apply military norms to civilian settings – was unpalatable to free people and, later, to those felons who became free. The situation was summarised in 1825 by outspoken barrister William Charles Wentworth as "the rude experiments of rude times," but the military retained a place in the NSW legal system for many years.[38] The debate over whether the small and fractious colony could uphold the ideals of civilian juries began as early as 1791 and raged until the 1830s.[39]

The *New South Wales Act 1823* (UK) allowed juries of 12 male civilians to hear certain civil cases, if the plaintiff and the defendant agreed.[40] The colony's first Chief Justice, Francis Forbes, "took the surprising view" that civilian juries could be empanelled for some criminal trials. Forbes also experimented, over 1824–28, with grand juries; "somewhere between 12 and 23 men" tasked with deciding if a matter should go to trial and be heard by a petit, or common, jury of 12.[41] This function was later fulfilled by committal hearings held in front of magistrates at Courts of Petty Sessions, now Local Courts. Legislation in 1828 "provided for trial by jury in the Supreme Court in civil cases and empowered the Governor to introduce general trial by jury in criminal matters."[42]

Military panels were dispensed with, for civilians, by the *Jury Trials Act 1839* (UK).[43] A jury of civilian peers could, though, be just as intimidating as a military tribunal in its swiftness. When John Knatchbull was tried for murdering Ellen Jamieson, a widowed mother of two, the jury declared him guilty "without leaving the box."[44] Around 10,000 Sydneysiders watched Knatchbull hang on 13 February 1844.[45]

The first civilians to sit on juries for trials in Australia were property holders. They were also men. In a twist, the first woman judicially hanged in NSW, saw a civilian jury composed entirely of women immediately after her trial. Ann Davis, guilty of theft and perjury, was sentenced to death but delayed her execution by saying she was pregnant. A group of women, selected from the cohort of convicts, was empanelled to assess the situation.[46] The forewoman, "a grave personage between sixty and seventy years old," stated: "Gentlemen! She is as much with child as I am."[47] Davis was executed on 23 November 1789.

Juries of matrons – a feature of English common law – could, in civil cases, support a new widow's assertion that she carried her deceased husband's heir. In criminal cases, these juries could defer an appointment with the hangman. These women were not supernumerary; juries of matrons wielded real power as their "verdicts were conclusive."[48]

The *Jury (Amendment) Act* 1947 (NSW) allowed women who were registered voters to put themselves forward as potential jurors. Gender equality was delayed as there were no "separate quarters" to accommodate women jurors in courthouses, with nobody rushing to build ladies' rooms as the Government did "not regard the innovation as urgent".[49] It was 30 years before the *Jury Act 1977* (NSW) ensured all enrolled electors were automatically inscribed on the jury roll.

Today, jurors are utilised across NSW, to "hear and determine more serious criminal matters" as well as to "hear and determine civil matters involving large monetary claims." Each year in NSW, approximately 150,000 people across the state receive a jury summons with around 9,000 selected to serve on a jury panel.[50] Juries are not perfect. Risks of bias, misconduct and tampering persist, while some eligible groups, such as First Nations peoples, remain underrepresented on juries.[51] The jury retains its place, regardless of difficulties, as a "critical decision making body," and to serve on a jury is to contribute to the transparency of an established legal system and its rule of law.[52]

PRIMARY SOURCE: PRISONERS FOR TRIAL, ADELAIDE, 1846

Proclaimed as a colony in 1836, South Australia was to be spared the convict taint, welcoming in only free emigrants of good character. This did not mean it escaped crime. To keep good order, the colony's court system began in 1837 when a Supreme Court was established. For lesser matters like those on this list from March 1846, there were minor courts presided over by paid resident magistrates. The details of the offences are revealing of life in the first years of a new colony, with several related to food and livestock. The telescope and glass eyes to be used in taxidermy reflect the scientific interests of some settler colonists, while the theft of a prayer book is open to interpretation. The outcome "no bill," or "*nolle prosequi*" in Latin, means that the court decided not to proceed with the charge, often because of a lack of evidence.

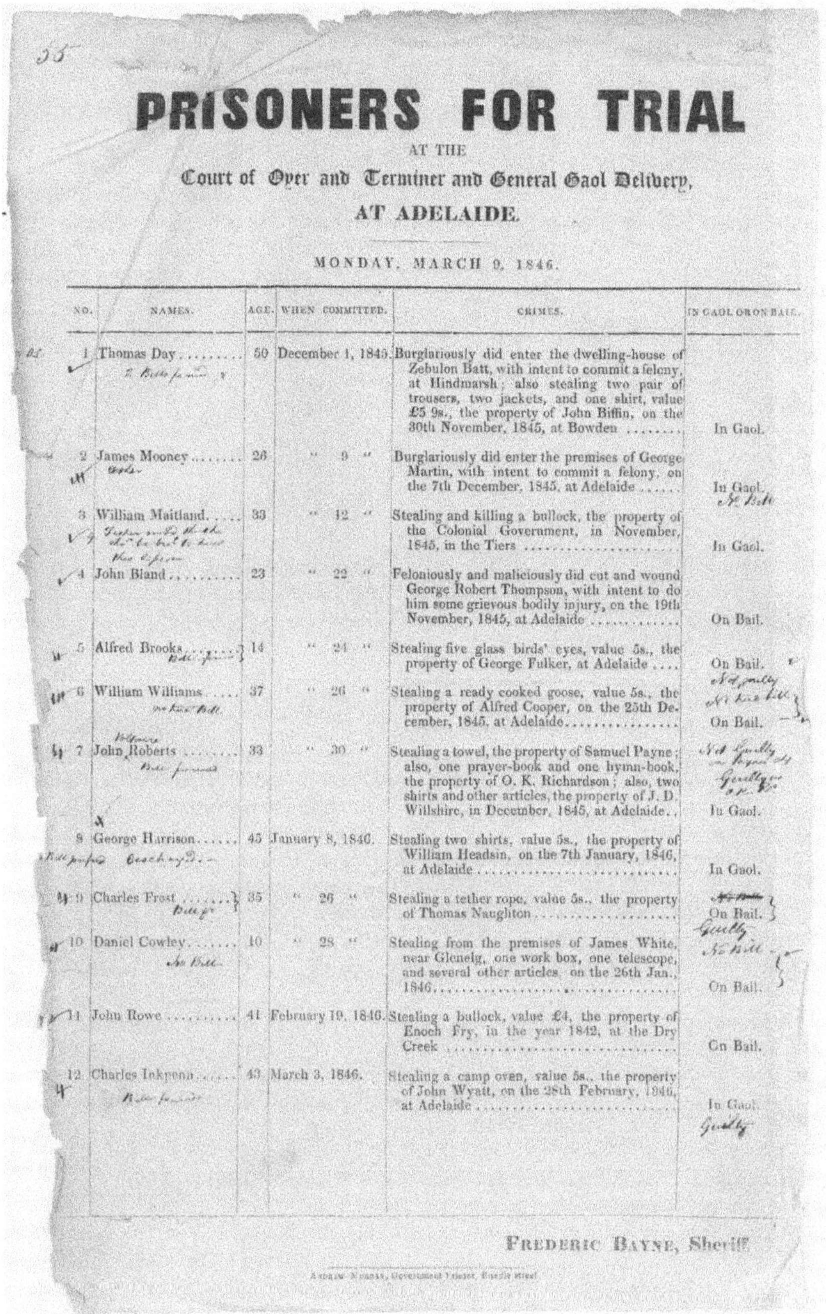

PRISONERS FOR TRIAL

AT THE

Court of Oyer and Terminer and General Gaol Delivery,

AT ADELAIDE.

MONDAY, MARCH 9, 1846.

NO.	NAMES.	AGE.	WHEN COMMITTED.	CRIMES.	IN GAOL OR ON BAIL.
1	Thomas Day	50	December 1, 1845.	Burglariously did enter the dwelling-house of Zebulon Batt, with intent to commit a felony, at Hindmarsh; also stealing two pair of trousers, two jackets, and one shirt, value £5 9s., the property of John Biffin, on the 30th November, 1845, at Bowden	In Gaol.
2	James Mooney	26	" 9 "	Burglariously did enter the premises of George Martin, with intent to commit a felony, on the 7th December, 1845, at Adelaide	In Gaol.
3	William Maitland	33	" 12 "	Stealing and killing a bullock, the property of the Colonial Government, in November, 1845, in the Tiers	In Gaol.
4	John Bland	23	" 22 "	Feloniously and maliciously did cut and wound George Robert Thompson, with intent to do him some grievous bodily injury, on the 19th November, 1845, at Adelaide	On Bail.
5	Alfred Brooks	14	" 24 "	Stealing five glass birds' eyes, value 5s., the property of George Fulker, at Adelaide	On Bail.
6	William Williams	37	" 26 "	Stealing a ready cooked goose, value 5s., the property of Alfred Cooper, on the 25th December, 1845, at Adelaide	On Bail.
7	John Roberts	33	" 30 "	Stealing a towel, the property of Samuel Payne; also, one prayer-book and one hymn-book, the property of O. K. Richardson; also, two shirts and other articles, the property of J. D. Willshire, in December, 1845, at Adelaide	In Gaol.
8	George Harrison	45	January 8, 1846.	Stealing two shirts, value 5s., the property of William Headsin, on the 7th January, 1846, at Adelaide	In Gaol.
9	Charles Frost	35	" 26 "	Stealing a tether rope, value 5s., the property of Thomas Naughton	On Bail.
10	Daniel Cowley	40	" 28 "	Stealing from the premises of James White, near Glenelg, one work box, one telescope, and several other articles, on the 26th Jan., 1846	On Bail.
11	John Rowe	41	February 19, 1846.	Stealing a bullock, value £4, the property of Enoch Fry, in the year 1842, at the Dry Creek	On Bail.
12	Charles Inkpenn	43	March 3, 1846.	Stealing a camp oven, value 5s., the property of John Wyatt, on the 28th February, 1846, at Adelaide	In Gaol.

FREDERIC BAYNE, Sheriff.

Figure 2.1 Criminal record books, Supreme Court of South Australia, Unit 1, p. 55, State Records of South Australia, GRS/12820/1.

Notes

1 I acknowledge Alana Piper who provided the original structure and material upon which this chapter is based.
2 Bruce Kercher, *An Unruly Child: A History of Law in Australia*, Sydney: Allen and Unwin, 1995, xi–xii.
3 "General Orders," *Sydney Gazette and NSW Advertiser*, 5 February 1804, 1. This was the Ticket of Leave system, whereby after having served a proportion of their sentence and displayed good behaviour, a convict was permitted to undertake paid employment within a restricted geographical area.
4 Bruce Kercher, "Colonial Settlement to Colony," Peter Cane, Lisa Ford and Mark McMillan, eds. *Cambridge Legal History of Australia*, Cambridge: Cambridge University Press, 2022, 90.
5 The final colony, Western Australia, only gained self-government in 1890, delayed in part because of the continuing transportation of British convicts there until 1868.
6 After long periods of administration by colonial, state and federal governments, the Northern Territory was granted self-government in 1978 and the Australian Capital Territory in 1988.
7 Louise Steding, *Forensics and Police through Time, Australian in Context, Nineteenth Century*, Sydney: In Focus Press, 2016, 8.
8 David Philips, "The Royal Bastard as Policeman? William Augustus Miles and the Sydney Police, 1841–1848," David Philips and Susanne Davies, eds. *A Nation of Rogues? Crime, Law and Punishment in Colonial Australia*, Melbourne: Melbourne University Press, 1994, 43.
9 Stefan Petrow, "The English Model? Policing in Late Nineteenth-Century Tasmania," Barry S. Godfrey and Graeme Dunstall, eds. *Crime and Empire 1840–1940: Criminal Justice in Local and Global Context*, London: Routledge, 2012, 125.
10 Tim Prenzler, "Change and Continuity in Australian Policing," Robyn Lincoln and Shirleene Robinson, eds. *Crime Over Time: Temporal Perspectives on Crime and Punishment in Australia*, Newcastle upon Tyne: Cambridge Scholars, 2010, 173.
11 Mark Finnane, "Police Rules and the Organisation of Policing in Queensland, 1905–1916," *Australia and New Zealand Journal of Criminology* 22 (1989): 96.
12 Amanda Nettelbeck, "'On the Side of Law and Order': Indigenous Aides to the Mounted Police on the Settler Frontiers of Australia and Canada," *Journal of Colonialism and Colonial History* 15, no. 2 (2014): Control through Conversion Section, p. 3 of 14.
13 H. Burke and L.A. Wallis, *Frontier Conflict and the Native Mounted Police in Queensland Database* (2019). https://frontierconflict.org/
14 Hilary Golder, *High and Responsible Office, A History of the NSW Magistracy*, Sydney: Sydney University Press, 1991, 8–9.
15 For an example of a Chinese witness breaking a plate in court as an affirmation of truth telling, see "Grafton Police Court," *Clarence and Richmond Examiner and New England Advertiser*, 19 January 1864, 2.
16 David Plater and Victoria Geason, "'The Prisoners Could Not Have that Fair and Impartial Trial Which Justice Demands': A Fair Criminal Trial in 19th Century Australia," *Canterbury Law Review* 25 (2019): n169.
17 Alana Piper and Mark Finnane, "Defending the Accused: The Impact of Legal Representation on Criminal Trial Outcomes in Victoria, Australia, 1861–1961," *Journal of Legal History* 38, no. 1 (2017): 28.
18 Piper and Finnane, "Defending the Accused," 30; 33. From a sample of 3341 defendants, they found that the rate of acquittal was 55.8% for the 1953 who were defended and 28.1% for the 908 who were not.
19 Michel Foucault, *Discipline and Punish: The Birth of the Prison*, trans. Alan Sheridan, London: Allen Lane, 1977.

20 Raymond Evans and William Thorpe, "Commanding Men: Masculinities and the Convict System," *Journal of Australian Studies* 56 (1998): 22–25.
21 Watkin Tench, *A Complete Account of the Settlement at Port Jackson*, London: G. Nicol, 1793, Ch. 13, https://gutenberg.net.au/ebooks/e00084.html.
22 On shaving women's hair, see Evans and Thorpe, "Commanding Men," 28. On the treadmill, see Graham Seal, *Great Convict Stories: Dramatic and Moving Tales from Australia's Brutal Early Years*, Sydney: Allen and Unwin, 2017, 106–08.
23 Robyn Lincoln and Shirleene Robinson, "When the Penalty was Death," Robyn Lincoln and Shirleene Robinson, eds. *Crime Over Time: Temporal Perspectives on Crime and Punishment in Australia*, Newcastle upon Tyne: Cambridge Scholars, 2010, 192.
24 R. Douglas and K. Laster, "A Matter of Life and Death: The Victorian Executive and the Decision to Execute, 1842–1967," *Australian and New Zealand Journal of Criminology* 24 (1991): 146.
25 Kercher, *An Unruly Child*, xiv.
26 Rachel Franks, *An Uncommon Hangman: The Life and Deaths of Robert "Nosey Bob" Howard*, Sydney: NewSouth, 2022, 38.
27 Lincoln and Robinson, "When the Penalty Was Death," 187; 197.
28 Mark Finnane, *Punishment in Australian Society*, Melbourne: Oxford University Press, 1997, 42–43.
29 Kay Daniels, *Convict Women*, Sydney: Allen and Unwin, 1998, Ch. 5 "The Female Factories: The Failure of Reform"; Joy Damousi, *Depraved and Disorderly: Female Convicts, Sexuality and Gender in Colonial Australia*, Cambridge: Cambridge University Press, 1997.
30 John Pratt, "'This Is Not a Prison': Foucault, the Panopticon and Pentonville," *Social and Legal Studies* 2, no. 4 (1993): 383–89.
31 Richard Tuffin and Martin Gibbs, "The Archaeology of the Convict Probation System: The Labor Landscapes of Port Arthur and the Cascades Probation Station, 1839–55," *International Journal of Historical Archaeology* 24, no. 3 (2020): 608–09.
32 The Fremantle institution was initially known as the Convict Establishment, built in the 1850s and renamed Fremantle Prison in 1867.
33 Alana Piper, "'I go out Worse Every Time' Connections and Corruption in a Female Prison," *History Australia* 9, no. 3 (2012): 132–53.
34 See, for example, the Western Australian Act to Permit the Conditional Release of First Offenders in Certain Cases (1892), https://www.legislation.wa.gov.au/legislation/prod/filestore.nsf/FileURL/mrdoc_14675.pdf/$FILE/Probation%20of%20First%20Offenders%20Act%201892%20-%20%5B00-00-00%5D.pdf?OpenElement and NSW First Offenders Probation Act (1894) https://jade.io/article/438518 (accessed 23 November 2021).
35 In R. Johns, *Trial by Jury: Recent Developments*, Sydney: NSW Parliamentary Library Research Service, 2005, 1.
36 D. Collins, *An Account of the English Colony in New South Wales*, vol. 1, Adelaide: Libraries Board of South Australia, [1798] 1971, 11.
37 Johns, *Trial*, 3.
38 In J.M. Bennett, "The Establishment of Jury Trial in New South Wales," *Sydney Law Review* 4, no. 3 (1961): 471.
39 Bennett, "The Establishment," 464–69.
40 Johns, *Trial*, 3.
41 G.D. Woods, *A History of Criminal Law in New South Wales: The Colonial Period, 1788–1900*, Annandale, NSW: Federation Press, 2002, 57–59.
42 "Australian Courts Act 1828 (UK)," Documenting a Democracy, Museum of Australian Democracy, 2011, https://www.foundingdocs.gov.au/item-sdid-72.html.
43 Bennett, "The Establishment," 476–77.

44 "Supreme Court – Criminal Side," *Sydney Morning Herald*, January 25, 1844, 2.
45 "Execution of John Knatchbull," *The Australian*, February 15, 1844, 3.
46 Johns, *Trial*, 3. J. Cobley, *Sydney Cove: 1789–1790*, Sydney: Angus & Robertson, [1963] 1980, 113–15.
47 W. Tench, T. Flannery, ed. *Watkin Tench's 1788*, Melbourne: Text, [1793] 2009, 268.
48 S.M. Butler, "More Than Mothers: Juries of Matrons and Pleas of the Belly in Medieval England," *Law and History Review* 37, no. 2 (2019): 367.
49 "No Women on Juries for About a Year," *Newcastle Sun*, July 17, 1924, 4.
50 "About Jury Service," NSW Government Communities & Justice, 2021, https://courts.nsw.gov.au/courts-and-tribunals/for-jurors/jury-service.html.
51 R. Goldflam, "The White Elephant in the Room: Juries, Jury Arrays and Race," *Indigenous Law Bulletin* 7, no. 26 (2011): 35.
52 Spigelman in Johns, *Trial*, 1.

3 The Criminal Class Theory and Its Enemies

If we are on a quest to find an Australian underworld, it might be expected that with the convicts, we have already reached our goal. That the people used to launch the settler colonisation of Australia had been convicted of crimes was long perceived to be a shameful birthstain. In this view, not only were the founders dishonest, violent and immoral, but the system developed to keep them in check was brutal and brutalising. The combined effects of bad people and a bad system were thought to be contagious, affecting all who shared the colonies with the convicts and particularly their own children, who carried an inherent tendency to crime which could emerge at any time. The English in particular like to keep alive the idea that Australians are still shaped by these origins. In 2018, after Australian cricketers were caught ball tampering in South Africa, Britain's Barmy Army of cricket fans sang a sledging ditty which included the phrase: "Those cheating Aussie convicts/ They'll never change at all!"[1]

In contrast, when I asked my Australian students to describe convicts, the words they chose included misunderstood, poor, unfortunate, disadvantaged, resilient and victims. They did not see the convicts as criminals by choice or nature, but as people who committed petty offences out of grim necessity and suffered a hugely disproportionate punishment. In this view, the prosperous country they helped to establish, with its high standard of living and an incidence of crime lower than that in Great Britain or the United States and comparable with non-convict Canada and New Zealand shows that they were innocent all along.

These differences of opinion do not just stem from national pride. They reflect long-term debates over who the convicts were and the legacy of their role in the founding of Britain's Australian colonies. These questions have remained open for two centuries not only because those trying to answer them had their own reasons for wanting to favour one position or another but also when it comes to the historians involved in the debates, in part because of their methodology. The term methodology, or research method, means how research is undertaken. Any historian when starting on a new project has to consider not only what questions they will ask but also how they will conduct their research in a way which allows them to develop an argument

DOI: 10.4324/9781003273561-4

and present a meaningful conclusion. Aspects of the methodology include what forms of evidence will be used (and which ones not used), how and where they will be sought and how their content will be analysed. There are many limitations that historians face in designing their methodology, including knowledge that specific evidence exists, access to that evidence and the analytical tools available to them, as well as restrictions on time and budget. This chapter will review how changes in historical methods influenced ideas about whether or not convicts were essentially criminal and whether their presence left Australians particularly oriented to criminal behaviour, before demonstrating how readily convict lives can now be reconstructed using online sources and tools.

Introducing Convicts

Convicts played a central role in the colonisation of Australia by the British from 1788. New South Wales received 80,000 men and women as transportees between 1788 and 1842; Van Diemen's Land 73,000 between 1803 and 1853; and Western Australia, almost 10,000 men only between 1850 and 1868. The areas which became Victoria and Queensland had populations of serving convicts while they were still part of NSW, with Brisbane (originally Moreton Bay) having its origins as a place of secondary punishment for reoffending convicts. South Australia did not directly accept convicts and its residents cultivated a reputation of being morally superior because of this, although former transportees did enter the colony after their sentences were served.

To understand why so many people were being transported to the Australian colonies in the nineteenth century, we need to go back to Great Britain 100 years earlier. Early eighteenth-century Britain was a parliamentary democracy in which only men with property could vote or be elected to sit in the House of Commons. The upper house, the House of Lords, was not elected at all but occupied by those with hereditary titles. The statute law passed by Parliament tended to protect the interests of this limited group of politicians and voters by punishing a wide range of crimes against property very harshly. Starting from some 50 capital crimes in 1689, they had added another 150 offences to what was called the "Bloody Code" by 1800, including stealing a sheep, shoplifting or picking a pocket.[2]

While having execution as the punishment for so many crimes was designed to make people law abiding out of fear for their lives, an unintended outcome was that ways were found to avoid having to kill so many offenders. Victims of crime sought direct compensation instead of pressing charges; partial verdicts could be given, finding the accused guilty of a lesser, non-capital crime; or juries could go against the evidence and deliver a not guilty verdict even if the case had been proven.[3] After conviction, an offender could receive a royal pardon which spared their life.

The other means by which execution was sidestepped after 1718 was using the new punishment of transportation, which sentenced offenders to a period of servitude outside of the country. While very serious crimes like murder continued to be punished by execution, lesser capital crimes became transportable offences, and some capital sentences could be commuted to transportation. Terms of transportation were 7 years, 14 years or for the term of their natural life (after 1813 defined as 15 years) according to the severity of the crime. Offences for which transportation became the punishment ranged widely, from destroying turnpike roads, cutting down trees and pickpocketing goods worth more than one shilling to being out at night with a blackened face, concealing the birth of a stillborn child and forgery.[4]

For imperial countries like Britain, France, Spain and Portugal, with surplus populations at home and labour shortages in their colonies, convict transportation solved several problems: punishment of offenders, deterrence of future offending and providing labour for the development of colonies.[5] The first destination for Britain's transportees were the North American Thirteen Colonies which received 50,000 British convicts between 1718 and 1775, with most going to farms in Maryland and Virginia. While Australian historians have been fascinated by convicts, American historians have not paid them much attention and they are generally not recognised as part of the national history of the United States.[6] Transportation across the Atlantic stopped with the American Declaration of Independence in 1776 and a decade later, with concern growing about the number of people sentenced to transportation who were being held in temporary facilities in Britain, it was decided to use convicts to establish a new colony at Botany Bay.

Although it was expensive and risky sending convicts to a such a far off place which had not been revisited since it was claimed for Britain by Lieutenant James Cook in 1770, the distance was counted as a positive. Not only would it be difficult for time-expired or escaping convicts to return to Britain, but the penal colony would serve as a trading and naval base from which British could extend its activity in the region.[7] The government took on responsibility for transporting, housing, clothing and feeding its convict workforce and providing them with basic medical care, and in return, convicts had to follow orders with regard to their behaviour, where they would live, who they could associate with and what work they would do for the term of their sentences.

With some variations in levels of freedom and compulsion over time and location, this was the model on which each of the Australian penal colonies operated over the next 80 years. Transportation was a punishment short of death but was still intended to be so harsh that it would operate as a deterrent to crime in Britain. For those who were transported, it was intended to have a reforming effect. Having laboured through their sentences and living in a place with work for all who wanted it, once free, former convicts could earn an honest livelihood for themselves and would not have to commit further crimes. But what if the convicts and former convicts did not want to work? What if transportation instead created a society in which crime was normalised? These questions have occupied historians for several generations.

Historians and Convicts

Writing about convict historiography (the study of histories and how they are written), Deborah Oxley referred to the "unlikely love affair of the past hundred years between historians and convicts."[8] She has a point, although it is a rather one-sided relationship, in which the convicts mean much more to the historians than historians do to convicts, and many historians did not show much love at all. The story of historians' changing views of convicts has been told many times, including by Oxley. Historiographers tracing the different understandings of convicts point to a number of factors which made ideas change over time, mainly stemming from the historian's wider research interests and how they reflected the values and priorities of their own times. As Manning Clark wrote, "Every generation writes its own history in its own image."[9]

Allowing that there are many other factors also at play, here I will focus in on the historians' methods and how these methods affected the kinds of research questions pursued and the answers developed. In the first years after the end of transportation, Australians tended to suppress knowledge of the convicts while fearing that their influence was negative and still present. As direct memory of convictism was lost, historians continued to minimise the role convicts had played in establishing the colonies and their characters, focusing instead on free settlers, explorers, gold seekers and the inland pastoral industry.

By the late nineteenth century, there were some alternative views being put forward, as Anna Clark explored in her review of how Australian history has been written.[10] The cause of the convicts was taken up by Frank Donohue in his *The Bulletin's History of Botany Bay* (1888). He interpreted them as blameless victims of a disgraceful criminal justice system and argued that the real villains of early settler colonial Australia were the agents of British imperialism. This suited the stance of the nationalist and republican *Bulletin*, which spoke on behalf of the more radical of the white, male workers who were the natural successors of the convicts.

This position was taken up again in the 1920s by University of Sydney Professor George Arnold Wood, himself an immigrant from Britain. Wood had access to original sources including the 1838 Molesworth Report to the British government which had recommended that transportation stop, government documents reproduced in the *Historical Records of Australia*, works by contemporary observers of convicts and memoirs from officials and free settlers.[11] He read them through the lens of work being published on the consolidation of land ownership in eighteenth-century Britain and how it left former small holders and rural workers without a livelihood.[12] By directing his attention to the convicts from rural areas who were transported for crimes like poaching or stealing food and to positive accounts of convict reform from figures like Governor Lachlan Macquarie, he concluded that while they might have been stupid and lazy, convicts were essentially innocent victims of elites whose efforts to survive left them criminalised by an excessively harsh legal system and subject to the monstrous punishment of transportation.

A new generation of historians in the post–Second World War period looked further into written records created during the convict period and reached differing conclusions. One was Russel Ward who added bush poetry and the words of folk songs to the more official sources used by Wood. Based in part on this evidence, he argued in his 1958 book, the *Australian Legend*, that the Australian national character was formed during the colonial period and that traits possessed by the convicts could be seen in it: being rough and ready in manners, quick to call out pretentiousness and sticking to their mates even if they were wrong. Hating officiousness and the exercise of authority especially in military officers and policemen were other traits Ward linked with convict influences.[13] He accepted that the convicts were a distinctive group with its own outlook and found they left cultural traces only lightly touched by criminality.

Ward's contemporary Manning Clark focused on the sources written by officials within the convict system, clergymen responsible for their spiritual guidance and landholders to whom convicts were assigned as workers. They said that the convicts were lazy, unskilled, uncooperative and generally the worst type of colonists imaginable. Many of the records the authorities created of course focused on troublesome convicts who resisted the terms of their servitude and broke the regulations imposed on them. Relying on sources like these, Clark followed a theory articulated in the mid-nineteenth century by so-called social explorers like Henry Mayhew who wrote about what he observed in the streets of London. Mayhew concluded that there was a large group of people there who were intellectually underdeveloped, immoral, loved cruelty and fighting, hated regular work and had no respect for property rights. Their involvement with crime was habitual or professional rather than casual or accidental and together they constituted a criminal class.[14] Accepting this premise, Clark concluded that many of the transported convicts were part of this criminal class and brought their distinctive outlook with them to Australia.[15]

Clark did not limit himself to traditional close readings of written sources but was amongst the first to supplement descriptive sources with sampling of the documents created to record the convicts from the time of arrest and charging, through their trial, sentencing and transportation. This information was consolidated in muster records (more frequently referred to as convict indents) as convicts disembarked from their transports and added to as they moved through the penal system, including any offences and punishments. They will be considered further in Chapter 6. Lloyd Robson took up this approach in the early 1960s to bring together a one in 20 sample of convict indents. The application of quantitative methodologies enabled historians for the first time to start to develop an overall view of the convicts which was somewhat less distorted by the biases of critics describing them, although still influenced by the historians' own interests and assumptions. When writing about the 25,000 female convicts transported to NSW and VDL, Robson assumed that since negative written assessments of them were so unanimous, they must be

Figure 3.1 There are not many images of serving convicts and this one of a grizzled assortment of male convicts, some in chains, being led out of Sydney's Hyde Park Barracks for their day's work in the late 1820s helps to support negative interpretations like those of Manning Clark.

Source: Augustus Earle, A Government Jail Gang, Sydney, N.S. Wales, from *Views in New South Wales and Van Diemen's Land. Australian Scrap Book.* London: Charles Hullmandel, 1830 held by State Library of NSW, Z/MRB/F981/E.

correct but sought to test them against the data from the indents.[16] His conclusions tended to echo the written sources, foregrounding sex work (recorded as being "on the town"), repeat offending and associations with the poor, overcrowded inner area of London explored by Mayhew. Robson quickly passed over contrary evidence, including that two-thirds of the women had no association with London; that only 13% were recorded as having been prostitutes; that "almost all of them" were said to have worked as domestic servants; and that many committed crimes he dismissed as pathetic or dull. His selective interpretation allowed him to conclude that convict women fit with the criminal class theory, what he called a *classe dangerouse*.

Work like this helped to fire up feminist historians to challenge what they saw as unfair characterisations. From the mid-1960s, they began their own research into convict women. Women historians went back to the written sources but read them against the grain, at first focusing in on the inequities which stemmed from women being allowed only two roles in the colonies: damned whores and god's police.[17] They found that women did reoffend in the colonies but argued that they had no choice as they had so few opportunities for legitimate employment. Ongoing research refined this early conclusion in part by applying a different methodology. Instead of drawing upon the sources which tended to focus on the most troublesome convicts, they examined cohorts of women, such as those who arrived on single ship or, in the case of Portia Robinson's work, all of the women transported to NSW.[18] This was an effective way of achieving a more balanced view of convicts, as it captured the lives not only those who reoffended but the often much less documented women who set up businesses, married or found steady employment, in contradiction to the expectations of members of a criminal class.

With the increasing access to computing in the 1980s, it became feasible to greatly expand the scale of projects analysing convict records. The Convict Workers project undertook a more ambitious study sampling data from the indents of 19,711 convicts who arrived in NSW between 1817 and 1840, one quarter of the total for that period, and using it to provide new insights into convicts as part of a global system of forced migration of workers rather than a peculiar Australianism.[19] This allowed them to answer new questions about these convicts, discovering their average age – 26, that they were more literate than the population in Britain and that 5 out of 6 were male. The heavy skew male is not unusual in criminal populations, as women are less likely to be convicted of crimes, for reasons that will be explored in Chapter 8. Most interestingly for the criminal class debate were the huge array of work-related skills reported by the convicts and attested to by the fact that many of their crimes occurred in their workplaces. These were not people who had lived by habitual crime but those who had committed opportunistic theft. They were young adults in their prime, with skills and basic education, along with what might generously be considered a drive to better themselves.

Having this quantitative picture of overall characteristics of convicts enabled historians of the turn of the millennium to drill down to very fine-grained studies of individuals or small groups of convicts. New types of evidence were used by applying methodologies relevant to visual and material sources, revealing novel perspectives on convicts. Two topics, tattoos and love tokens, drew attention to how convicted people and those who cared about them created means of remembrance.[20] The tendency of this research was to show that convicts were not disconnected outcasts before or after their sentences but valued members of partnerships, families and communities.

The digital revolution of the twenty-first century gave historians access to powerful new analytical tools to apply in methodologies which can drill down from high-level statistical averages to the experience of a single individual. This began with the digitisation of official records, newspapers and private papers, greatly expanding access to evidence previously only available by visiting libraries and archives in person. For printed documents, the process of finding references to a topic was reduced from days to seconds. Handwritten records required the additional step of transcription. This role was taken on in some cases by researchers themselves but increasingly by citizen social scientists who volunteered their time to read and write down the words and figures in these documents and enter them into data fields.[21] The second stage was the use of computer programs to analyse these data, drawing out averages and extremes, and revealing change or continuity over time. Leading projects including the Digital Panopticon and Founders and Survivors have greatly advanced understandings of convict life courses.

These projects have also been able to address some of the remaining uncertainty around the criminal class theory, as Hamish Maxwell-Stewart demonstrates in the essay accompanying this chapter. Once their sentences had expired and they regained the freedoms enjoyed by other citizens, most convicts used their prior skills or those they had acquired in the colony to support themselves and did not reoffend. Those who had children did not raise them with a distorted morality which launched them on their own criminal careers.[22] The experience of transportation and forced labour, with systematic progress towards freedom with the ticket of leave system (a form of parole), is now viewed as having been much more effective at achieving reform than other approaches to punishment, including modern incarceration. Hamish Maxwell-Stewart and Michael Quinlan argue that the idea of the criminal class was kept alive by those who found it useful to devalue and degrade the convicts to keep them as an almost sub-human group who could be brutalised into providing cheap labour. This seems to be a final definitive answer to the criminal class question. British historians have argued that such a group did not exist there, and the evidence now available for Australia does not support its emergence out of the convict system.

Testing the Handkerchief Hypothesis

Disproving the criminal class theory does not mean that my students were right in thinking that all convicts were innocent victims who went on to lead law-abiding lives in Australia. Some had extensive criminal records and broke not just the additional rules imposed on them as convicts but the general criminal law both during their sentences and after they regained their freedom. This sometimes stemmed from difficulties finding employment or from alcoholism but once the cycle of law breaking in the colonies began, it was hard to escape, not only because of the usual interplay of factors which entrench disadvantage, but because of assumptions about convicts in the wider society. Former convicts did not enjoy any of the leniency offered to first offenders. When they were incarcerated, their dependents suffered from the loss of income and children could be placed in care, with its high correlation with future offending. This scenario plays out in the Jenny Green case treated in Chapter 7. For those observing at the time, it was easy to blame intergenerational patterns of crime on inherited characteristics or attitudes learned in the home, but a more considered view must also take into account the structural factors which can lead to crime.

But what if we focused in on those who were transported for very minor crimes? Surely, they would not reoffend. Using the online database of crimes prosecuted at London's Central Criminal Court, the Old Bailey Online, we can test my students' understanding that convicts transported for stealing a loaf of bread or a handkerchief were not really criminal at all and so did not bring any tendency to crime with them which might have remained within the Australian national character.

Honing in on the theft of a handkerchief, although we now think of this theft as inconsequential, it was treated seriously in the pre-throw-away society of late-eighteenth and early-nineteenth-century Britain. While the less well-off might make do with a rag, or use their shirt sleeve for wiping their noses, the better off carried large handkerchiefs made of expensive materials like linen and silk. Handkerchiefs were given as gifts and personalised with initials or tokens of affection. A handkerchief was not an insubstantial piece of property and it had a resale value on the second-hand market, meaning that they were considered worth stealing. Further, this was not a theft of unattended goods, but stealing from the person, which was an affront to bodily integrity and the physical separation of classes, as well as the sanctity of private property. Victims often reported feeling the offender's hands on them as the crime was committed. Finally, pickpocketing was viewed in this period as an entry-level crime from which boys and youths would graduate to more serious criminal activity.[23] By decisively punishing those who picked pockets, it was thought that the escalation of crime could be avoided.

Entering handkerchief in the Keyword box of the Old Bailey Online's search page and restricting the search to the Time Period "1787 to 1868" (the years during which transportation to Australia was undertaken), the Verdict to "Guilty > all subcategories" and the Sentence to "transportation" identifies over 6000 people whose presence in Australia was linked with having stolen a handkerchief, out of 160,000 transported (3.8%). Reading the accounts of these convictions quickly reveals that few of them had *only* stolen a handkerchief. In many cases, the handkerchief was just one item in a larger suite of goods taken from their lodgings, their workplace or a shop. The charge these people faced was grand larceny.

We can drill down to those who stole only a handkerchief by refining the search to just the Offence "Theft > pocketpicking." This reduces the total to some 2700. To take one example, 19-year-old William Gullen was caught stealing a handkerchief from Frederick Burnett in London in 1838. Burnett was walking in the street and "felt something at my pocket." He turned and found Gullen close behind him, grabbed him and drew the attention of policeman Joseph Winter who was standing nearby. Gullen was quick to drop Burnett's handkerchief on the ground, but when he was searched, two silk patterned handkerchiefs were found in the seat of Gullen's trousers and one in his hat. Both Gullen and his companion 18-year-old Thomas Baker who was in the area but played no direct role in the theft were found guilty of stealing from the person and sentenced to transportation for seven years.

Having been convicted of the minor crime of stealing a handkerchief worth two shillings and sixpence might suggest that Gullen would be one of the transportees who served his sentence with little incident and then embraced the greater life opportunities available in the colonies as compared with the streets of London. Reference to his life archive on the Digital Panopticon site, which follows the convicted from the Old Bailey to Australia, quickly shows that this was not the case.[24] The first detail it reveals is that this theft was not his first offence. He already had two convictions, at least one for pickpocketing, before his 1838 trial and transportation to NSW on the ship *Portsea.* Convict records for this colony are available in the NSW State Archives and Records, but fragments of a convict's life can also be found in the National Library of Australia's Trove online newspaper database. Using his name as the search term and limiting the years to his conviction year of 1838 and a possible life span up to 1900, it soon becomes apparent that Gullen continued to offend in NSW.

The early years of Gullen's sentence did not leave any traces in the newspapers. He was issued with a Ticket of Leave in 1847 allowing him to work on his own account as long as he remained in the Windsor District northwest of Sydney. When he was found 50 km to the south in Liverpool in July, his Ticket of Leave was revoked, before being reinstated for the Sydney district later that year, only to have it once more cancelled for disorderly conduct in June 1848.[25] Despite these infractions, Gullen's Certificate of Freedom was issued in August 1848, his sentence having been extended to 10 years. This was Gullen's opportunity to leave behind his criminal associations. However, within a month, he was apprehended by a police constable at the Hope tavern in the Barrack Lane area of Sydney and charged with burglary in company with two others.[26] Gullen was sentenced at the next sitting of the court of Quarter Sessions to 3 years in an ironed gang. He absconded from the Woolloomooloo gang in December before being recaptured early the following year.[27]

There is no further record of William Gullen in the newspapers until 1865, when he was charged with manslaughter after a drunken brawl with Marrickville quarryman John Craig at the Napoleon Inn in Kensington Street, Sydney.[28] Based on the victim's reputation as a quarrelsome drunk, his greater size and strength and Gullen's remorse, the jury in the coroner's inquest found that Gullen was incited to fight and the coroner recommended that he face a charge of manslaughter rather than murder in the Central Criminal Court at Darlinghurst.[29] At his trial in October, his employers said that having known Gullen for 15 years (i.e., since he was released from jail) they found him to be a quiet, hard-working and sober married man with a large family.[30] Gullen was found guilty with the jury strongly recommending mercy and he was sentenced to just three months in jail, being listed in the *NSW Police Gazette* as having been discharged from Darlinghurst Gaol in December.[31] Gullen was in trouble again in 1869, this time appearing in Sydney's Central Police Court for damage to a premises in Pitt Street.[32] Two years later, Gullen was ordered by the Police Court to keep the peace for six months and pay £40 in fines and sureties for using threatening language and then fined 20 shillings or a week in jail for assaulting a Sarah Woods.[33]

It was notable that none of the references to Gullen in the newspaper mentioned his status as a time-expired convict as might have been expected given the general suspicion of current and former convicts as potential reoffenders. Specific laws had been put in place in the 1830s to control former "Transported Felons," including requiring them to register with the police.[34] This omission suggests a delicacy around revealing this information publicly which also contributed to these acts lapsing in 1853. Former convicts were to be allowed to get on with their lives without a label, although the public often attributed ongoing crime to them.

In 1880, a funeral notice appeared, not of William but of his beloved wife Ann, aged just 51, starting from the home of their married daughter.[35] In his early 60s, Gullen was still working, appearing in an account of a case of smallpox in Glebe Point in 1881 as a person employed to look after a property and an Aboriginal man named Jemmy who was found to be suffering with the disease.[36] Gullen lived until 1896.

In terms of historical research, Gullen was a good choice to try to follow because his name was unusual. There was another convict named William Gullen sent to Van Diemen's Land and so care had to be taken not to mistake events from his life for those in our William Gullen's biography. With his more common name, Gullen's co-accused Thomas Baker would be much more difficult to follow with any confidence. In this case, he was transported to Van Diemen's Land, ensuring the former accomplices were well separated, and he can be found on the Digital Panopticon.[37] Records there show that Baker also had a previous conviction, for hawking (street selling) without a licence and was sent out on the *Layton* arriving in December 1839. Just a few months later, he died in the hospital at Hobart. Although there is no information on the cause of death, this was during an outbreak of the highly infectious disease, typhus.[38] Cases like this show the random nature of the impact of transportation that was of concern to the Molesworth enquiry. Baker was an accomplice rather than a perpetrator of the crime and yet his sentence became death at just 20 years old, while the leader went on to have a family and live into his 70s.

Having followed William Gullen through the records, it is tempting to draw more general conclusions about our question of whether being established by convicts meant that the Australian colonies were particularly marked by crime. In this case, it is clear that while Gullen built a life for himself, he did continue to reoffend, committing crimes of greater seriousness than his original theft of a handkerchief. This single case does not overturn the work of the dozens of historians who have shown that reform was the usual outcome of the convict system. Factors drawing Gullen back to crime could include habit since his theft of the handkerchief was not his first but his third prosecution. Involvement in burglary very soon after the end of his sentence in 1848 could indicate that it was not easy for him to find honest work at the end of the decade of Australia's first deep economic depression, especially in light of the prejudices against former convicts. Gullen's long period without any recorded offences through the 1850s and early 1860s again follows the economic cycle with the boom years of the gold rushes, during which his employers found him to be a reliable worker and good family man. Although described in court as usually quiet and sober, he was very drunk on the night of the fight and was known to the publican, suggesting he was a regular customer. Later charges of threatening language and assault of a woman also hint at intoxication. Many former convicts drank to excess in what was then seen as a character flaw but now could be understood as a way of coping with past trauma. Reading the newspaper accounts for fine details like these and placing Gullen in a wider context helps to explain why some who passed through the convict system were able to successfully reintegrate into civil life while others remained on its margins. At times, either could re-offend. A close study of individual lives enriches and nuances understandings of the past, but general conclusions must be much more broadly based.

Conclusion

Australia is distinctive in having so many of its original settler colonists being unwilling emigrants. They were sent halfway around the world as a punishment, most commonly for theft. Opinions about whether having this distinctive founding population has had a lasting impact on Australia have varied over time. Convicts have been considered victims of a harsh legal system, members of a criminal class, workers and as people who were part of families and networks, before the scale at which they were studied again expanded in the twenty-first century, making individual convict experience into data points which can tell new, often more positive stories about their contribution to Australian society.

All of these contrasting views of convicts make one thing clear, and that is that convicts have had a long-term impact on Australia and Australians, and how we are viewed by the rest of the world. While the current understanding is that they did not constitute a criminal underclass and did not generally continue to commit crimes once they had left the convict system, there has always been anxiety that they did, and we will see this played out in the later chapters of this book.

Suggested Readings

Nicholas, Stephen ed. *Convict Workers, Reinterpreting Australia's Past*. Melbourne: Cambridge University Press, 1988.

Duffield, Ian and James Bradley, eds. *Representing Convicts: New Perspectives on Convict Forced Labour Migration*. London: Leicester University Press, 1997.

Anderson, Clare, ed. *A Global History of Convicts and Penal Colonies*. London: Bloomsbury Academic, 2018.

Maxwell-Stewart, Hamish and Michael Quinlan. *Unfree Workers: Insubordination and Resistance in Convict Australia, 1788–1860*. Singapore: Palgrave, 2022.

Maxwell-Stewart, Hamish, Kris Inwood and Jim Stankovich. "The Prison and the Colonial Family." *History of the Family* 20, no. 2 (2015): 231–48.

ESSAY: BRITISH AND IRISH CONVICTS AND THE IDEA OF A CRIMINAL CLASS

Hamish Maxwell-Stewart

The notion that the convicts lagged to Australia constituted a criminal class gained currency in the nineteenth century largely because it was useful to characterise these unwilling migrants as less than fully human. As quintessential members of the idle poor, those who chose to live by crime and crime alone rendered themselves fitting objects of punishment. As James Mudie, a prominent New South Wales settler put it, convicts were "lower than the brutes, a disgrace to all animal existence."[39] It might even be argued that colonial labour exploitation conferred a benefit on those who had "left their country for their country's good," equipping the transported with an aptitude for future work. As such, "convictism," the ideology that underpinned penal transportation, had much in common with arguments used to justify slavery. Both forms of unfreedom, it was said, constituted a form of tutelage designed to rescue Africans and criminals from their former state of barbarism.[40]

The colonial administration's passion for record keeping – convicts were documented in extraordinary detail – provides opportunities to test such characterisations. Analysis of confessional data elicited on arrival reveals that most convicts did indeed confess to a history of prior interaction with the courts. This was especially true for those convicted in Scotland and by the Northern, Midland and Norfolk circuit courts. In these jurisdictions, judges and jurors were reluctant to sentence first-time offenders to transportation, while the Old Bailey, the Oxford and Western circuits and courts in Ireland had fewer scruples.[41] Convicts were certainly not innocent nor, in the majority of cases, were they strangers to criminal justice systems. This does not, however, mean that they were career criminals. Nearly all reported an occupation. While some undoubtedly lied about levels of skill, cross-reference to other recorded attributes suggests that most spoke the truth. Those who confessed to skilled work were more likely to bring money to Australia, and to be literate.[42] Many convict bodies were marked with the signs of work. A disproportionate number of cotton spinners had broken fingers (an occupational hazard associated with working with power looms) while miners were marked with scars stained blue from coal dust.[43] Ironically, the details of the offence that sent many into exile confirm their engagement with the legitimate economy. Thousands of women and men were transported for stealing objects associated with the occupations that they claimed.[44] Thus, while far from innocent, the vast majority were skilled in more than theft and as such did not fit the nineteenth-century definition of a professional criminal which hinged on failure to engage with work.

While it was common to argue that the transported lacked a history of employment, the care taken to allocate skills to appropriate work settings illustrates the extent to which prior work experience was both acknowledged and valued in practice.[45] That the demand for assigned servants regularly outstripped supply attests to the profits that could be made by hiring bond over free workers. As the opponents of transportation pointed out, however, a focus on skill meant that punishment fell unevenly across convict bodies. Some were in a better position to bargain than others and as a result were less likely to be dragged before a colonial court. Prosecution rates also fluctuated according to market demand. When the cost of maintaining an assigned servant rose, prosecutions increased, as did the number of sentences to hard labour. The magistrates' bench effectively operated as a labour bureau directing surplus convicts to the public works whenever the marginal benefit of hiring the unfree over free workers was reduced. The idea that convicts constituted a criminal class helped to disguise the vagaries of such state-sanctioned punishments.

While the length of a punishment record was widely interpreted as a measure of criminality, less than 10% of the 446,000 charges brought against serving convicts in Van Diemen's Land were for assaults and thefts. The remaining prosecutions were largely for work-related charges. Many of these were collective, an indication of the extent to which convict attempts to combine in order to protest against working conditions were savagely punished.[46]

The rate at which convicts reoffended post-release also requires some contextualisation. A study of subsequent reoffending by former convicts estimates that 21% of emancipists were reconvicted, although just under half of these arrests were for public order and other non-indictable offences. The majority of convicts appear to have avoided the courts post-release, reflecting colonial employment opportunities. Rates of rearrest were highest for those with a significant record of punishment under sentence. While this might reflect a proclivity to offend across the life course, it also suggests that attempts to extort compliance through high levels of punishment were counter-productive.[47] Other studies have failed to provide evidence that the children of convicts were at greater risk of prosecution than those whose parents had arrived free.[48] In short, despite societal fears that the convict stain would continue to permeate the courts long after the arrival of the last transport vessel, there is little evidence that this was in fact the case.

PRIMARY SOURCE: FEMALE CONVICT INDENTS, 1845

Indents were created for each newly transported convict. The range of information recorded was added to over time. By 1845, a wide-ranging biography was recorded, including their useful skills, past offences and relationships. Their "Callings" show that the women had experience in housekeeping, food preparation, childcare, washing and making clothing, which could readily be applied as they served their sentences in Van Diemen's Land. The "Relations" column suggests the impact of transportation on families, noting parents, siblings, partners and children left behind. You can find out more about the women as recorded in conduct records, description lists and muster rolls by entering their names in the search box of the Tasmanian Names Index: https://linctas.ent.sirsidynix.net.au/client/en_AU/names/

If you have trouble with this handwritten version of the indents, see advice on reading script provided by NSW State Records and Archives: https://www.records.nsw.gov.au/archives/collections-and-research/guides-and-indexes/handwritten-documents.

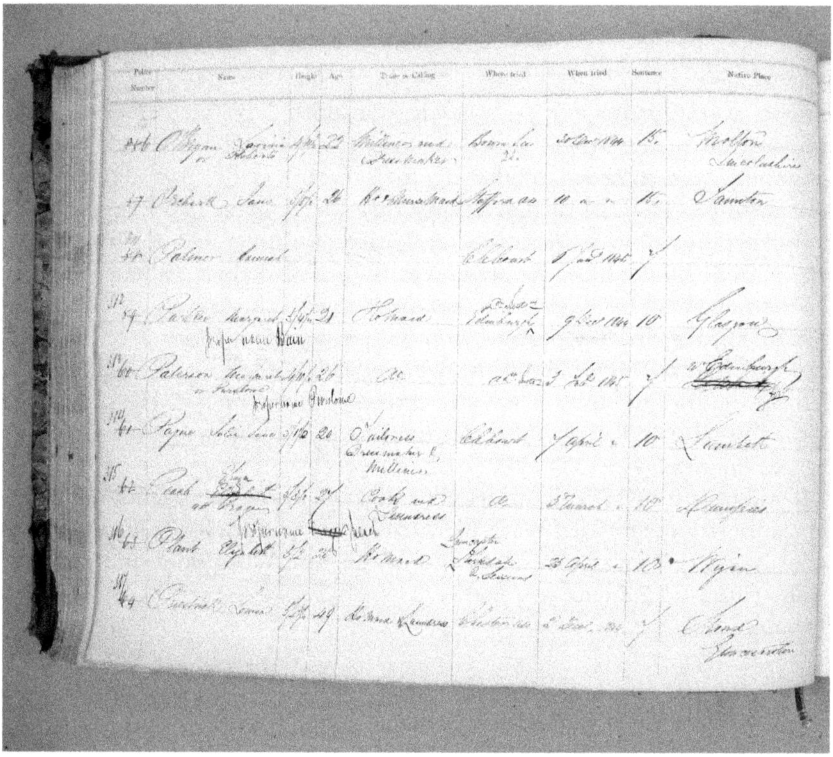

Figure 3.2 Indents of Female Convicts for the ship Lloyds, arrived 7 November 1845, Convict Department, Tasmania. Tasmanian Archives, CON15/1/3, images 212 and 213. (*Continued*)

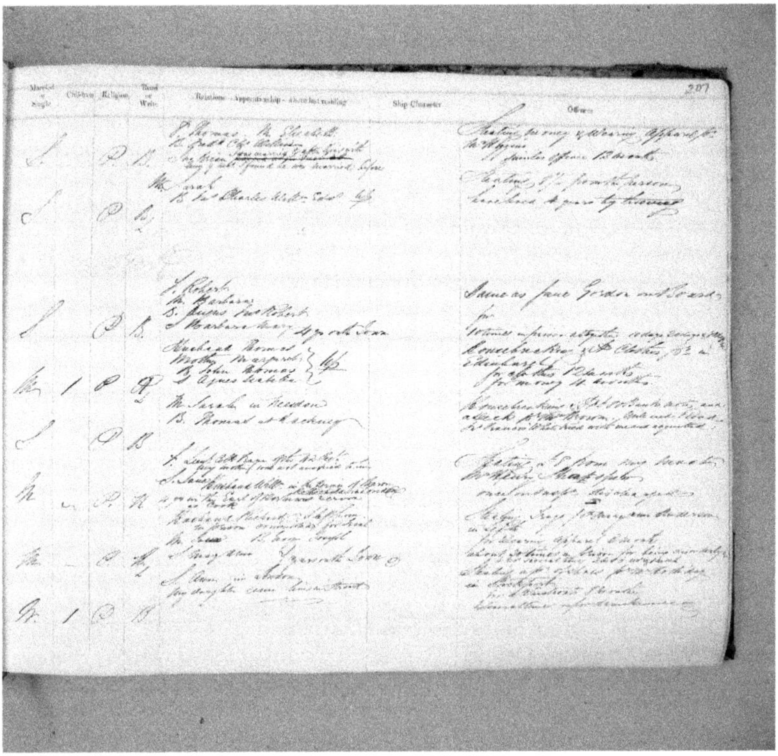

Figure 3.2 (*Continued*)

Notes

1 Staff writers, Fox Sports, "Australia Cricket Cheating Scandal: Barmy Army's Vile Sledge Targets Steve Smith, David Warner," Fox Sports, March 27, 2018, accessed28February2022,https://www.foxsports.com.au/cricket/australia-cricket-cheating-scandal-barmy-armys-vile-sledge-targets-steve-smith-david-warner/news-story/6f4a3ebc73e3f23e1ea97daea53ddcfa.

2 Michael R. Weisser, *Crime and Punishment in Early Modern Europe*, Brighton: The Harvester Press, 1982, 138–39.

3 Peter King and Richard Ward, "Rethinking the Bloody Code in Eighteenth-Century Britain: Capital Punishment at the Centre and on the Periphery," *Past & Present* 228, no. 1 (2015): 159–205.

4 A list of crimes for which people were transported to Australia is available here: Convict Records of Australia, https://convictrecords.com.au/crimes with links through to the individuals who committed those crimes.

5 For accounts of how other European nations used convict transportation, see Clare Anderson, ed. *A Global History of Convicts and Penal Colonies*, London: Bloomsbury Academic, 2018.

6 A. Roger Ekirch, *Bound for America: The Transportation of British Convicts to the Colonies, 1718–1775*, Oxford: Oxford University Press, 1987; Gwenda Morgan and Peter Rushton, *Eighteenth-Century Criminal Transportation: The Formation of the Criminal Atlantic*, New York: Palgrave Macmillan, 2004.

7 Angus R. McGillivery, "Convict Settlers, Seamen's Greens, and Imperial Designs at Port Jackson: A Maritime Perspective of British Settler Agriculture," *Agricultural History* 78, no. 3 (2004): 261–88.

8 Deborah Oxley, "Counting the Convicts: The Unlikely Love Affair between Convicts and Historians," Deborah Gare and David Ritter, eds. *Making Australian History: Perspectives on the Past since 1788*, Melbourne: Thomson, 2008, 115.

9 Manning Clark, foreword to *The Women of Botany Bay* by Portia Robinson, Melbourne: Penguin, 1993 [1988], vii.

10 Anna Clark, *Making Australian History*, Melbourne: Vintage, 2022, 66–7.

11 *The Historical Records of NSW* (https://nla.gov.au/nla.obj-343230396) and the *Historical Records of Australia* (https://nla.gov.au/nla.obj-442186184) can be accessed via the National Library of Australia's Trove database: https://trove.nla.gov.au/.

12 David Roberts in "'More Sinned Against Than Sinning': George Arnold Wood and the Noble Convict," Deborah Gare and David Ritter, eds. *Making Australian History: Perspectives on the Past Since 1788*, Melbourne: Thomson, 2008, 125. See footnotes in G.A. Wood, "Convicts," *Royal Australian Historical Society Journal and Proceedings* VIII, no. IV (1922): 177–208 (http://nla.gov.au/nla.obj-595105133).

13 Russel Ward, *The Australian Legend*, Melbourne: Oxford University Press, 1983 [1958], 1–2.

14 Henry Mayhew, *London Labour and the London Poor: Cyclopaedia of the Conditions and Earnings of Those That Will Work, Those That Cannot Work and Those That Will Not Work*, London: Charles Griffin, c1861, 29. https://collection.sl.nsw.gov.au/record/74VKPJJW5k6y

15 Manning Clark, "The Origins of the Convicts Transported to Eastern Australia, 1787–1852, Part I," *Historical Studies: Australia and New Zealand* 7, no. 26 (1956): 121–35; Part II, 7, no. 27 (1956): 314–27.

16 L.L. Robson, "The Origin of the Women Convicts Sent to Australia, 1787–1852," *Australian Historical Studies* 11, no. 41 (1963): 43–53.

17 Anne Summers, *Damned Whores and God's Police: The Colonisation of Women in Australia*, Sydney: NewSouth, 2016.

18 Babette Smith, *A Cargo of Women: Susannah Watson and the Convicts of the Princess Royal*, Sydney: Allen and Unwin, 2008; Portia Robinson, *The Women of Botany Bay*, Melbourne: Penguin, 1993.

19 Stephen Nicholas and Peter R. Shergold, "Convicts as Migrants," Stephen Nicholas, ed. *Convict Workers, Reinterpreting Australia's Past*, Melbourne: Cambridge University Press, 1988, 44.

20 Michele Field and Timothy Millett, eds. *Convict Love Tokens: The Leaden Hearts the Convicts Left Behind*, Adelaide: Wakefield Press, 1998; Simon Barnard, *Convict Tattoos: Marked Men and Women of Australia*, Melbourne: Text Publishing, 2016; Ian Duffield and James Bradley, eds. *Representing Convicts: New Perspectives on Convict Forced Labour Migration*, London: Leicester University Press, 1997.

21 An ongoing project at the time of writing is Criminal Characters, Investigating the Lives of Historical Offenders in Australia (https://criminalcharacters.com/). It provides an introduction and training on transcription and the opportunity to work with jail records from a number of Australian archives. Another opportunity is available on the Trove database where users are invited to become "Voluntroves" to correct text which has been inaccurately rendered by the computer transcription process (https://trove.nla.gov.au/help/become-voluntrove/text-correction).

22 Hamish Maxwell Stewart, Kris Inwood and Jim Stankovich, "Prison and the Colonial Family," *History of the Family* 20, no. 2 (2015): 241; 244.

23 Peter K. Andersson, "'Bustling, Crowding, and Pushing': Pickpockets and the Nineteenth-Century Street Crowd," *Urban History* 41, no. 2 (2014): 296.

24 William Gullen, Life Archive, *Digital Panopticon*, Version 1.2.1, accessed 30 October 2021, https://www.digitalpanopticon.org/life?id=obpdef1-1143-18380514.

25 "Tickets of Leave," *NSW Government Gazette* 65, July 30, 1847, 809; *NSW Government Gazette* 111, December 24, 1847, 1422; *NSW Government Gazette* 61, June 9, 1848, 734.

26 "Daring House Robbery," *Sydney Daily Advertiser*, September 18, 1848, 2.

27 Sydney Quarter Session, *Sydney Morning Herald*, November 6, 1848, 2; "Runaways Apprehended," *NSW Government Gazette* 12, January 19, 1849, 113.

28 "Fatal Encounter," *Empire* (Sydney), September 27, 1865, 5.

29 "Fatal Occurrence in Kensington-Street," *Sydney Morning Herald*, September 28, 1865, 4.

30 "Second Court," *Empire* (Sydney), October 3, 1865, 5.

31 *NSW Police Gazette and Weekly Record of Crime* 49, December 6, 1865, 427.

32 Central Police Court, *Sydney Morning Herald*, January 8, 1869, 5.

33 "Police Courts, This Day," *Evening News* (Sydney), January 10, 1871, 3; "Central Police Court – Tuesday," *Empire* (Sydney), January 11, 1871, 2.

34 These include, in NSW, the 1834 Transported Offenders and Suspected Robbers Apprehension Act and the 1838 An Act to facilitate the Apprehension of Transported Felons and Offenders Illegally at Large and of Persons found with Arms and suspected to be Robbers. Michael Eburn, "Outlawry in Colonial Australia: The Felons Apprehension Acts 1865–1899," *Australian and New Zealand Law and History* E-Journal 6 (2005): 86, note 47 (https://www.austlii.edu.au/cgibin/viewdoc/au/journals/ANZLawHisteJl/2005/6.html?context=1;query=outlawry;mask_path=au/journals/ANZLawHisteJl).

35 "Funerals," *Sydney Morning Herald*, October 4, 1880, 10.

36 "Smallpox," *Sydney Morning Herald*, September 20, 1881, 6.

37 Thomas Baker, Life Archive, *Digital Panopticon*, Version 1.2.1, accessed 31 October 2021, https://www.digitalpanopticon.org/life?id=obpdef2-1143-18380514

38 "The Fever – Official Report," *Colonial Times*, March 24, 1840, 4.

39 J. Mudie, *The Felonry of New South Wales: Being a Faithful Picture of the Real Romance of Life in Botany Bay. With Anecdotes of Botany Bay Society*. London: Whaley and Co, 1837, 122.

40 L. Ford, "Reconfiguring the Old South: 'Solving' the Problem of Slavery, 1787–1838," *The Journal of American History* 95, no. 1 (2008): 95–122.
41 Tasmanian Archives, Conduct Records, Con 31, 33, 40 and 41.
42 H. Maxwell-Stewart, "The State, Convicts and Longitudinal Analysis," *Australian Historical Studies* 47, no. 3 (2016): 420–3.
43 H. Maxwell-Stewart and J. Bradley, "'Behold the Man': Power, Observation and the Tattooed Convict," *Australian Studies* 12, no. 1 (1997): 71–97.
44 S. Nicholas and P. R. Shergold, "Convicts as Workers," S. Nicholas, ed. *Convict Workers*, Cambridge: Cambridge University Press, 1988, 66–7.
45 K. Reid, *Gender, Crime and Empire*, Manchester: Manchester University Press, 2007, 134.
46 H. Maxwell-Stewart and M. Quinlan, *Unfree Workers: Insubordination and Resistance in Convict Australia 1788–1860*, Singapore: Palgrave, 2022, 287–302.
47 R. Kippen and H. Maxwell-Stewart, "'What Is a Man That is a Bolter to Do? I Would Steal the Governor's axe Rather Than Starve': Old Lags and Recidivism in the Tasmanian Penal Colony," James Campbell and Vivien Miller, eds. *Transnational Penal Cultures*, London: Routledge, 2014, 165–83.
48 H. Maxwell-Stewart, K. Inwood, and J. Stankovich, "The Prison and the Colonial Family," *History of the Family* 20, no. 2 (2015): 231–48.

4 Aboriginal People and Settler Colonial Law

In Chapter 3, I argued against the idea that the people transported to Australia were a criminal class, an underworld who replicated their lawless and immoral lives in a new setting. Transportees *were* convicted lawbreakers, but most were not career criminals. Rather, they were opportunists who took a chance (or perhaps several chances) to steal, were caught and ended up on the other side of the world. If we shift our focus, taking a step back from these individuals to the imperial endeavour which brought them to Australia, there was a much more serious crime being perpetrated. The convicts can be seen as mere pawns in a larger game, as their labour was being used to steal land on a massive scale. Like other offenders, the British government took what they wanted for their own purposes, without negotiation or payment, and then found ways to justify their actions. As part of their crime, they not only disrupted Aboriginal Law but incrementally imposed their own foreign law on people who at first had no understanding of it. The results were predictable and familiar from other colonised places. Aboriginal people were accorded limited protection by the English law but came to be disproportionately prosecuted under it.

From this perspective, the rural poachers, light-fingered maids and London pickpockets may have begun as a cross-section of the British working class but were made into more serious criminals in Australia. More than a criminal class, they were representatives of a thieving nation, taking land, resources, autonomy and well-being from Indigenous Australians. Focusing on the first 50 years of colonisation, it will be shown that Aboriginal people were sometimes protected by the imported legal system but more often treated as though they were outside of it, being subjected to violence by civilians and the state without the legal protection provided to other British subjects. Over time, efforts were made to bring Aboriginal people under the discipline of the criminal law, processing them through a legal system they did not fully understand. In this, we can see very clearly how systems of laws which purport to be fair, neutral and as the image of Justice suggests, blindly applied to people regardless of their gender, skin colour, religion or language, were actually "instrument[s] of domination" used to establish and maintain authority.[1] This chapter will consider what happened when Aboriginal people became subject to English laws.

DOI: 10.4324/9781003273561-5

Introducing English Law

As soon as possession of NSW was officially taken on 26 January 1788 and the commissions establishing the authority of the governor and English law there were read out on 7 February, everyone who lived in the eastern half of the continent of Australia nominally became a British subject, ruled over by George III, the current British monarch.[2] Since this was a colony established by occupation, in a land deemed to be *terra nullius* – that is, claimed by no one, with no pre-existing system of law or even public order – it was considered a blank slate, where British law could be imposed.[3] Notionally, military officers, convicts and Aboriginal people all had the protection of British law and were subject to it from that time.

However, this did not really apply. Early relations between Aboriginal people and colonists were cautious, but each group inevitably broke the laws of the other. The British entered into people's Country without permission, not performing correct ceremonies, disturbing sacred sites, and using soils, plants and animals in disrespectful ways, without sharing. Further, convicts and the official parties broke what would be their own laws if the victims were British: stealing Aboriginal people's tools and weapons as curiosities, trespassing and kidnapping both adults and children.

In some instances, convicts were prosecuted for theft from Aboriginal people. In 1789, sixteen convicts armed with clubs and tools went from Sydney to Kamay (Botany Bay) with the intention of stealing fishing gear and spears. Having been previously subjected to such raids, the Kameygal people defended themselves, killing one and wounding seven.[4] Marines were sent to force the would-be thieves back to Sydney where they were flogged, as was a man who stole a fishing line from an Aboriginal person in 1791. Generally, however, the British people did not see their laws as restricting their behaviour towards Aboriginal people. Even for more serious matters, as in 1799 when several men were found guilty of murdering two Aboriginal boys by the Court of Criminal Jurisdiction, uncertainty led the governor to seek advice from London. He was directed not to punish the offenders as settlers had a right to protect their property.[5]

Subjects But Outside the Law

On the other side, Aboriginal people were also rarely prosecuted for assault or theft from the settler colonists in these early years. In 1805, Judge Advocate Atkins ruled that Aboriginal people did not understand the English language or law sufficiently to be brought before the courts for trial. While this was logical, it meant that those who felt themselves to be wronged by Aboriginal people found other means of retaliation, deterrence and punishment, often through direct action.[6]

These attempts to manage relations between invaders and invaded through the application of imported law were set aside in each colony when acts of violence between settlers and Aboriginal people escalated, sometimes very soon after the arrival of settler colonists, but more generally after a period of uneasy coexistence. When the violence became too disruptive to settler society, Aboriginal people were placed outside of the legal system and treated as internal enemies of the state. Governors declared martial law in defined regions. Used in cases of rebellion, martial law meant that the usual civil and criminal law were suspended and troops could be sent in against civilians.[7] Stephen Gapps, author of the *Sydney Wars*, has shown that between 1788 and 1817, both the British authorities and Aboriginal people understood their hostile relations as a state of war and organised their actions accordingly.[8] This warfare continued as colonists advanced into the interior. In the Bathurst district in 1824, 75 troops were sent in after a series of cattle killings. Strong resistance from the Wiradjuri people, led by Windradyne, escalated into a guerrilla war and massacres of Wiradjuri women and children.[9] Under martial law, not only could Aboriginal people be directly attacked, but magistrates were allowed to dispense summary justice, having them punished without any formal charges being laid or hearings undertaken.

A similar situation developed in lutruwita (Van Diemen's Land, abbreviated to VDL) where, if anything, the violence between the settlers and the palawa people was more extensive. Palawa warriors acquired firearms which they used along with spears and clubs against settlers on farms, killing colonists and their livestock and frightening some back to the towns.[10] Trying to get on a better footing, a four-strip pictogram was produced in the late 1820s by surveyor general George Frankland to distribute the message that laws were to be applied equally. The message was painted on some 100 boards which were attached to trees where they would be seen both by the Palawa and by settler colonists, many of whom were illiterate. In the images on these proclamation boards, settler and Aboriginal men, women and children could be seen interacting on equal terms (see Primary Source 4). When a member of one group killed a member of the other, he was shown as facing justice and being punished with execution. The message about equality before the law was not honoured and government orders to capture rather than kill Aboriginal people were ignored. The armed conflict known as the Black Wars which had been raging since 1824 continued until 1831, aided by the declaration of martial law over the whole colony in 1830.

The same pattern was repeated as each colony was established. Crimes by Aboriginal people were considered not to be able to prosecuted under the ordinary British law and were therefore countered with direct violence. The new settlement started in 1829 at the Swan River in Western Australia was a free enterprise colony, peopled by those with capital and workers they had contracted to come with them. It was no less dangerous or lawless than the convict colonies for the local Whadjuk people. As in the east, their resistance to the theft and occupation of their country, driven by hunger as they were denied access to yam beds and as animal populations were decimated, was met with a mixture of military and police action.[11] In 1832, the leading defenders of the land, Yagan, Munday and Midgegooroo were declared outlaws who could be captured or shot on sight. When Yagan was shot by a 13-year-old settler colonist seeking reward money in 1833, his head was removed, smoked to preserve it and ultimately (like the remains of many other Indigenous people) sent to Britain. There it was put on display, beginning a period of exile which only ended after a long campaign by descendants for its return, being buried in 2010 in a memorial park on the Upper Swan River.[12] Clashes continued after Yagan's death, with one to the southwest of Perth in 1834 given the name the Battle of Pinjarra leading to the deaths of up to 35 Whadjuk people as well as the superintendent of police.

Back in NSW, a mounted paramilitary-style police force was established in 1826 to be used to keep order outside of the settlements. Consisting of soldiers paid by the army but with horses and equipment provided by the colonial government and supplemented by local civilian volunteers, the deployment of mounted police reflected the uncertainty about whether Aboriginal people should be dealt with as lawbreakers or enemies of the state. A detachment of the mounted police commanded by Lieutenant Nathaniel Lowe was deployed to the Hunter Valley in 1826 to put a stop to a series of violent raids on huts and farms and robberies of travellers by Wonnarua people, most likely working with Wiradjuri allies.[13] Although suspects were to be taken into custody so they could face trial, the mounted police instead proceeded as if at war, shooting them during encounters or as they tried to escape. In August, Lowe shot dead a suspect known as Jackey-Jackey who was being held in the Wallis Plains (later Maitland) watch house. While earlier actions of this type had been tolerated by the Sydney authorities, such a clear deviation from official orders led to the prosecution of Lowe for murder, the first time in the colony that a military officer had been tried for killing an Aboriginal person.[14] At his trial in 1827, his counsel tried to have the case dismissed, arguing that Lowe had no option but to shoot Aboriginal people because they could not be prosecuted for their offences. This argument was rejected but the testimony of witnesses was undermined and Lowe was found not guilty by the military jury, which deliberated for just 5 minutes.

The issue of whether Aboriginal people could face trial for offences was raised again in 1829, when Chief Justice Francis Forbes decided not to proceed with a case against an Aboriginal man named Ballard who had killed another Aboriginal man at the Domain in Sydney. Forbes ruled that crimes between Aboriginal people (referred to as *inter se*) remained outside of the colonial law if the actions could be understood as being part of their own customs for addressing wrongs. While describing such practices as both barbarous and shocking, Forbes recognised their validity, stating that they were founded in natural justice and comparable with the ancient law of England.[15] Further, he argued that it would be unjust to subject Aboriginal people to a legal process in which they did not have any knowledge of the language, law or social practices. However, in cases which involved a settler colonist either as victim or perpetrator, he said that an Aboriginal person should be subject to the English criminal law, assuming, rather optimistically, that it would afford equal protection to all.

Extending the Reach of the Law

An experiment in responding to Aboriginal resistance using legal processes took place in the mid-1830s in the Brisbane Water District of NSW, between Sydney and the Hunter Valley, now known as the Central Coast. By this time, introduced disease, disruption of food sources and violence had reduced the Aboriginal populations of the settled areas of New South Wales and VDL to perhaps 5% of what they had been before 1788. The population of convicts and free settlers had risen to almost 70,000 in the two eastern colonies, plus another few thousand in the Swan River Colony around Perth. While settler colonists in peripheral areas were still committed to violence against Aboriginal people, those at the centre, guided by advice from Britain, preferred to attempt to apply the law to try to force them into alignment with the settler society.

In the 1830s, the number of Darkinjung and Dharug survivors in the Brisbane Water District was low, at only about 100 people.[16] Timber getters had come through their country, followed by more permanent intruders in the 1820s, who were determined to turn the forests into open agricultural land with labour provided by assigned convict workers and casually employed Aboriginal people. In 1833, relatively harmonious relations were upset when a group of Aboriginal men, including both locals and people from the Hunter region, began a series of raids on local farms. They were armed with firearms and spears, demanded food and property with menace, stole and in one case, committed a rape. At Jaques' farm at Wyong, up to 60 warriors were said to have attacked armed with spears and waddies (heavy pointed clubs), calling for tea, sugar and meat. Jaques later testified that he knew many of the attackers, and one, Hobby, had told him that their aim was to take back their rightful place in control of the region. Jaques' version of what he was told was: "black fellow turn out everybody. White fellow eat bandicoots and black snakes now." Other settlers, like James Smith of Blue Gum Flat (now Ourimbah), blamed the individuals who were attacked for having drawn hostility through their own actions, revealing the understanding also expressed elsewhere that much of the violence perpetrated by Aboriginal people was not random or treating all settlers as enemies but retribution for specific wrongs, as their Law prescribed.

The settler colonists of Brisbane Water called for help, hoping that a detachment of soldiers could be sent to sort out the problem as had been done in the Bathurst District and the Hunter Valley, by killing some and driving the rest away – what was called euphemistically "dispersal." However, the new governor, Sir Richard Bourke (1831–37) was influenced by the humanitarian and anti-slavery movements and he decided to try to use the law to settle the issue. Mounted Police and a detachment of soldiers were sent to assist magistrate Jonathan Warner, their task being to arrest the offenders rather than shoot them. They failed to find anyone to arrest. As attacks on farms continued, Bourke resorted to posting rewards of £10 each for the apprehension of 24 named Aboriginal men wanted in relation to the series of "Robberies and other Outrages." See Figure 4.1

Colonial Secretary's Office, Sydney,
December 15th, 1834.

ONE HUNDRED AND EIGHTY POUNDS REWARD.

WHEREAS the undermentioned BLACK NATIVES have been reported to the Government as Ringleaders in various Robberies and other Outrages which have been recently committed in the District of Brisbane Water; Notice is hereby given, that any person who shall apprehend or cause to be apprehended, and lodged in any of His Majesty's Gaols, the whole or either of ths said Offenders shall receive a REWARD of TEN POUNDS for each of them who shall be so secured :—

MOLLY MORGAN, HOBBY, LITTLE JACK, } Brothers, and very bad characters.
JACK JONES, TOM JONES, JUGO, } **Brothers, and ditto.**
ABRAHAMS, PADDY, } **Brothers, and ditto.**
YOUNG DICK, **always carries a gun,**
BIG JIMMY, **speared a white man.**
WHIPUNUP, **ditto.**
KURUNGBONG JIMMY, EMU, MONKEY, NIMBO, BIG HARRY, } **Bad characters.**
LITTLE DICK, **Principal agent and messenger.**
OLD JOHN, **Bad character, and father to Abrahams and Paddy.**

By His Excellency's Command.

Figure 4.1 Advertisements placed in the newspapers and *Government Gazette* to encourage settler colonists to assist in the apprehension of the suspected Brisbane Water District raiders show that the adversaries were not strangers but were known to one another. "One hundred and eighty pounds reward,"

Source: "One hundred and eighty pounds reward," *NSW Government Gazette*, 146, 17 December, 1834, 881.

The names given to the men are revealing. They show that the family relationships and past offences of the Aboriginal men were known and their characters had been judged. In most cases, there was no effort made to provide their actual names. They were referred to by the English names they had been given to ease their integration with settler society. Most were not conventional names but were derogatory or descriptive, linking them with animals (Emu, Monkey, Jemmy Jackass) or differentiating them from others given the same narrow range of names (Little Jack, Big Jimmy, Young Dick, Miserable Billy).

The rewards were effective and over a period of months, 21 of the men were arrested by local convicts and settlers, and brought to Sydney for 9 separate trials in the Supreme Court. *Although Bourke's intention was to be fair and to replace disordered frontier violence with regular legal proceedings, this was a terrifying and bewildering ordeal for the men, as Laurie Allen explores in the essay accompanying this chapter.* In court facing charges of robbery, stealing, putting in fear and rape, they had a limited understanding of what was being said, no capacity to defend themselves or offer evidence which would assist in defending their associates, and were subject to decisions on guilt or innocence made not by a jury of their peers, but by settler colonists.

Some of the defendants did have a translator, Reverend Lancelot Threlkeld, who had studied the Awabakal language as a missionary at Lake Macquarie. They were also assigned lawyers. One, Roger Therry, tried to put a sympathetic case. He acted for Legome, who was accused of having stolen a pipe and tobacco with menace. Therry asked in cross-examination whether the victim, Patrick Sheridan, was aware that he had been a squatter for some time on Legome's ground and hunted his kangaroos. Sheridan was confused by this proposition and said he was on government land and had no interest in kangaroos. He did not see himself as living on unceded Aboriginal Country because he had accepted the word of his government that the land was previously unclaimed and had passed into their control. The outcome of this trial was similar to when the same line of argument was used by barrister G.R. Nichols in his defence of Wong-ko-bi-kan, a Hunter Valley man charged with murder in 1834. Nichols argued that his client should be acquitted because settler colonists had no right to disturb the natural rights of Aboriginal people as the primary tenants of the soil.[17] These arguments held little weight inside or outside of court.

Unsurprisingly, most of the Brisbane Water men were found guilty. Mickey, who was convicted of the rape of a female servant near Wollombi, was executed. Fourteen of the men had sentences of death recorded which were commuted to up to four years of imprisonment with hard labour in irons. They spent this time quarrying rock at the prison on Goat Island in Sydney Harbour, while receiving a basic education in English, arithmetic and Christianity from a clergyman employed for the purpose. Six died during their servitude. In 1836, the eight survivors were transferred to Threlkeld's mission at Lake Macquarie where it was expected that they would settle, applying their new understanding of colonial culture to become a productive part of the settler society. Hopes were dashed when, within 48 hours, all of them had run away from the mission. Their experiences of arrest, prosecution, imprisonment and forced labour had not made them more willing to be part of settler society.

These were not the only Aboriginal people to be subjected to trial and punishment in this period. Kristyn Harman and Hamish Maxwell-Stewart found 60 Aboriginal prisoners were punished with transportation between 1805 and

1860.[18] Prosecution was an advance on the military-style reprisal parties of the mounted police in that most of the men's lives were initially spared, although almost half died in custody. They were also effective. In the Brisbane Water District, locking the men away achieved the aim of stopping their raids.

Once drawn into the legal system, however, Aboriginal people became disproportionately caught up with it, sometimes being harshly treated and, at other times, relatively leniently. From 1836, crimes committed by one Aboriginal person against another formally became the business of colonial law in NSW, according to a ruling in the murder trial *R v Jack Congo Murrell* who was accused of killing another Aboriginal man, Pat Barey, at Windsor in 1835.[19] The Supreme Court rejected the defence argument heard before, that since Aboriginal people did not understand English legal processes they could not be subject to them but remained under their own law, ruling that there could be only one law in a British territory and everyone was both protected by it and subject to it.[20] Having clarified that Aboriginal people would be held accountable for their transgressions, the next step was to ensure that the protection of the law was extended to them as well, as was tested in a landmark case in 1838.

Massacre in the Colonial Landscape

An instance of settler colonists being held accountable for crimes against Aboriginal people was the Myall Creek Massacre which occurred just a few years after the Brisbane Water Trials, in 1838. That settler colonists murdered large numbers of Aboriginal people was long denied or minimised, leading to the so-called History Wars at the turn of the twenty-first century, but acceptance has grown in recent years.[21] After some historians dismissed the idea of being able to provide evidence of massacres or how many Aboriginal people were killed in them, historian Lyndall Ryan began a project to document and map every Australian massacre, whether of Aboriginal people or settler colonists.

The online Colonial Frontier Massacres in Australia map provides the location and descriptions of massacres across Australia from the time of colonisation until 1930.[22] Events are included as massacres if sufficient evidence exists that six or more people were deliberately and unlawfully killed in one event. Six is not an arbitrary number but was chosen as constituting a fractal massacre, which means one which would leave other members of a typical Indigenous group of twenty active members unable to continue to thrive, having less capacity for food gathering, child rearing, self-defence and ceremonial obligations. By killing six members of such groups, their further disintegration was almost guaranteed. So even while it may be the case that only relatively small numbers of Aboriginal people were killed in massacres compared with the numbers who died of introduced diseases and other causes, mass killings had serious implications for the ongoing well-being of Aboriginal populations as well as reflecting the attitude of settler colonists towards Aboriginal people.

The vast majority of these massacres were not prosecuted as crimes. Indeed, there was no crime of massacre. In some cases, this lack of a legal response was because they were state sanctioned violence. This was the case for the 1816 Appin massacre committed under orders from Governor Macquarie (1810–21) to capture or kill Aboriginal people as a reprisal for what he called "sanguinary Outrages and Barbarities," ignoring the settler violence which triggered them. After weeks of searching the Appin and Airds district south-west of Sydney, soldiers on foot under the command of Captain James Wallis attacked a camp at night, killing at least 14 Muringong and Gandangarra men, women and children by gunshot and by driving them over the edge of a river gorge.[23] Three of the dead had their heads severed and put on display, later being given to the University of Edinburgh's Anatomy Department for study. In addition to massacres by military and police forces, mass killings were undertaken by settler colonists without official sanction. These were often responses to local hostilities and were framed as either retaliation for specific acts of violence by Aboriginal people or a means of intimidating them into withdrawal or compliance. The status of these unsanctioned massacres was uncertain. If Aboriginal people were truly protected by the introduced law, they were serious crimes. Alternatively, they could be seen as part of an unofficial but legitimate frontier war in which both sides used violence to punish and intimidate the other. Finally, they were viewed by some as of no significance at all, as parallels of the killing of native animals to make way for the colonists' herds, flocks and crops.

The Myall Creek Massacre

The Myall Creek Massacre is remembered because it was made a test case for the view that massacres were crimes. The massacre took place on 10 June 1838 when 12 pastoral workers brutally murdered thirty Wirrayaraay old men, women and children. The Wirrayaraay group had been living amicably on country with workers from Henry Dangar's Myall Creek cattle station in what is now northern New South Wales. With the Wirrayaraay people suffering from the widespread drought of the period, they had come to an agreement on exchanging labour for food, and the two groups lived side by side, socialising together.[24] These harmonious arrangements were not achieved on some other stations. Instead, there was a belief that Aboriginal people frightened livestock, making them anxious and hard to manage, and that sheep and cattle and Aboriginal people should be kept separate.

On a day when both the station overseer William Hobbs and the younger Wirrayaraay men were absent, the latter doing work on a nearby station, 10 convict and ex-convict stockmen and drovers from at least seven properties in the region rode into Myall Creek, led by a free settler colonist, John Fleming.[25] The group rounded up the Wirrayaraay people who were present, roped them together and forced them to walk a short distance from the station to a stockyard, which they were ushered inside. Dangar's employee Charles Kilmeister mounted his own horse and joined in. Using swords and pistols, the men brutally attacked the Wirrayaraay, decapitating some, severing limbs and killing all but one woman, who was kept alive to be raped by the offenders over the next 24 hours. They set a fire and piled the bodies on it in an effort to hide some of the evidence of their crime. Telling those on a neighbouring station what had happened, the group replied in the oblique language of the time that they had "settled the blacks."

George Anderson, a stockman at Myall Creek who had refused to join in the violence and extended protection to those he could help, told his overseer what had happened on his return. A young man who had hidden during the massacre, Yintayintin (also known as Davey), took Hobbs to the site, where they were able to identify 28 bodies. Hobbs wrote to his employer, Henry Dangar, and to the Colonial Secretary to report what he understood as a crime. Police magistrate Edward Denny Day, based 240 kilometres away in Invermein (now Scone), investigated with eight mounted police troopers at the end of July, almost two months later. They found the by then much disturbed human remains, took depositions from witnesses and arrested the stockmen who were sent to Sydney for trial, along with Anderson as a witness for the prosecution. The leader of the attack, Fleming, fled and evaded any responsibility, later returning to public life.[26]

Although it is easy to assume that everyone in the past shared the same beliefs, the running of the case drew out the range of opinions on whether Aboriginal people should have the protection of the law. Governor Gipps (1838–46), who had only arrived in NSW in February, had been sent out with a brief from the British government to better protect Aboriginal people's rights and so endorsed the prosecution of the offenders. Gipps was supported by others who believed in individual liberty, equality and the universal right to legal protection. Many longer term colonists whose livelihoods were connected with rural industries disagreed, arguing that they had the right and even a duty to use any means to clear Indigenous people from the land so they could use it productively. Many were surprised when the case was prosecuted in November 1838 with 11 men standing trial for wilful murder.

As only one murder case was then permitted to be heard in any single trial, it was the killing of the most identifiable victim, a large man termed in the indictment "'Daddy' or an Aboriginal male to the Attorney General unknown," which was prosecuted. With the punishment for those found guilty being death, there was no need to secure a conviction for more than one murder. If this case failed to secure a guilty verdict, the accused could be tried for killing another of the victims.[27] Assisting with the defence were Dangar, and other landholders from the Hunter River and Liverpool Plains regions who wanted to continue to be able to use violence to remove Aboriginal people from their land. Forming a defence fund called the Black Association, they raised money to provide the defendants with the colony's best legal counsel. The prosecution relied on evidence from Hobbs and Anderson, while Dangar gave evidence in support of Kilmeister and undermining Anderson's credibility. The jury found that the identity of the victim was not sufficiently proven in Daddy's case and the accused were found not guilty.

Attorney General Plunkett ran a second case just over a week later, this time focusing on only seven of the defendants and on the murder of a boy named "Charley, or of an unidentified child." There was trouble finding enough men to serve on the jury, with some suggestion that the Black Association was intimidating people to keep them away. This case was stronger as new evidence was heard from Magistrate Day and Dangar's attempts to discredit his employees rebounded onto him when his own dismissal from his role as government surveyor for misappropriating land was revealed to undermine his credibility. The jury found all seven of the accused guilty. The verdict was unsuccessfully appealed, and a review by the Executive Council confirmed the punishment. The men were hanged in December 1838. The remaining four men were kept in custody to face charges at the next court session but were released the following February when Yintayintin (the admissibility of whose evidence was uncertain) could not be located to testify against them. It was said that Dangar had "put him out of the way."

The Myall Creek case was followed closely around the colony. J.H. Bannatyne of Sydney wrote about it to his friend in England. His words are quoted here in full to show how well the case was known and what a recent immigrant based in Sydney thought of it:

> By the bye, writing of sentiment, I must not forget to tell you of a circumstance which has agitated the public mind in the Colony lately. You may perhaps see something of it in the newspapers – A quantity of stockmen in the interior having had their masters' cattle speared by the Native Aborigines were determined on revenging themselves the first opportunity – falling in with a tribe of strange Blacks 30 in number – men, women & children, a tribe they apparently never saw before, totally innocent of the charge, for which they were slaughtered without having given the slightest provocation and unsuspecting by confiding in the protection of one of these wretches were enticed to the huts of the Stockmen, where having bound their hands and having fastened them together, took them into a remote part of the Bush, and then in cold blood murdered every soul of them, after which, they piled them in a heap and burnt their bodies – the remains were however discovered by persons attracted to the spot by seeing birds of prey hovering about in great numbers over the scene of the massacre – information was forwarded to Government – the men were brought to justice tried twice by separate juries and the second time found guilty – Some escaped but the 7 who were tried are all to be hanged on Tuesday 18 inst.; their trial created an extraordinary sensation in the Colony and will be the subject of gossip for many a long day yet. The Greenacre Murder was nothing to this – "quite a rush light to a mould candle."
>
> [Postscript]
>
> I have just returned from seeing the seven men all launched into eternity at the same moment it was an awful sight and has made me feel quite sick – I shall never forget it.[28]

The Greenacre murder he referred to took place in London in 1836 before Bannatyne emigrated, when a grocer killed his fiancée and cut her body into pieces which were soon discovered in various canals and ditches. The reference shows how knowledge of crimes of particular note or significance circulated around the British Empire, carried by individuals and in newspaper accounts, just as the news of the Myall Creek massacre travelled back to Britain in this letter, in government reports and in newspaper articles.[29] Bannatyne clearly sided with the Aboriginal people, with his references to their innocence and trusting natures in contrast with the cold-blooded actions of the murderous stockmen. Even in these circumstances, he found the mass execution sickening, showing that capital punishment still had a powerful impact.

This chapter has up to this point considered the most serious crimes committed by and perpetrated against Aboriginal people in the first half of the nineteenth century. Of course, high-level crimes were less frequent points of intersection between people and the criminal justice system than other, more everyday offences. At the more minor end of the scale, Aboriginal people were, in some cases, treated more leniently than others by the law. One example of this was the commonly prosecuted offence of public drunkenness.[30] Many people drank excessively and publicly in the colonial period and Aboriginal people seeking solace from the multiple traumas they had experienced were amongst them. To try to address this perceived offence to good order and progress, the NSW Licensed Publicans Act of 1838 took a paternalistic position and made it an offence to supply alcohol to Aboriginal people.[31] After that, while Aboriginal people were still arrested if found drunk in the streets, they were not charged, fined or made to serve a jail sentence like non-Aboriginal people. Instead, they were considered to be the victims of the illegal actions of those who sold them the alcohol. Charges only followed if they exhibited offensive behaviour or committed an assault. Similarly, while the NSW Vagrancy Act forbade people of European heritage "wandering" with Aboriginal people, it specifically excluded Aboriginal people from being prosecuted for moving from place to place, recognising their right to do so.

Changes on the east coast did not necessarily transfer to other areas of settlement across the continent. Indeed, each colony had to tread its own path as the new legal framework was superimposed over the old Law. In Western Australia, frustrated by the difficulty of keeping Aboriginal people in legal custody, a "Place of Confinement for Native Prisoners" was established on Rottnest Island in 1839.[32] Located 22 kilometres off the coast of Fremantle, it was considered a place from which no one could escape. Following the same method as the Brisbane Water trials a few years earlier, in July 1839 advertisements were placed drawing attention to warrants for the arrest of 14 Aboriginal men for murder or aiding and abetting murder in the York district.[33] Two of the men listed, Yughite or Doodjep and Bunabong, were tried in 1840 for killing a woman and her infant. They were provided with a public interpreter through whom both men confessed to the spearing, something rarely done in a capital crime. Giving them the opportunity of a hearing, not guilty pleas were entered on their behalf before the Advocate General described the crime in the worst of terms, as wanton, savage, unprovoked and treacherous. The pair was found guilty and became the first people to be formally executed in that colony, three years before the first settler colonist was hanged there.[34] In South Australia, two Aboriginal men held accountable for the murder of survivors of the wreck of the *Maria* near Encounter Bay in South Australia were summarily executed at the site in 1839 by order of the Commissioner of Police. It was decided that punishing them there, in sight of their people, would have more deterrent power than taking them to Adelaide for trial and execution.[35] With regard to *inter se* crimes between Aboriginal people, in South Australia in 1840, the sole Judge Charles Cooper ruled that it was impossible to attempt to prosecute those of "a wild and savage tribe" whose lands were not yet occupied by settler colonists and who had not submitted to "domination."[36]

Conclusion

While the Brisbane Water trials did put an end to Aboriginal resistance on the Central Coast, the trial of the Myall Creek murderers did not have the intended impact of stopping settler violence on the more distant frontier, or even of ensuring that those who harmed Aboriginal people were brought to justice. In only three other cases were settler colonists executed for murdering Aboriginal people on the frontier, and none of them occurred after the Myall Creek Massacre. As the Massacre Map shows, massacres continued, although they were increasingly well concealed, and some used less obvious methods such as poison. The undeclared frontier war on Indigenous people continued with a culture of secrecy and a language of cover-up even as Aboriginal people in more settled districts were increasingly being controlled through the criminal justice system. We will return again to this issue of how Aboriginal people were treated under the supposedly colour-blind system of British laws, but the next chapter turns to another instance of rural lawlessness: bushrangers and in particular, the iconic Ned Kelly.

Suggested Readings

Colonial Frontier Massacres in Australia, 1788–1930, https://c21ch.newcastle.edu.au/colonialmassacres/map.php

Douglas, Heather and Mark Finnane. *Indigenous Crime and Settler Law: White Sovereignty after Empire*. Basingstoke: Palgrave Macmillan, 2012.

Harman, Kristyn and Hamish Maxwell-Stewart. "Aboriginal Deaths in Custody in Colonial Australia, 1805–1860," *Journal of Colonialism and Colonial History* 13, no. 2 (2012), np.

Lydon, Jane and Lyndall Ryan, eds. *Remembering the Myall Creek Massacre*. Sydney: NewSouth Publishing, 2018.

Owen, Chris. *Every Mother's Son Is Guilty: Policing the Kimberley Frontier of Western Australia 1882–1905*. Perth: UWA Publishing, 2016.

ESSAY: ENTANGLED IN THE COLONIAL JUSTICE SYSTEM

Laurie Allen

From mid-November 1834 when Governor Sir Richard Bourke first authorised rewards for the Aboriginal men said to have raided settlers in the Brisbane Water District of NSW, bounty hunters sprang into action.[37] On 21 November, Brisbane Water magistrate Jonathan Warner wrote that of four prisoners he had in the local watchhouse, "three have been brought to us by men working in the bush."[38] Whip-em-up (also called "Whipunup") was caught by a free man, Miles McGrath, and a convict, Thomas Swan, and in forwarding their claim for compensation, Warner wrote that others had already received "rewards of a similar nature."[39] Corporal McKnight of the Mounted Police received a £10 reward for capturing Old John, despite it presumably being his official duty to arrest wanted men.[40] Emu was pursued by William Clarke and Michael Riley at Rev. Lancelot Threlkeld's mission on Lake Macquarie. According to Threlkeld, they made friendly overtures to Emu, then tried to seize him. When Emu ran, Clarke shot and wounded him and compelled him to row towards Newcastle where he was jailed and placed in irons, but later released.[41] While some settlers no doubt wanted only to have disruptive Aboriginal men leave their District, the promise of a monetary reward set at the equivalent of three months of a police constable's wages must have been a strong motivation to turn them in.

Despite their leaders being gradually secured, the Darkinjung remained defiant. Abrahams, for instance, warned farm overseer Adam Rainey in December that "white fellows must be very quiet now … or the blacks would kill them all."[42] This spirit of resistance was no doubt heightened when some of the wanted men escaped custody. Six Aboriginal men, including Nimbo and the two brothers Jack and Jugo Jones, attempted to rob Rainey's hut on 2 January 1835, only to find Rainey had enlisted the help of a constable and two other settlers to defend his property.[43] Several of the Aboriginal men fled but Nimbo and the Jones brothers were overpowered and conveyed to the Brisbane Water watchhouse. Despite Jack being severely wounded in the neck, the three escaped two days later. All were subsequently recaptured and sent to Sydney.

Transport of prisoners between Brisbane Water and Sydney was normally by sea, but in the case of these Aboriginal men, the operation sometimes became complicated. In January 1835, for example, Long Dick (called Young Dick in the reward notice), Joe the Marine and Monkey were initially sent to Windsor on the Hawkesbury River, then forwarded on to Sydney Gaol. They remained there for eight days until sent to the Police Office, where the magistrates ordered that they be returned to Brisbane Water for trial, since "it [was] the usual course to send prisoners to the place where a charge exists against them."[44] These magistrates were clearly unaware of the plans for a series of demonstration trials in Sydney.

After the bureaucratic tangle was unravelled, Long Dick was sent to Sydney yet again with five others on the sloop *Betsy* on 2 February.[45] For some undiscovered reason Long Dick was then sent back to Brisbane Water for a third time – or perhaps he escaped – since he travelled to Sydney again with Abrahams, arriving on 2 April.[46] This was Long Dick's final entry into Sydney Gaol and he stood trial in mid-May.[47] Thus Long Dick made at least five, and possibly six, escorted trips back and forth between Brisbane Water and Sydney before his case was heard, greatly adding to the trauma of his situation. The voyages would have been painful for the men, who were made to wear leg irons to prevent their escaping overboard.[48] Leg irons could produce deep wounds, particularly in Aboriginal people who had little or no access to cloth to protect their flesh.[49] Other men also made repeated journeys, which shows not only that the justice system was not yet ready to deal with trying Aboriginal people from outside Sydney, but also that the whole exercise was a costly and time-consuming one, particularly as a constable had to accompany all travelling prisoners.

Many of these difficult journeys were clearly unwarranted. One man, for example, was brought before the court in Sydney for a robbery he could not have committed, since he was in the Brisbane Water watchhouse on the day of his alleged crime.[50] He was acquitted of the charge in February 1835 but continued to be held in Sydney Gaol until August, when a second charge against him failed because he could not be positively identified. He was finally returned home in September, having been imprisoned for almost 12 months on the basis of flawed evidence.[51] Nevertheless, he experienced a better outcome than did others in his cohort, a number of whom did not survive.

The official letters reporting the tracking, capture and movement of Aboriginal men from the Brisbane Water District to Sydney for trial provide a glimpse into the lives of the men taken into custody and those who put them there. A close reading of these letters calls into doubt whether the harm caused by this experiment in extending the reach of the colonial law to cover the actions of Aboriginal people outweighed any improvement in justice done.

PRIMARY SOURCE: "PROCLAMATION TO THE ABORIGINES," C. 1828–30

This pictogram produced in lutruwita (VDL) in the midst of their Black Wars (1824–31) shows an idealised version of relations between the Palawa people and settler colonists. It portrays equality on an individual, family, state and legal basis. However, having the Palawa people dressed in British clothing in the first sequence and the governor presiding over the executions in the final two without the presence of elders underscores that this equality was only imagined by the settler colonists on their own terms. Up to 100 of these boards were made and placed on trees in contested areas in the hope that they would help to end the conflict. Instead, violence continued until the island's original population had been reduced to a small remnant.

Figure 4.2 "Proclamation to the Aborigines," c. 1828–30.

Source: "Governor Arthur's Proclamation to the Aborigines," c. 1828–30, oil on Huon Pine board, Mitchell Library, State Library of New South Wales, SAFE/R 247.

Notes

1. Heather Douglas and Mark Finnane, *Indigenous Crime and Settler Law: White Sovereignty after Empire*, Basingstoke: Palgrave Macmillan, 2012, 6.
2. This excluded visitors and immigrants of other recognised nationalities who had to be naturalised to become British subjects.
3. Bruce Buchan and Mary Heath, "Savagery and Civilization: From Terra Nullius to the 'Tide of History,'" *Ethnicities* 6, no. 1 (2006): 7–9.
4. Watkin Tench, *A Complete Account of the Settlement at Port Jackson*, London: G. Nicol and J. Sewell, 1793, March 1789, https://gutenberg.net.au/ebooks/e00084.html (accessed 18 February 2022).
5. Golder, *High and Responsible Office*, 21–22.
6. Douglas and Finnane, *Indigenous Crime and Settler Law*, 56.
7. Bruce Kercher, *An Unruly Child, A History of Law in Australia*, Sydney: Allen and Unwin, 1995, 8.
8. Stephen Gapps, *The Sydney Wars, 1788–1817*, Sydney: NewSouth, 2018.
9. Stephen Gapps, *Gudyarra: The First Wiradyuri War of Resistance—The Bathurst War, 1822–1824*, Sydney: NewSouth, 2021.
10. Nicholas Clements, *The Black War: Fear, Sex and Resistance in Tasmania*, Brisbane: University of Queensland Press, 2014, Ch. 4, Experience.
11. Douglas and Finnane, *Indigenous Crime and Settler Law*, 16–22.
12. R. H. W. Reece, "Yagan (1795–1833)," *Australian Dictionary of Biography*, National Centre of Biography, Australian National University, https://adb.anu.edu.au/biography/yagan-2826/text36984, published online 2019 (accessed 30 May 2022).
13. Mark Dunn, *The Convict Valley, The Bloody Struggle on Australia's First Frontier*, Sydney: Allen and Unwin, 2020, Ch. 8 "Resistance and Reprisals."
14. Dunn, *The Convict Valley*, 177–80.
15. "Commercial Intelligence, *Sydney Gazette and New South Wales Advertiser*, April 23, 1829, 2.
16. This account draws on the work of Laurie Allen in his thesis, "A History of the Aboriginal People of the Central Coast of New South Wales to 1874" (University of Newcastle, 2021), Ch. 7.
17. Paul Irish, *Hidden in Plain View, The Aboriginal People of Coastal Sydney*, Sydney: NewSouth, 2017, 100.
18. K. Harman and H. Maxwell-Stewart, "Aboriginal Deaths in Custody in Colonial Australia, 1805–1860," *Journal of Colonialism and Colonial History* 13, no. 2 (2012), DOI: 10.1353/cch.2012.0023.
19. Supreme Court (Criminal Side), *Commercial Journal and Advertiser*, May 21, 1836, 2.
20. Kercher, *An Unruly Child*, 9–10.
21. Stuart Macintyre and Anna Clark, *The History Wars*, Melbourne: Melbourne University Press, 2003.
22. Colonial Frontier Massacres in Australia, 1788–1930, https://c21ch.newcastle.edu.au/colonialmassacres/map.php (accessed 19 February 2022).
23. Grace Karskens, *The Colony, A History of Early Sydney*, Sydney: Allen and Unwin, 2009, 507–14.
24. The details about these events come from Lyndall Ryan, "'A Very Bad Business': Henry Dangar and the Myall Creek massacre 1838," Jane Lydon and Lyndall Ryan, eds., *Remembering the Myall Creek Massacre*, Sydney: NewSouth Publishing, 2018, 15–37.
25. Patsy Withycombe has written about Fleming in "The Twelfth Man: John Henry Fleming and the Myall Creek Massacre," Jane Lydon and Lyndall Ryan, eds. *Remembering the Myall Creek Massacre*, Sydney: NewSouth Publishing, 2018, 38–51.
26. Withycombe, "The Twelfth Man," 41.
27. Mark Tedeschi, *Murder at Myall Creek*, Sydney: Simon and Schuster, 2016, 134–35.

28 State Library of New South Wales, Letter from J. H Bannatyne to Other Windsor Berry Esq. relating to the Myall Creek Massacre, pg. 117 December 1838, https://www.sl.nsw.gov.au/collection-items/letter-j-h-bannatyne-other-windsor-berry-esq-relating-myall-creek-massacre-pg-1 (accessed 6 June 2022).
29 "Law Reports," *Sydney Gazette and New South Wales Advertiser*, August 24, 1837, 4.
30 Matthew Allen, "Policing a Free Society: Drunkenness and Liberty in Colonial New South Wales," *History Australia* 12, no. 2 (2015): 143–164.
31 Paul Irish, *Hidden in Plain View*, 42–43.
32 "The Government Gazette," *Perth Gazette and Western Australian Journal*, August 31, 1839, 138.
33 "The Government Gazette," *Perth Gazette and Western Australian Journal*, July 6, 1839, 105; August 31, 1839, 138 and subsequently.
34 "Quarter Sessions," Perth *Gazette and Western Australian Journal*, July 4, 1840, 3.
35 "Execution of Two Natives", *Adelaide Chronicle*, September 9, 1840, 2.
36 Bruce Debelle, "Aboriginal Customary Law and the Common Law," Elliott Johnston, Martin Hinton and Daryle Rigney, eds. *Indigenous Australians and the Law*, Sydney: Cavendish, 1997, 88.
37 Governor Sir Richard Bourke to Lieutenant Campbell, 11 November 1834, State Archives of NSW (SANSW): NRS 905, [4/2251.2].
38 Jonathan Warner to Colonial Secretary Alexander McLeay, 21 November 1834, 3, SANSW: NRS 905, [4/2289.4].
39 Warner to McLeay, 7 April 1835, 1, SANSW: NRS 905, [4/2289.4].
40 Thomas Harington to Commandant, Mounted Police, and Harington to Lieutenant-Colonel Snodgrass, both 14 February 1835, SANSW: NRS 989, [4/3837].
41 N. Gunson, ed. *Australian Reminiscences and Papers of LE Threlkeld, 1824–1859*, Canberra: AIAS, 1974, 121.
42 Warner to McLeay, 17 December 1834, 2, SANSW: NRS 905, [4/2249.5].
43 Warner to McLeay, 15 January 1835, 1–3, SANSW: NRS 905, [4/2289.4].
44 Wilson to McLeay, 24 January 1835 (with enclosures), SANSW: NRS 905, [4/2293.4].
45 Warner to McLeay, 16 February 1835, SANSW: NRS 905, [4/2289.4].
46 Warner to Attorney-General, 25 March 1835, 18, SANSW: NRS 3016, [4/5525].
47 SANSW: NRS 13477, [T40].
48 Warner to McLeay, 15 January 1835, 3, SANSW: NRS 905, [4/2289.4].
49 K. Harman and H. Maxwell-Stewart, "Aboriginal Deaths in Custody in Colonial Australia, 1805–1860," *Journal of Colonialism and Colonial History* 13, no. 2 (2012), no page numbers, DOI: 10.1353/cch.2012.0023.
50 Warner to McLeay, 24 October 1834, 3, SANSW: NRS 905, [2249.5].
51 "Quarterly Abstracts," 58, SANSW: NRS 3025, [4/5525].

5 The World of Ned Kelly

Australian readers will know a lot about Ned Kelly, or think you do. His life has been portrayed in plays, novels, children's stories and films, including the world's first feature-length narrative film, *The Story of the Kelly Gang* which premiered on Boxing Day 1906 in Melbourne's Town Hall. The film was toured around Australia and then to New Zealand and Great Britain, but the Victorian government banned its screening in Kelly's home district of north-eastern Victoria to avoid inspiring copycats.[1] Many more film depictions of Ned Kelly followed, including by Mick Jagger in 1970, Heath Ledger in 2003 and George MacKay in the *True History of the Kelly Gang* (2019), based on the 2001 Booker Prize–winning novel by Peter Carey. Bushrangers in helmets inspired by Sydney Nolan's 1947–48 Ned Kelly series of paintings were part of the Sydney 2000 Olympics opening ceremony, and in the following decade, Ned Kelly was named as Australia's greatest folk hero on an official government website.[2] Many people so identify with Kelly that they have an image of him on a t-shirt, a poster, a bumper sticker or even tattooed on their body.

This focus on Ned Kelly warrants attention. He was neither the first nor the last of the bushrangers. Others stole more money and had larger gangs and longer periods of activity. He was described when still alive as a wretch, murderer, traitor, liar and coward. Still, Kelly retains a status and a profile that other bushrangers, many of whom were very famous in their day as well, do not. A 2010 study found he was not just the best-remembered bushranger but "perhaps the only 19th-century Australian still recognized nationally."[3] This chapter will investigate why.

Ned Kelly's Family and Community Context

To best understand Ned Kelly, popular and mass media depictions must be set aside in favour of viewing his life in its historical context. He is seen most clearly not as an individual but as part of an Irish Australian family.

That family had its start when Ned Kelly's father, Irish farm worker John Kelly, arrived in Van Diemen's Land in 1842 as a convict.[4] John Kelly had been transported for stealing and then selling two pigs. He was tall for the period at 173 cm (5′ 8″), and his red hair and beard led to his nickname

DOI: 10.4324/9781003273561-6

"Red." Red Kelly served out his seven-year sentence, receiving his ticket of leave in 1845 and certificate of freedom in 1848. He started a new life by moving to the Port Phillip district of NSW, soon to become the separate colony of Victoria. There he met Ellen Quinn, aged 18, in 1850.

Ellen Quinn had come from Ireland as a free immigrant in 1841. She and the rest of her large family benefitted from the program of assisted immigration then in place to reduce the so-called surplus population of the UK while building up the settler population of Australia. The Quinn family rented a small rural property outside of Melbourne, where Red and Ellen met and married. Red worked splitting timber for fences, gold seeking and horse trading, and the couple saved enough to buy land at Beveridge, 55 kilometres north of Melbourne. Their third child, Edward, known as Ned, was born there in 1854 or 1855, although his birth was not formally recorded. The gold rushes had brought general prosperity to the colony, but not to the Kelly family which grew to include six children by 1865. They moved to a smaller property and then became tenant farmers at Avenel where Red was jailed for having a cow hide in his possession, which was taken as evidence of cattle theft. He died in 1866, in his mid-40s, his health damaged by the time in jail and chronic alcoholism.

Ellen then moved with her children to northeastern Victoria, where her father had leased a large tract of land known as the Glenmore run. They initially lived in a former hotel with two of her sisters, whose husbands were in jail for stock theft. In 1868, Red's brother Jim Kelly burned the building down, leading to a conviction for attempted murder and a 15-year prison sentence served in a psychiatric facility.

Ellen became a free selector in May 1867, taking up land at Eleven Mile Creek, about half-way between the towns of Greta and Glenrowan in a lightly populated area surrounded by low mountain ranges and dense bush. Free selection was a means of achieving land ownership without having the purchase price in full. It was put in place by the government of Victoria after the expansion of voting rights to include all white male British subjects of European descent over the age of 21. While this manhood suffrage was achieved in NSW, Victoria and South Australia in the 1850s, in Britain it was not granted until 1918. Although considered radical at the time, it still meant that men of colour including Aboriginal people and all women had no voice in government.

A priority for the parliaments elected by these new working class voters was to expand land ownership. Much of the Crown (public) land appropriated from Aboriginal people was held from the 1820s on very cheap long-term leases and used to graze sheep and cattle. Having originally occupied the land without permission from the government, these land holders were known as squatters but by the 1860s they held formal leases, in some cases of vast tracts of land and many had become very wealthy from their pastoral enterprises. Largely free settlers from England and Scotland and followers of the Protestant forms of Christianity, squatters formed a rural elite, serving as magistrates and in the upper houses of parliament, the Legislative Councils. The Land Acts passed in the 1860s in Victoria sought to create a settled agricultural population by enabling working class men and women to take possession of and farm a parcel of crown land as free selectors.[5] This was another blow for Aboriginal people who had managed to stay on Country when it was lightly used for pastoralism. To governments, it was a means of economic development. For Ellen Kelly, free selection offered a chance to provide a secure home and source of income for her family.

There were several obstacles to realising these aims. The size of the blocks allocated for free selection, between 40 and 640 acres (up to 260 hectares), tended to be too small to be capable of providing a living, meaning that selectors and their family members still had to take off-farm work to make ends meet. The squatters resisted what they saw as intrusions onto their land, and threats to their prosperity, blocking selectors by buying up the best land and harassing them, including by having their livestock impounded if it strayed onto the squatter's holdings, so they would have to pay to have it released. To try to reduce the ability of the squatters to distort the intended outcomes of free selection, three new land acts were passed in Victoria in the 1860s. The one in effect when Ellen took up her land required her to live on her block for three years and make improvements to the value of £1 an acre. She added to the family income by illegally selling alcohol to travellers and locals.

Ned Kelly was vocal about how the conflict with squatters made him feel unjustly treated, but he had other grievances as well. Kelly carried the legacy of both sides of his family's experience of grinding poverty in Ireland, his father's transportation and his parents' mixed fortunes in Australia, for which he had been taught to blame the English as a foreign power that had dominated Ireland for centuries. Kelly's life was shaped by these larger forces and they provided a context for his criminal activity.

Beginning a Life of Crime

As much as he identified as Irish, Ned Kelly also took pride in having been born in Victoria. Many around Kelly were immigrants who had had to acquire the skills of living in a new environment, but he had always been immersed in the colonial landscape. He knew no other life and he excelled at it. When he was eleven, Kelly saved a younger boy from drowning in a flooded creek and was awarded a green sash with gold trimmings for his bravery by the appreciative family. Throughout his life, he was praised for bush skills including riding, accurate shooting and living off the land.

These skills were useful when he began to participate in his extended family's questionable dealings in livestock. Throughout Ned's childhood, various Kelly and Quinn relatives and the Lloyd family with whom they had intermarried were in trouble with the law, mainly for stealing cattle or horses. It was suggested that the reason that Kelly's grandfather James Quinn had relocated to the northeast was to escape a reputation for livestock theft and to go to an area on the "borders of settlement and civilization" where he would have more scope for illegal activity.[6] Reflecting the political power of the squatters, sentences for stock theft were severe in Victoria's Criminal Law and Practice Statute (1864).[7] Stealing cattle was punishable by up to 10 years imprisonment, while for other forms of theft to any value the maximum sentence was 5 years. In 1863, when Ned was 8, he provided an alibi for his uncle Jim Kelly who was accused of cattle theft. It didn't work. The uncle was convicted in one of 16 times he was arrested and charged. In 1868, at 14, Ned began to spend time with bushranger Harry Power, perhaps serving an informal apprenticeship.

In 1869, Ned again provided an alibi to a person who was later convicted and was himself arrested for the alleged assault of a Chinese miner and held for 10 days on remand before the charge was dismissed. In May 1870, Ned was arrested and held in custody in Benalla for a week on suspicion of committing highway robbery with Power, but again the charge was dismissed. An article covering his court appearance called him a bushranger, perhaps for the first time: "Bushranger Kelly," the juvenile highwayman. The journalist said Kelly had a jaunty air and seemed to see himself as someone to be admired.[8] He was already developing the flash persona which was so prominent in his final years.

Ned Kelly's first prison term came late in 1870 when he was convicted of summary offences and sentenced to 6 months after a fight with a married couple who lived near his mother's house. Even his own version of events as recounted in the Jerilderie Letter, featuring him sending a package containing a pair of calves' testicles, revealed his guilt. Soon after release, Kelly was sentenced to a more serious term: 3 years in Pentridge prison for receiving a stolen mare. By then 182 cm tall and sturdily built, Kelly violently resisted his arrest but during his sentence, he became a model prisoner. He made good use of the prison library and was allowed incremental increases in freedom before being discharged in 1874. See Figure 5.1 Ned found legitimate work, staying out of trouble for 2 years. In 1876, this came to an end when he joined his mother's new husband George King in a well-organised scheme of "wholesale and retail" cattle and horse stealing, taking advantage of rewards posted for lost livestock and the impounding system.[9]

Outlawed

With all of this illegal activity, the Kelly family drew regular attention from the police. Directed from Melbourne, the Victorian police force favoured stationing staff in places where they had no local connections, to avoid corruption, so many of their officers were immigrants, with very little experience of the bush, horses or firearms. Blaming past offenders for recent crime was a easy way to solve crime and often warranted in cases like that of the Kellys. They perceived this as harassment. Ned Kelly suggested that the police took pride in convicting the Kellys for crimes they had not committed: "it is a credit to a policeman to convict an innocent man but any muff can pot a guilty one."[10] Searching the Prosecution Project database for the surname Kelly in the 1860s and 1870s in Victorian trials held at Beechworth and Benalla shows three convictions for James Kelly and one each for Mary Ann and Ned's younger brother Daniel Kelly.

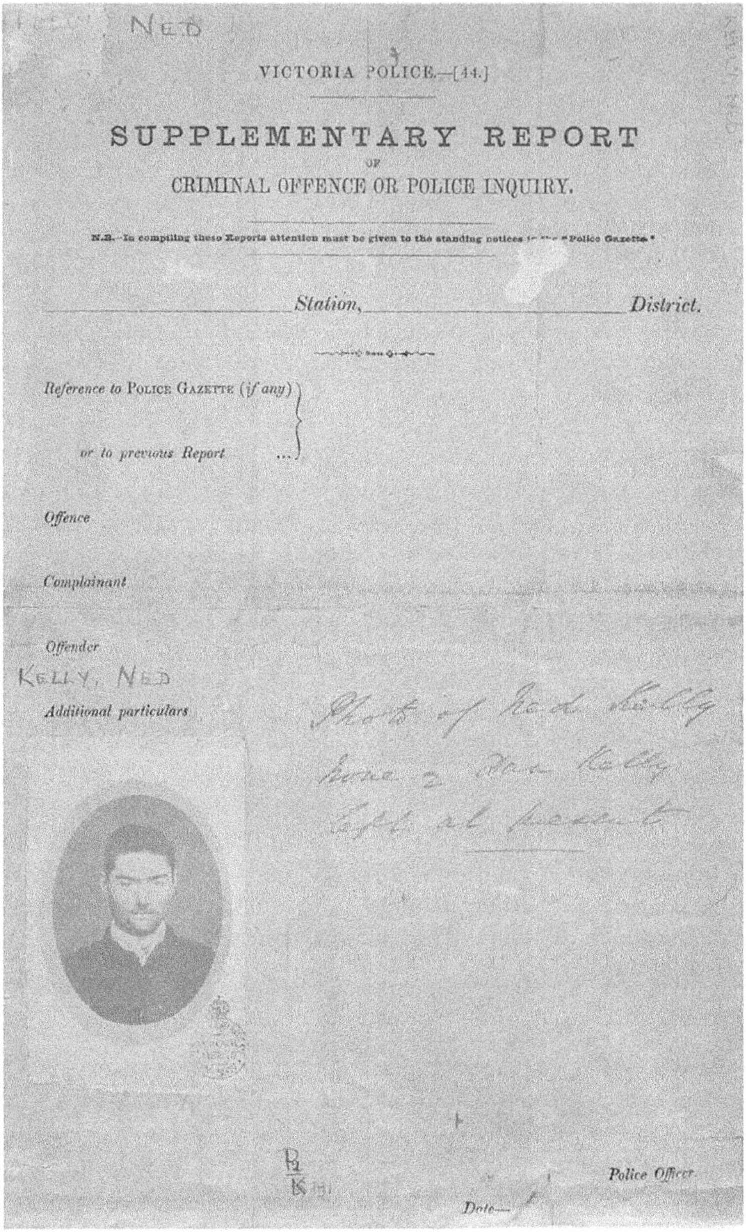

NED

VICTORIA POLICE.—[44.]

SUPPLEMENTARY REPORT
OF
CRIMINAL OFFENCE OR POLICE INQUIRY.

N.B.—In compiling these Reports attention must be given to the standing notices in the "Police Gazette."

Station, District.

Reference to Police Gazette (*if any*) *or to previous Report*

Offence

Complainant

Offender

KELLY, NED

Additional particulars

Photo of Ned Kelly

Police Officer.

Date—

Figure 5.1 The photograph of Ned Kelly attached to this Supplementary Report form was taken prior to his release from jail in 1874. Kelly has resisted the process, not raising his eyes to meet the camera. The bureaucratic nature of the form reflects the centralisation of the Victorian Police, while the lack of information entered suggests the inattention to detail which plagued the hunt for the Kellys.

Source: Victoria Police, Supplementary Report of Criminal Offence or Police Inquiry form, with portrait of Ned Kelly [1874], State Library of NSW, P2/191.

What the Kellys saw as an instance of this police harassment triggered the formation of the Kelly gang. In mid-April 1878, Alexander Fitzpatrick, a mounted police trooper based at Benalla, saw in the *Police Gazette* an outstanding warrant for horse stealing for Ned's brother Dan, then aged 17, and went to the Kelly house at Greta to arrest him. While he was there, Ned Kelly appeared and an altercation occurred during which Fitzpatrick said he was shot in the arm by Ned and struck with a shovel by Ellen Kelly. Ellen and two men were charged for the shooting and its intent to prevent Dan's arrest, being sentenced to three years for Ellen, with her newborn baby, and 6 years in the case of the men.[11] Ned and Dan escaped, hiding out in the nearby Wombat Ranges, where they were joined by two mates, Joe Byrne and Steve Hart. The four men were considered to be the core of the Kelly Gang, but other associates also came and went, including Ned's cousin Tom Lloyd. According to Ned, they lived illegally but peacefully in the bush, occupying a house with twenty acres of land on Bullock Creek, running a still to make whiskey and doing some gold seeking.[12]

Police Superintendent John Sadleir was assigned the task of apprehending the Kellys but for five months no active attempt was made to find them. In October, Chief Commissioner of Police F.C. Standish agreed that efforts should be stepped up and approved of a reward of £100 being posted and two armed search parties being established.[13] One of these parties, made up of four police officers of Irish origin, was attacked by the Kelly gang at their Stringybark Creek camp. Exactly what happened is not clear. According to Ned, when they approached, one of the two policemen present, Thomas Lonigan, drew his revolver and Ned shot him dead in self-defence. Countering this, there was evidence to suggest that Lonigan did not manage to remove his firearm from its holster. The second policeman, Thomas McIntyre, surrendered. When the other police officers returned, they would not surrender to the gang, so Ned shot both, again lethally. In the confusion, McIntyre escaped and raised the alarm, while the gang stripped the camp of food, weapons, horses and even took a ring and pocket watch from the dead bodies.

The murder of three policemen in this ambush raised the Kelly gang to a high priority not only for the police force, but for the Victorian government. Based on an act which had been in effect in NSW in 1865 and 1866 to counter an earlier wave of bushranging, a Felons Apprehension Act (1878) was passed by the Victorian parliament, which declared to be an outlaw anyone who had committed a capital crime and wilfully avoided apprehension after a summons requiring their surrender had been published in the *Government Gazette*. If armed, these outlaws were outside of the protection of the law.[14] They could be captured, alive or dead, by anyone. As was stated during the parliamentary debate, they could be shot like a kangaroo.[15] Rewards for catching the Kellys increased over time, ultimately reaching £8000 with contributions from both the Victorian and NSW governments. NSW re-enacted its Felons Apprehension Act to help with its own actions against the Kellys and left the legislation in place until 1976.[16] Taking advantage of the new railway line to northeastern Victoria (opened in 1873), Standish despatched reinforcements from Melbourne, reaching a peak of 217 men in December 1878 and maintaining over 150 in the district for the next year, arming them with Spencer repeating rifles and breech-loading double-barrelled guns.[17] Special trains were put on to rush police anywhere the Kellys were thought to be and parties of armed police travelled the roads and towns, searching houses and interrogating occupants. In 1879, trackers from the Queensland Native Police were brought in to assist, including Butchulla people from K'gari (Fraser Island).

With little left to lose, the Kelly gang went on a crime spree around the Riverina region. After taking 22 hostages at Faithfull's Creek Station, they robbed the National Bank at nearby Euroa of £2000 in December 1878. Police command decided to step up the firepower against the Kellys and artillery pieces began to be sent to the towns of Kelly Country. The Kelly Gang's crimes and their style of committing them brought attention from the press, the public and the authorities, who all started to follow their every move with great interest. They were young and foolhardy, confident in their own skills and cleverness and they began to perform their bushranger characters for the audience, some of whom looked on in admiration and some in fear and disgust.

Bushrangers

The young men of the Kelly gang, born in the 1850s, had grown up with stories of bushrangers, past and present. The origins of bushranging in Australia go back to the first years of colonisation. John "Black" Caesar who ran away from the Sydney settlement in 1790 is said to have been the first bushranger.[18] Some of these fugitives were accepted by Aboriginal groups and others formed self-sustaining camps, but most turned to stealing goods and livestock to support themselves. They were hunted down by the penal authorities not only as absconders and thieves, but also because of their potential to inspire other convicts to run away by demonstrating that life outside of the convict system was possible. Already in 1814, people in NSW were being reminded that it was their duty to assist with the capture of "Runaways and Bushrangers" who were said to be infesting the country and "rendering the necessary Intercourses of Life full of Danger."[19] Large rewards were posted for the apprehension of bushrangers or information leading to the conviction of anyone who provided supplies or shelter to a bushranger, each set at 50 guineas (£52 10s) in VDL in 1815.[20] The hanging of bushrangers contributed to the high number of executions in the island colony, which reached 103 in 1826–27.[21] They remained such a problem in NSW that in 1830, a Bushranging Act was passed making bushranging a specific crime which was punishable by execution within 2 days of a guilty verdict. The Act put the onus on individuals to prove they were *not* escaped convicts, had *not* committed robberies and did *not* use their firearms illegally, as well as setting life imprisonment as punishment for those who received goods obtained by robbery.[22] This legislation was not enough to stamp out the crime and bushranging became a consistent presence in the Australian colonies, shifting over time from serving convicts to others who preferred, or were driven, to live outside of social bounds and earn their living through crime.

The new wealth of the 1850s gold rush period encouraged more bushranging as gangs held up stagecoaches, stole from pubs and banks and robbed the homesteads of the well to do. As Sue West argued, while some cultivated a flamboyant and chivalrous reputation, most were rather ordinary offenders, committing small crimes around their local area. What made bushrangers distinctive was operating in rural settings, on horseback, carrying firearms, and with an audience. Taking goods from an empty homestead or vacant shop was simple theft, but the bushranging crimes required victims to be present and offered opportunities for eyewitness accounts.[23] As a boy, Ned Kelly would have known of Mad Dan Morgan who was active in the Riverina district of Victoria in the 1860s as a horse thief, house robber and murderer of three men, including two police officers. He was shot by a member of a vigilante group while holding up a station near Wangaratta. Some 300 people gathered to witness the inquest into his death. Once his killing was determined to have been a justifiable homicide, his beard was cut from his face as a souvenir and his body put on display before his head was sent to Melbourne to be examined by a professor of comparative anatomy.[24] One of Kelly's contemporaries as a bushranger was Captain Moonlite, a name taken by Andrew George Scott, an Irish immigrant, engineer and clergyman, who started as a conventional bank robber but turned bushranger in 1879.[25] After a shootout with police near Wagga Wagga, he was tried for murder and executed in Sydney in January 1880. Attesting to the public interest in bushrangers, death masks were made of many of them, including Morgan, Scott and Kelly, for study and public amusement.[26]

Without any property likely to make him a target, bushrangers would have been attractive figures for young Ned Kelly. Their exploits were the subjects of newspaper articles, songs and stories and a relief from the tedium of daily life. Kelly likely modelled some of his own actions on what he had heard about other bushrangers. Like him, they rejected the conventional life of labour for little reward set out for working class men and instead lived off the fortunes of others.

The Jerilderie Letter

Another shared feature of bushrangers was mobility and the Kelly Gang took pleasure in surprising people with their presence. In February 1879, they were some 200 kilometres north of their usual haunts in the NSW town of Jerilderie. In one of the reversals of the usual order in which they delighted, they captured the two policemen stationed in the town, shut them up in the police cell and then walked around the town in police uniforms, before holding up the local bank. Ned took the opportunity to pass on to the bank's accountant a long manifesto, dictated by him and written down by Joe Byrne, who made a copy on the bank's stationery. This was the second time Ned had put his own case in written form. An earlier letter, signed "Edward Kelly, A Forced Outlaw," had been sent to journalist and politician Donald Cameron in December 1878 and is known as the Cameron Letter. From Jerilderie, instead of having the letter published as Kelly had wanted, the letter was sent to the bank's headquarters in Melbourne. Newspapers published summaries of it but it was suppressed by the police and not allowed to be published in full until 1930.[27] This Jerilderie letter (an excerpt which is the Primary Source for this chapter) provides historians with a great deal of information not only about Kelly's motivations, and self-justifications, but his language, and his world view.

Kelly's anti-English stance is clear in the letter. Drawing upon stories told by his grandfather, he called England a "nation that has destroyed, massacred and murdered [Irish people's] forefathers by the greatest of torture as rolling them down hill in spiked barrels, pulling their toes and fingernails, and on the wheel and every torture imaginable." He perceived this persecution as being continued in Australia, referring to Irish people, including his own father, being:

> transported to Van Dieman's Land to pine their young lives away in starvation and misery among tyrants worse than the promised hell itself … [or] were doomed to Port McQuarie, Toweringabbie [Toongabbie, near Sydney] and Norfolk Island and Emu Plain. And in those places of tyranny and condemnation, many a blooming Irishman rather than subdue to the Saxon yoke were flogged to death and bravely died in servile chains, but true to the Shamrock and a credit to Paddy's land.[28]

Knowledge of the names and reputations of these places was passed on to people with little formal education like Ned Kelly through folk ballads, in this case "Moreton Bay."[29] This hatred of the English extended to the Victorian government and to the colony's police. He saved his worst (or best) insults for the Irish immigrants who joined the police force, calling them:

> a parcel of big ugly, fat necked, wombat headed, big bellied, magpie legged, narrow hipped splaw-footed sons of Irish bailiffs or English landlords which is better known as officers of justice or Victorian police.

Kelly's words also reveal his own experience as he uses metaphors drawing upon the sights and sounds of his rural upbringing and the birds and animals of the Australian bush.

Australian Bushrangers and Their Supporters

The long title of the Felons Apprehension Act was "An Act to facilitate the taking or apprehending of persons charged with certain felonies and *the punishment of those by whom they are harbored.*" This made it clear that one of the concerns of the authorities was that the Kellys, like earlier bushrangers, were not acting alone, but with the support and collusion of others. Anyone found to have aided a felon by providing shelter, firearms or horses, of having provided them with information or withheld intelligence on their movements from police, could be imprisoned for up to fifteen years, with hard labour. Within a few months of the passage of the act, it was being used to hold fourteen men in the Beechworth gaol on suspicion of having provided support to the Kelly gang. As there was no evidence, they were soon released, feeling even more hostile to the police than before.

As they established themselves as bushrangers, the Kelly gang crafted an image which would draw attention and admiration. They were flash. They dressed flamboyantly, rode handsome stolen horses and used better saddlery than anyone else, and the Kelly gang deliberately committed their crimes in showy ways. They issued grand threats that they would attack the leading authority figures, dressed up as policemen and as women and held up whole towns. They would sometimes track those who were tracking them, just to show off. The gang enjoyed reading the newspaper coverage of their exploits. Daily updates on where they had been seen and what they had done gained them supporters in the cities as well, where larrikins sang Kelly ballads to taunt the police.

The appeal of the bushranger ran deeper than entertainment, however. In the divided society of nineteenth-century Australia, for some, they also represented the powerless striking out at the powerful. Historians John McQuilton and Sue West have both argued that a sub-group of high-profile bushrangers were social bandits, using a concept developed by Eric Hobsbawm to describe peasants who refused to accept their lot and instead earned a living by acting against those with power, influence and wealth, using the fictional Robin Hood as an exemplar.[30] These good bandits were admired by people of the same class, who suffered from oppression but had no institutional way to express their grievances.[31] *Meg Foster in her essay reminds us that the social bandit argument overlooks the bushrangers who did not benefit from community support, in particular drawing attention to those other bushrangers who were not white or male.*

In the case of Ned Kelly, some of the free selectors of northeastern Victoria saw him as correcting the inequities with which they lived, where the squatters were rich and they were poor, and the squatters seemed to control the police and manipulate the legal system against them. The Kelly gang were careful to cultivate this image. Bushrangers needed all sorts of assistance, from food supplies to information about the movements of police, as well as for their own locations not to be revealed, so it was very much in their best interests to act the role of social bandits. The Kellys avoided harming those from their own social stratum, and provided them with hospitality, at the expense of the publicans whose premises they held up. In NSW in the 1860s, West found that almost half of all bushranging crime was committed against innkeepers, storekeepers and squatters. There were examples of the Kelly gang returning things they had taken, from horses to watches, when they realised that they belonged to a poor person or a woman; befriending fellow travellers on the roads without revealing their identity; and destroying mortgage papers when robbing banks so there was no record of loans needing to be repaid.[32]

For their part, many people in what the subsequent Royal Commission termed the "disturbed district" or Kelly Country, extending from Mansfield, Benalla and Beechworth to the Murray River, supported the gang. The Victorian police force struggled to track the Kellys through the thick and hilly bush, broken up by ravines and rivers and expected them to be sick and starving after almost two years on the run. However, the doctor who examined Ned Kelly after his capture reported that he was in splendid physical condition, well-nourished and clean. This was because the gang had not been living off the land and camping out all of this time but were being taken in and hidden by friends and supporters.

Other scholars have challenged the idea that the Kellys can be regarded as social bandits. They draw attention to the violence and brutality they displayed and argue that the dominant responses to them were disgust and fear of being attacked or robbed.[33] Police Commissioner Standish believed that many people only aided the Kellys out of fear:

> [They] were intimidated by a fear of the consequences from giving any information whatsoever to the police. Not only their lives and those of their families were in danger, but their cattle, and sheep, and horses, and property were liable to be stolen or destroyed.[34]

One person who did provide the police with information was Bricky Williamson, who had been jailed for his role in the wounding of Constable Fitzpatrick. From Pentridge prison, he provided a statement about the gang members, where they were likely to be hiding and even drew a sketch map of the area around the Kelly house.[35] Safely out of reach of the gang, he was able to try to ingratiate himself to the authorities. Confirming that retribution for informing was a genuine concern, the gang's final victim, in June 1880, was a former friend named Aaron Sherritt who was shot dead by Joe Byrne in the doorway to his hut for colluding with police, four of whom were inside, on watch for the Kelly gang.

Newspaper articles about the Kelly outbreak often reflect this hostile perspective as the newspapers were produced by and for the respectable classes who stood to lose from the disruption the Kelly Outbreak caused. The large, urban newspapers also staunchly supported law and order. Reporting the murder of the policemen at Stringybark Creek, the *Age* decried this revival of bushranging, blaming the continuing unsettled nature of the colony for enabling "monsters" like Kelly to commit daring "atrocities" and condemning any "romantic sympathy" for them.[36] Some local newspapers from areas near the Kelly's home base like the *Benalla Standard* did portray the Kellys more sympathetically. The power of the large newspapers to frame not only understandings at the time but those of historians is evident in the absence of the *Benalla Standard* for this period from the Trove database. Careful historians must still go to the State Library of Victoria to access microfilm copies of newspapers like this which may dissent from the more commonly published point of view.

While cultivating community support was important to the Kelly gang, some have suggested that Ned Kelly developed grandiose ideas that went well beyond what those around him aspired to. Certainly, the Jerilderie letter contains some big claims, including that he would slaughter his enemies through an unstated stratagem that would shock the British army. His vision was of an independent region which was not subject to interventions from Melbourne where an idealised egalitarian rural society could thrive. Recognising the role of the telegraph in imposing the colonial government's authority on the regions, including for police communications, telegraph lines were cut and offices targeted by the Kellys. Similarly, the railway was understood as both a symbolic and practical means of asserting central control, including in tracking the gang. It was not a coincidence that one of Kelly's last acts as an outlaw was to tear up the railway tracks outside of Glenrowan.

Catching the Kellys

As they evaded police with the help of supporters and continued their crime wave, the reward for the capture of the Kelly gang was increased to £2000 each. In total, the Victorian government invested over £50,000 into hunting the Kellys, using all of the resources they had available, including mounted military-style search parties, a spy system and Aboriginal trackers. The Royal Commission on the Police Force of Victoria held in 1881 to investigate why bringing the Kellys to justice had been so difficult noted poor leadership, favouritism, procrastination, inefficiency, cowardice, confusion, lack of training and excessive bureaucracy.

The final showdown was orchestrated by the gang rather than the police. They anticipated that after the murder of Aaron Sherritt, a large force would be sent from Melbourne by special train to capture them. Their plan was to make the train derail outside Glenrowan, killing so many police that the gang could rob another bank without being apprehended, giving them funds to continue their outlaw lives, or perhaps to depart the colonies altogether. Having overseen the destruction of a section of track on 27 June 1880, they gathered 60 residents of Glenrowan into a pub, to await the expected derailment. The plan was frustrated when school teacher Thomas Curnow was permitted to leave the pub. He walked along the railway line with a light to warn the driver who was able to stop the train. The police, trackers, journalists and women who had come to spectate disembarked safely and the police prepared to do battle.

Meanwhile, the gang members put on the heavy suits of armour made from plough mould boards (the sheets of metal which lift and turn soil during ploughing) which had been reported as going missing around the region over the previous 6 months.[37] Once they were tracked to the pub, shots were exchanged over a 14-hour period, with 2 of the hostages killed. Ned escaped from the battle for a time, but returned, calling for his mates. As he did, he added to the mystique around him by appearing in the morning mist like a very tall, black apparition which, covered in armour, was apparently bulletproof. His unprotected arms and legs became the targets, and he was captured. With Ned Kelly in custody, it was decided to set fire to the pub to force the remaining gang members out. It is likely they were already dead, Byrne having been shot standing at the bar and Dan Kelly and Hart thought to have shot each other to avoid capture. Byrne's corpse was rescued from the flames and then tied to a window of the Benalla Police station, where the press took photographs of it to use as the basis of wood-cut illustrations for their newspapers.[38] Displaying the bodies of bushrangers was a common practice which Gilmour notes not only reassured a nervous public that the feared figure was really dead (and confirmed the loss to their supporters) and allowed for ghoulish observation of the state of the bullet-riddled body but further punished the offender by denying them the respectful treatment generally accorded to human remains.[39] Postmortem photographs published in newspapers or printed on cards extended this opportunity to savour the victory over wrongdoing or to mourn a romanticised anti-hero.

Ned Kelly was taken to Beechworth for an initial hearing and then to Melbourne to be tried in the Central Criminal Court for the murder of Constable Lonigan. He was found guilty and sentenced by Judge Redmond Barry to be executed. Although over 4000 people gathered in Melbourne to show their support for him, and 32,000 people signed petitions asking that he be granted a reprieve, mercy was not extended, and Ned Kelly was hanged in Melbourne Gaol on 11 November 1880, with a crowd of 6000 people described as loafers and larrikins assembled outside and two Irish Roman Catholic priests by his side to administer last rites. His final words are often said to have been "Such is life" but more reliably he said, "I suppose it has come to this."[40] A death mask was made and put on display the next day. It was used by phrenologist A.S. Hamilton to provide the insights that Kelly's skull showed overdeveloped tendencies to high self-esteem, combativeness and destructiveness and underdeveloped cautiousness and conscientiousness.[41] Kelly's mother was still in jail serving her 3-year sentence for the incident that started the Kelly Outbreak and was permitted to see Ned the day before he died. She lived into her 90s, in a small house near Greta, dying in 1923.

Conclusion

Placing Ned Kelly in his social context helps with understanding why he has become Australia's most famous offender. His crimes grew out of larger issues including the Irish resentment of the English and the tensions between squatters and free selectors. His stand against authority was admired by many in similar situations even as much as it was decried by those who felt at risk of becoming victims of the gang. There is no doubt that Kelly was a career criminal, starting with perjury as he protected family members in court, progressing to cattle stealing, assaults, bank robberies and murder. Over time, the crimes themselves have tended not to be discussed or remembered. Ned Kelly's reputation for courage, flamboyance, standing up to authority and sympathy with the oppressed have remained, and it is those qualities with which many Australians identify.

In terms of Australian underworlds, in the history of the Kelly Gang, we can see something of one here. The Kellys were part of a large group of disadvantaged people in rural areas, some with convict ancestry and some of Irish ethnicity, who consistently engaged in crime throughout their lives. They operated to a different and distinctive moral code, within which it was acceptable to take from those who had more than they did, and they were supported in this by friends, neighbours and relatives. The judge who sentenced Ned Kelly to be executed certainly saw them in this way. He said Kelly was a member of a class which disregarded the evil consequences of crime and that such a class was particularly likely to emerge in a new community which did not have the strong social bonds of older countries. The determined, if somewhat ineffective, response of the Victorian government to what they called the Kelly Outbreak showed the concern those in authority had about the potential impact this underworld could have in creating a disordered and unsettled society. In particular, Judge Barry declared that these "self-made heroes" had to be punished to encourage other foolish, unprincipled youths to change their behaviour. These youths feature prominently in Chapter 7, but we now turn to a topic which explains why the heads of bushrangers like Ned Kelly were of such interest to scientists and the public: the issue of what an underworld might look like.

Suggested Readings

Cormick, Craig, ed. *Ned Kelly: Under the Microscope*. Canberra: CSIRO Publishing, 2014.

MacFarlane, Ian and Russ Scott. "Ned Kelly: Stock Thief, Bank Robber, Murderer, Psychopath," *Psychiatry, Psychology and Law* 21, no. 5 (2014): 716–46.

McQuilton, John. *The Kelly Outbreak 1887–1880: The Geographical Dimensions of Social Banditry*. Melbourne: University of Melbourne Press, 1979.

Tranter, Bruce and Jed Donoghue. "Ned Kelly: Armoured Icon," *Journal of Sociology* 46, no. 2 (2010): 187–205.

West, Susan. *Bushranging and the Policing of Rural Banditry in New South Wales, 1860–1880*. Melbourne: Australian Scholarly Publishing, 2009.

ESSAY: THE OTHER BUSHRANGERS

Meg Foster

Bushrangers are Australian national icons. We know them from folklore and popular culture, merchandise and films and songs. And although a couple of hundred years separate real bushrangers from their likeness in the present day, historians usually start their research from the same point – they begin with bushrangers' popularity.

The most common framework that historians use to understand Kelly and his bushranging brethren is that of "social banditry."[42] By looking at a bushranger's popularity with their supporters, historians seek to use these men to understand the social group to which bushrangers belonged and the world of which they were a part. Although this method can be useful, it can also conceal more than it reveals about Australia's past.

The "social bandit" model overlooks bushrangers who did not receive support from white settlers. There were "other" bushrangers, who were not white men and who did not receive support from colonists as a result. Aboriginal, African-American, Chinese and female bushrangers did not fit the bushranging mould created by colonists. Bushranging has long been associated with white settler masculinity. Other bushrangers often committed the same crimes and operated at the same time as white, bushranging men, but they never entered mainstream folklore or popular culture, experienced no groundswell of support and they were never lauded as national heroes in the same way as white, male bushrangers.[43]

Aboriginal bushranger Jimmy Governor robbed settlers almost the length and breadth of New South Wales in 1900. He taunted the police with their missteps, and evaded capture for 3 months, despite being the target of the "largest manhunt in Australian history."[44] Like the Kellys, Governor also committed murder. Although he claimed to be a bushranger and was inspired by white bushranging tales, Governor is remembered as a mass murderer rather than a bushranging legend.[45] African-American bushranger "Black Douglas" was renowned as the "terror of the goldfields" in his own time of the 1880s, but he was never heroised for robbing diggers or escaping the clutches of the Victorian police. He was an object of fear and anxiety who has since been forgotten.[46]

Although there were never as many other bushrangers as there were white bushranging men, this is not the reason for their exclusion from our histories. It was other bushrangers' race and/or gender that meant there was no space for them in colonial myth-making and later our understanding of the nation's past.

However, other bushrangers were not completely friendless – they had supporters of their own. In some instances, settlers may have downplayed other bushrangers' networks to make them appear less threatening. Colonists claimed that the Chinese bushranger Sam Poo was "unfriended," but this appears unlikely.[47] Not only were other Chinese people spotted in the vicinity of Sam Poo's capture (casting grave doubts as to whether Sam Poo was the Chinese man who committed these crimes) but it was by far the norm for Chinese men to be working and living together in the Australian colonies.[48]

The extent of other bushrangers' support varied from individual to individual. In some instances, such as that of "Black Douglas" or Worimi woman Mary Ann Bugg, there is evidence of local or familial support. Douglas was part of a criminal gang of white ex-convicts while Bugg appears to have gained assistance from Aboriginal people, possibly her Indigenous kin.[49] In other instances, such as the case of Jimmy Governor, colonists feared that other bushrangers were not alone and would incite others to join them. Governor's Aboriginal family was illegally locked up in the rural town of Wollar and later Mudgee Gaol for fear that they would join Governor in his criminal exploits.[50] Just as there were elements of physical and imagined support for white, male bushrangers, there were for other bushrangers too. The difference is that other bushrangers' advocates were not from the ranks of otherwise law-abiding white colonists. Their race placed these supporters outside the bounds of white society.

Studies of bushranging in Australia currently privilege white colonists' perspectives. The nation's archives were created by settlers and enshrined their ideas, and so the "public opinion" that social banditry refers to is that of the *white, colonial* public. Local or familial groups who supported other bushrangers are a lot harder to see than white settlers, and we often do not have enough material to bring these people squarely into view. It is difficult to push beyond the colonial frame of reference, especially when social banditry is premised on substantial evidence of popular support. Colonial ideas of difference continue to shape ideas about bushranging and social banditry. They influence who we believe garnered popular support and by extension, who warrants our attention, remembrance and understanding.

PRIMARY SOURCE: THE JERILDERIE LETTER, 1879, EXCERPT

In the last two pages of the letter authored by Ned Kelly and copied out by Joe Byrne in a bank in the NSW town of Jerilderie in February 1879, Kelly makes his demands. Referring to those who joined together in a Stock Protection Society, pooling their funds to offer rewards for stolen livestock, he directs them to instead distribute their money to the poor. Going further, Kelly commands all with reason to fear him to sell their properties, distribute some of their profits to widows and orphans and then leave the colony or face terrible consequences. His words capture his sense that he is on the side of right, working on behalf of the poor and vulnerable, and his belief that his actions have placed him in a position from which he can deliver orders which "must be obeyed."

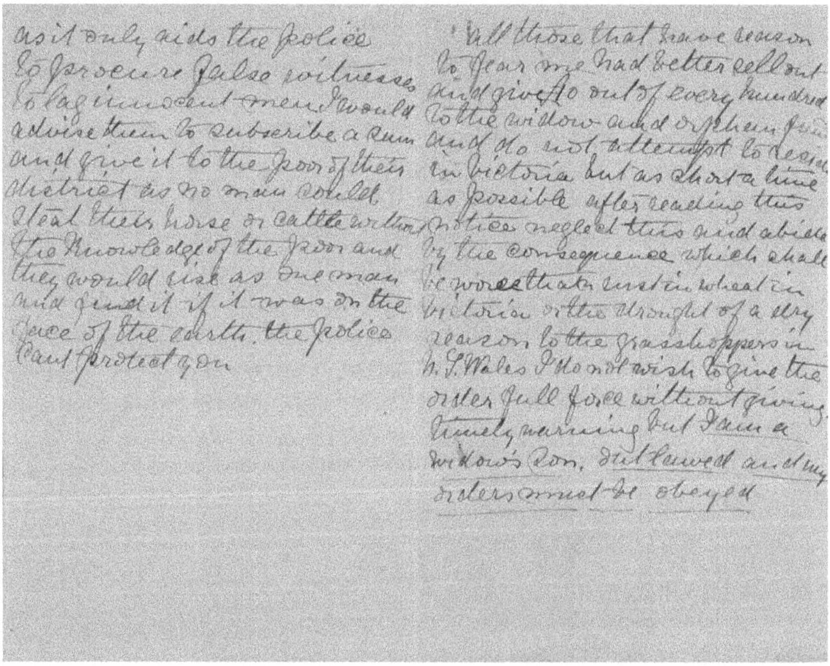

as it only aids the police
to procure false witnesses
to lag innocent men I would
advise them to subscribe a sum
and give it to the poor of their
district as no man could
steal their horse or cattle without
the knowledge of the poor and
they would rise as one man
and find it if it was on the
face of the earth. the police
cant protect you

All those that have reason
to fear me had better sell out
and give 10 out of every hundred
to the widow and orphan fund
and do not attempt to reside
in Victoria but as short a time
as possible after reading this
notice neglect this and abide
by the consequence which shall
be worse than the rust in wheat in
Victoria or the drought of a dry
season to the grasshoppers in
N. S. Wales I do not wish to give the
order full force without giving
timely warning but I am a
widow's son, outlawed and my
orders must be obeyed

Figure 5.2 Ned Kelly, Jerilderie Letter, handwritten, 1879. National Museum of Australia.

Notes

1 Sally Jackson and Graham Shirley, "Restoring the world's first feature film," *National Film and Sound Archive*, https://www.nfsa.gov.au/latest/story-kelly-gang (accessed 6 June 2022).

2 Thank you to Meg Foster for the example from the Sydney Olympics. The reference to Kelly as a folk hero has since been removed from the government site. See a critique here: Melissa Davey, "Ned Kelly expert accuses government of pushing biased view of bushranger," *The Guardian*, 9 January 2017, https://www.theguardian.com/australia-news/2017/jan/09/ned-kelly-expert-accuses-government-of-pushing-biased-view-of-bushranger (accessed 28 January 2022).

3 Bruce Tranter and Jed Donoghue, "Ned Kelly: Armoured icon," *Journal of Sociology* 46, 2 (2010): 199.

4 This account is informed by several accounts of Ned Kelly's life, including John McQuilton, *The Kelly Outbreak 1887–1880: The Geographical Dimensions of Social Banditry*, Melbourne: University of Melbourne Press, 1979; John Molony, *Ned Kelly*, Melbourne: Melbourne University Press, 2001 and Grantlee Kieza, *Mrs Kelly: The Astonishing life of Ned Kelly's mother*, Melbourne: Harper Collins, 2017.
John Kelly's convict records can be viewed on the Digital Panopticon website: John Kelly, *Prince Regent* (2), Record ID fasai39279, https://www.digitalpanopticon.org/life?id=fasai39279 (accessed 9 November 2021).

5 Richard Waterhouse, *The Vision Splendid, A Social and Cultural History of Rural Australia*, Perth: Curtin University Books, 2005, 24–6.

6 Police Commission, *Second Progress Report of the Royal Commission of Enquiry into the Circumstances of the Kelly Outbreak, the Present State and Organisation of the Police Force, etc.*, Melbourne: Government Printer, 1881, vii.

7 Victoria. No. CCXXXIII. An Act to consolidate the Law relating to Crimes and the Practice in Criminal Courts, 2 June 1864, available at http://www5.austlii.edu.au/au/legis/vic/hist_act/tclaps1864316/ (accessed 31 May 2022).

8 "The Bushranger Kelly," *Ovens and Murray Advertiser*, May 10, 1870, 2.

9 Police Commission, Second Progress Report of the Royal Commission of Enquiry into the Circumstances of the Kelly Outbreak, viii–ix.

10 Ned Kelly, Letter, known as the Jerilderie Letter, in Joe Byrne's handwriting, February 1879, manuscript, State Library Victoria, MS 13361.

11 Angus McIntyre, "Ned Kelly, A Folk Hero," John Carroll, ed. *Intruders in the Bush, The Australian Quest for Identity*, Melbourne: Oxford University Press, 1982, 39.

12 "Statements in the Gaol," *Leader* (Melbourne), November 13, 1880, 22.

13 Chief Commissioner of Police FC Standish's account of the Kelly Outbreak can be read in the Minutes of Evidence of the Royal Commission on the Police in Victoria, Melbourne: Government Printer, 1881, available at https://ironicon.com.au/the-royal-commission-kelly-outbreak.html (accessed 12 November 2021).

14 "Felons Apprehension Act 1878" (Victoria), http://www.austlii.edu.au/au/legis/vic/hist_act/faa1878214.pdf (accessed 10 November 2021).

15 Michael Eburn, "Outlawry in Colonial Australia: The Felons Apprehension Acts 1865–1899," *Australian and New Zealand Law and History E-Journal* 6 (2005): 82, https://www.austlii.edu.au/cgi-bin/viewdoc/au/journals/ANZLawHisteJl/2005/6.html?context=1;query=outlawry;mask_path=au/journals/ANZLawHisteJl.

16 Eburn notes that only ten offenders were ever declared outlaws in the colonies with this legislation: John Gilbert and John Dunn of bushranger Ben Hall's gang; Thomas Clarke, Patrick Connell and Jimmy and Joe Governor in NSW; the four members of the Kelly gang in Victoria; and no one in Queensland (Eburn, "Outlawry in Colonial Australia," 85).

17 Police Commission, Second Progress Report of the Royal Commission of Enquiry into the Circumstances of the Kelly Outbreak, xviii.

18 Murray Johnson, "Australian Bushrangers: Law, retribution and the public imagination," Robyn Lincoln and Shirleene Robinson, eds. *Crime Over Time: Temporal Perspectives on Crime and Punishment in Australia*, Newcastle upon Tyne: Cambridge Scholars, 2010, 192.

19 "Government and General Orders, Civil Department," *Sydney Gazette*, July 30, 1814, 1.

20 No title, *Sydney Gazette and NSW Advertiser*, May 20, 1815, 2.

21 Robyn Lincoln and Shirleene Robinson, "When the Penalty was Death," Robyn Lincoln and Shirleene Robinson, eds. *Crime Over Time: Temporal Perspectives on Crime and Punishment in Australia*, Newcastle upon Tyne: Cambridge Scholars, 2010, 192.

22 Bruce Kercher, *An Unruly Child: A History of law in Australia*, Sydney: Allen and Unwin, 1995, 106.

23 Susan West, *Bushranging and the Policing of Rural Banditry in New South Wales, 1860–1880*, Melbourne: Australian Scholarly Publishing, 2009, 3–4.

24 Joanna Gilmour, *Sideshow Alley: Infamy, the Macabre and the Portrait*, Canberra: National Portrait Gallery, 2015, 77–78.

25 "Scott, Andrew George (1842–1880)," *Australian Dictionary of Biography*. National Centre of Biography, Australian National University, https://adb.anu.edu.au/biography/scott-andrew-george-4546/text7451, published first in hardcopy 1976 (accessed 28 January 2022).

26 Death masks are held in many Australian collections including those of Sydney's Justice and Police Museum and Australian Museum, the National Portrait Gallery in Canberra and Melbourne's Old Melbourne Gaol.

27 An example of the edited version made available is "The Autobiography of Kelly" published in the *Leader* on 13 November 1880, 22.

28 You can read or listen to the Jerilderie letter on the National Museum of Australia website: https://www.nma.gov.au/explore/features/ned-kelly-jerilderie-letter (accessed 10 November 2021).

29 Many versions of the ballad "Moreton Bay" exist, but some have the chorus (the most memorable element of a song) as "Moreton Bay you'll find no equal/Norfolk Island and Emu Plains/At Castle Hill and cursed Toongabbie/And all time places in New South Wales" (Moreton Bay, Frank the Poet – Francis MacNamara, 1811–1861, frankthepoet.blogspot.com (accessed 24 February 2022)). Frank the Poet and the use of ballads in history making are discussed by Anna Clark in *Making Australian History*, Melbourne: Vintage, 2022, 68–72.

30 Eric Hobsbawm, "Social Bandits: Reply," *Comparative Studies in Society and History* 14, 4 (1972): 504.

31 McQuilton, *The Kelly Outbreak 1887–1880*, especially Ch 8 "Twenty months of untrammeled freedom"; Sue West, "'The Thiefdom': Bushrangers, supporters and social banditry in 1860s New South Wales," *Journal of the Royal Australian Historical Society* 101, 2 (2015): 134–155.

32 McIntyre, "Ned Kelly," 42–43.

33 Ian MacFarlane and Russ Scott. "Ned Kelly: Stock thief, bank robber, murderer, psychopath," *Psychiatry, Psychology and Law* 21, no. 5 (2014): 716–746.

34 Evidence of F.C. Standish. *Minutes of Evidence taken before Royal Commission on the Police in Victoria*, Melbourne: Government Printer, 1881, 23 March 1881, 2.

35 Police Commission, Second Progress Report of the Royal Commission of Enquiry into the Circumstances of the Kelly Outbreak, viii.

36 "Murder of Two Constables," *The Age*, 29 October 1878.

37 McIntyre, "Ned Kelly," 50–51.

38 Wendy Morgan, *Ned Kelly Reconstructed*, Melbourne: Cambridge University Press, 1994, 103–07.

39 Gilmour, *Sideshow Alley*, 80–81.

40 "Ned Kelly Sympathy," *Manaro Mercury*, 10 November 1880, 3; "Execution of Ned Kelly," *Victorian Express*, 1 December 1880, 3.
41 Dean Wilson, "Reading Ned's head: Colonial phrenology, popular science and entertainment," Craig Cormick, ed. *Ned Kelly: Under the Microscope*, Canberra: CSIRO Publishing, 2014.
42 Eric Hobsbawm, *Bandits*, London: Abacas, 2001; Eric Hobsbawm, *Primitive Rebels*, London, Abacas, 2017.
43 Meg Foster, *Boundary Crossers: The Hidden History of Australia's Other Bushrangers*, Sydney: NewSouth, 2022.
44 Laurie Moore and Stephan Williams, *The True Story of Jimmy Governor*, Sydney: Allen & Unwin, 2001.
45 Foster, *Boundary Crossers*, Chs. 5 and 6.
46 Foster, *Boundary Crossers*, Ch. 1.
47 "Summary," *Sydney Mail*, February 25, 1865, 4.
48 Foster, *Boundary Crossers*, Ch. 3.
49 Foster, *Boundary Crossers*, Chs. 1, 2 and 4.
50 Meg Foster, "The Forgotten War of 1900: Jimmy Governor and the Aboriginal People of Wollar," *Australian Historical Studies* 50, no. 3 (2019): 305–320.

6 Identifying Underworlds

Identifying the offender is a key focus in investigating crime and prosecuting criminals. Much time is taken with having witnesses describe offenders, police searches for them and formal identification, which can then be contested in court. For their part, lawbreakers want to hide their appearance. A range of strategies are employed to avoid being identified. Offenders may commit their illegal acts at night under cover of darkness, wear masks or disguises, alter their voices or pass notes instead of making verbal commands, or make changes to their appearances after committing a crime such as cutting their hair, shaving a beard or dressing in a different style.

This chapter will examine the means by which law enforcement officers in settler colonial Australia kept track of those who had committed crimes or were thought likely to do so. This started with careful written records of convicts, which were continued for later offenders, in which tattoos played an important and perhaps unanticipated role. Photographs were added to these written records for those entering jail from the 1870s. Sets of images of offenders supported the application of emerging pseudoscientific concepts about physical traits shared by criminals which could be used to identify likely offenders, even before a law was broken. In the twentieth century, new technologies led to greater sophistication of identification techniques, reducing the scale from the whole person down to the level of their microscopic traces.

Looking at this issue historically, the need to establish identity is a problem of modernity. In earlier times, whether in Europe or in Australia before invasion, most people lived in stable communities, where everyone knew everyone else. Any stranger who entered such communities was immediately identifiable as an outsider and was often viewed with suspicion as a potential lawbreaker. In Aboriginal societies, protocols existed by which outsiders approached a group. Their identity was established to reveal their place in webs of relationships, situating them within the Law. This was less well managed in Europe where many folk tales rely on the arrival of the stranger to set up situations of mystery, intrigue and conflict which are only resolved when the newcomer is either incorporated into the group or ejected.

DOI: 10.4324/9781003273561-7

Consider the potential chaos then, from 1788, as thousands of people arrived in Australia who were not only strangers to the original inhabitants but for the most part to one another as well. It was just the sort of environment lawbreakers would relish. No one knew about their past beyond their criminal record and few knew them by name or appearance. The response was to keep careful records of transported convicts and others who offended in the colonies. The types of records created have changed over time as new technologies of photography, fingerprinting and biological testing were applied to identifying offenders. While offenders might seem to be people who "slip under the historian's radar, then vanish silently, like particles of sand dropping through the hourglass, from the historic record," the careful documenting of their lives by those hostile to them has, ironically, made them amongst the most visible people in Australian history.[1]

Convict Indents

Great Britain in the late eighteenth century was building up a range of bureaucratic processes to enable the government to better keep track of its citizens. The Transportation Act of 1784 included guidelines on how those sentenced to transportation would be documented, in addition to their court records.[2] As they were confined awaiting transportation, overseers collected their names, ages, offences, in which court they were convicted, sentences, physical description and behaviour. When their ship was ready to depart, a legal indenture was created to formally transfer the "Property in the Service" of the offenders to the entity shipping them to their destination. The indentures, generally shortened to indents, included for each convict on a ship, their names, ages, offences, courts of conviction and sentences. These documents were passed to the Governor when the ship arrived in the colony of NSW or VDL, transferring legal custody of the convicts to the local administration.

Before leaving the ship on which they had arrived in Australia, each convict had an interview with a colonial Muster Master who wrote down a physical description of them along with their answers to a series of questions which could then be compared with the information in the indents. At first, the information recorded was limited to name, trial place and date and length of sentence, excluding even age and the crime committed. From 1814 to 1815, the convict's age, trade and place of birth were added to the records. In the 1820s, as the usefulness of being able to identify convicts became better understood, more details were added including skin tone or complexion; hair colour; eye colour; particular marks or scars; and height (in feet and inches), as well as the crimes committed by English convicts (from 1826). The name of the ship on which they arrived became part of their record, and in VDL, a police number was allocated to each convict in one of the earliest attempts on the British Empire to link individuals with a unique identifier as a means of keeping track of them, as seen in Figure 3.2.[3]

Every time a convict came into contact with the authorities, for having committed a new crime, for example, these descriptions were reviewed and updated. If a convict ran away, the description would be printed in the newspaper, often with a reward for their return. As one example, the NSW *Government Gazette* for 13 November 1833 included rewards posted for men who took part in an assault and robbery at the property of James Mudie in the Hunter Valley which became known as the Castle Forbes revolt. In contrast with most other crimes committed by convicts, this one directly attacked the property and the life of their assignment master and is understood as an act of protest against ongoing bad treatment by him.[4] Amongst those sought for these offences was John Poole. He was described as having arrived on the ship *Claudine*, aged 22, from Dublin, where he was a joiner (woodworker). He was 5 feet 5½ inches tall, with a ruddy freckled complexion, dark brown hair and blue eyes. Another suspect was 17-year-old James Ryan, transported on the sixth voyage to Australia made by the ship *Eliza* (recorded as *Eliza* (6)). Ryan was from County Tipperary in Ireland, where he had worked as a shoemaker's apprentice. He was 5 feet ¼ inch tall with a fair freckled complexion, brown hair, grey eyes and warts on the back of his right thumb and left hand. Clothing worn at the time of the offence or typically worn by the suspect was often included in these descriptions. Convicts on assignment did not wear uniforms but their public-issue clothing was mass produced and ill fitting. The Castle Forbes men were said to be wearing clothes stolen from Mudie to help them escape detection.

For historians, convict records provide a verbal portrait of Australia's early settler colonists which is rarely matched amongst other populations. The Digital Panopticon site notes that "Convict Indents are one of the most detailed record sets on non-elite people in British history."[5] One aspect which has proven to be revealing is height. An individual's height is an outcome of their genetic inheritances and factors they have experienced in utero and during their lifetimes. Poor nutrition, disease, stress, lack of exposure to sunlight and hard physical labour from a young age all tend to stunt growth, leading to a lower adult height.[6] Finding the average height of convicts transported to Western Australia and comparing them with inmates of Wandsworth Prison in London in the same time period, Nicholas Meinzer found no significant difference, suggesting that those selected for transportation were neither the most disadvantaged people in the prison system nor those considered most healthy and able. Further work comparing British convicts with locally born prisoners in Fremantle Prison found the Australian-born to be on average two centimetres taller, reflecting better living conditions in the colonies.[7]

Another feature of the descriptions which has caught historians' attention is tattoos. Although tattooing was frowned upon by polite society in Britain in the late eighteenth and early nineteenth century, being banned in the Bible (Leviticus 19:28), the practice had grown in popularity amongst the urban working classes after being rediscovered in the Americas and Polynesia. One-third of convict men and one in ten of the women had a tattoo, some acquired before departure from Britain and others on the voyage out. There was a language of tattoos which could be read by those within their cultures. Anchors, for example, meant hope, safety and good luck but their meaning was altered if they were presented with other images. An anchor with a set of scales represented hope for justice; an upside-down anchor signalled no hope. Initials were common, either asserting one's own identity or love for someone else. Other common images were human figures, crosses and mermaids. Colour was unusual, with most tattoos consisting of black outlines made using lamp black, the soot created when oil was burned in a lamp. Tattoos enabled convicts to continue to show who they were as they moved through criminal justice processes which insisted on conformity in behaviour, hair and clothing.

David Kent argues that tattoos are of particular value to historians because of this capacity to reveal how the bearers understood and projected their own identity.[8] Ironically, this exercise in self-expression was also used by the authorities to build up their own power. Permanent marks on the body, including branding and tattooing, had been used in Britain and elsewhere as part of punishment regimes, causing pain as they were administered, a reference point during sentence and a long-lasting visual warning that a person was a past offender. Tattoos acquired voluntarily could also be used for identification. In the Castle Forbes revolt mentioned earlier, while other details supplied about John Poole's appearance would have helped the authorities to narrow down a search, knowing that he had a tattoo of a fish on his left arm, a circular mark and the sun on the back of one hand, a small scar under his left eyebrow and JP tattooed on the upper part of his right arm would permit a confident identification. An instance in which tattoos led to an otherwise unlikely conviction was the case of William Hill who in 1835 was caught after having lived as a free man under a new identity for two years. The written description of Hill made when he arrived as a convict, which included his numerous tattoos, confirmed his convict status and he was returned to servitude.[9]

Tattooing continued to be characteristic of criminals in the colonies. One man born in the 1860s named Arthur Riley, "a well-known larrikin", was a violent thief imprisoned multiple times in the late nineteenth century.[10] He entered Goulburn Gaol in 1894 with no tattoos and left two years later with a long list: many figures of women, a man fighting a lion and several patriotic symbols including a coat of arms with the motto Advance Australia 1867. The tattoos might have provided him with way to pass the time as his behaviour there was recorded as good while it had been deemed very bad in other prisons. Mary Ann Sullivan, who spent time in the Toowoomba Gaol in the last decades of the nineteenth century, had a similar experience. Sullivan entered prison without any tattoos and by 1903 was marked with initials, a year, "Brisbane," a male figure, a cross and a chain.[11] We know this because police and those administering prisons continued to see the value in providing written descriptions of the appearance of offenders, including their tattoos.

As policing was professionalised in the 1830s and 1840s, one man took the idea of keeping written descriptions of offenders a step further. He was commissioner of police for Sydney, William Augustus Miles. In 1840, Miles set up a system of cross-referencing known offenders and their associates in what he called a Registry of Flash Men.[12] The Registry contained information about names, aliases, appearance, address, associates, character, previous convictions, sightings and circumstances of the individuals he considered an underworld.

The Registry of Flash Men was an aid to hands on policing. Miles and his police force were out in the city streets watching and listening. They believed that they knew who likely offenders were and how they were interconnected to one another. The assumption that this knowledge could be useful in crime prevention and apprehending offenders was carried forward from this single registry to a *Police Gazette* for each colony, starting from the 1850s in Victoria and in New South Wales, where the full title was the *NSW Police Gazette and Weekly Record of Crime*. In the 1860s, other colonies followed suit with the Tasmanian *Reports of Crime, etc., etc. etc. for Police Information* and the *South Australian Police Gazette. Police Gazettes* contained information about crimes committed, criminals wanted, criminals apprehended, persons on good behaviour bonds, missing persons, and police appointments and promotions. Assuming that former offenders would again break the law, they included written descriptions of individuals released from police custody. In Tasmania, this included name, age, place of birth, ship of arrival, height, hair colour, distinguishing physical features, date of trial, offence, length of sentence, and place and date of discharge. Those currently being sought were described as fully as possible, and these descriptions were shared between the *Gazettes*. For example, in 1864, the NSW *Police Gazette* reprinted an item from the *Victorian Police Gazette* stating that Matthew Barron (or Barrow) was wanted for assault with intent to rob Constable Arthur Gribbin on the Victorian side of the border with NSW in late June. Barron was described as a 30-year-old Victorian native, a bullock driver who was 5 feet 7 inches with brown hair, a sandy complexion, long visage, pockmarked, little or no beard or whiskers and wearing a waist-length red-lined monkey jacket and an old cabbage tree hat.[13] *The essay by Catharine Coleborne discusses how those charged with vagrancy in Victoria in the following decades were portrayed in the Victorian Police Gazette and how these descriptions made visible people who often sought to be invisible.*

Written descriptions of British convicts transported to Australia and of those who offended in the colonies were an important resource for keeping track of known offenders, whether they were serving convicts who ran away from custody or free people who committed an offence in the colony. The attention to them reflected a belief that crime was largely committed by a small group of repeat offenders, so in trying to solve a crime, those with a prior conviction were a likely starting point. This assumption meant that the same people did come in for investigation and likely that on occasion, past offenders were successfully prosecuted for new crimes which they had not committed. For historians, the detailed records of offenders and suspects provide an unparalleled source of information about the appearance of these otherwise largely undocumented people, which reveals how their life experiences of illness, accident and work, and their cultures of dress and adornment were recorded on their bodies.

The Introduction of the Camera in Policing

Much more rare than these word pictures of offenders were sketches or paintings of them. As Joanna Gilmour found, few colonial images contained convicts, and when they did, the convicts often only served as background details intended to situate a landscape in the penal colonies.[14] When convicts received more attention from an artist, they were often caricatured to play up expected characteristics, as in Augustus Earle's image of a battered work gang of convicts outside the Hyde Park Barracks published in 1830 (see Figure 3.1). There were some exceptions for offenders who became well known because of their identities, activism or their crimes. These included the notorious pickpocket and author George Barrington, and lawyer and political campaigner Thomas Muir. These images were not intended to aid in identification but to give wide audiences a chance to see infamous characters.

The process of identification in law enforcement gained a new element in the 1870s with the introduction of the photographic mug shot. Photography was developed in the late 1830s in France and arrived in Australia in 1841 in the form of the daguerreotype. These were small images printed on a polished silver surface which were easily damaged and had to be kept under a protective glass cover. Experimentation led to alternative image making and fixing processes including the calotype, ambrotype and tintype before exposure on a glass negative which could be used to make large numbers of prints became the standard form.[15]

Photography was and is part art (in terms of composition, framing and lighting) and part science (developing the images and printing from the negatives). The first professional photographer in Australia, George Goodman, set up his daguerreotype portrait studio in Sydney in 1842, later moving on to Bathurst, Hobart, Melbourne, Newcastle, Maitland, Goulburn and Adelaide, and the novelty spread as photographers took their cameras across the countryside. Initially, photographs were produced as a means of providing accurate images of members of well-to-do families, but as it became more familiar, the usefulness of these images for other purposes was explored. From the 1870s, it was decided that photographs would be used to keep track of criminals in prisons and after their release, as had been done in Belgium from the 1840s, in Britain from the 1850s and suggested by Sydney photographer James Freeman in 1859.[16] He wrote that photography could be a detective: "a prisoner escapes, copies of his photograph accompany the hue and cry and his identification is rendered easy."[17] In NSW in 1871 and in Tasmania in 1872, but not until 1892 in Queensland, the process of admission to prison was expanded from making a written account of a person's appearance and background to include the taking of a photograph. In Hobart, Municipal Police Office, Mayor's Court and Hobart Gaol photographs were taken in the

1870s and 1880s by Thomas Nevin, who also ran a business as a commercial portrait photographer in collaboration with his brother, who was a police constable.[18] Over time, these photographs became more systematised, moving from portraiture styles to requiring subjects to pose both squarely facing the camera and in profile. In most jurisdictions, images taken after conviction and again two weeks prior to release were collected into what were known as jail photographic description books and kept on hand to use in identifying suspected reoffenders.

These jail photos are now highly valued by descendants, having captured and preserved images of people often not in a position to create and pass on their own family albums. As the vogue for exchanging small photographic portraits called carte de visit (visiting cards) grew in the 1860s, people who were already offending or would in the future were amongst those who voluntarily had photographs taken.[19] In some cases, somewhat in parallel with tattoos, these images made for personal reasons and intended to show a person at their best were secured and circulated for law enforcement purposes and were reproduced, often as line drawings, in newspapers, as we will see in the cases of two women on trial in Chapter 8.

Police were slower to take up photography than their prison-based colleagues. An early use of police photography was in Switzerland, where photographs were taken of each person arrested for vagrancy in Bern for several years from 1852 and distributed to police around the country to track and obstruct their mobility.[20] Similarly, in Australia, photographs were a particular aid in identifying the highly mobile across jurisdictions. Around 1910, police in Sydney took a new approach, taking what they called "Special Photographs" of those under suspicion but who had not been convicted. One report from the 1930s said the subjects of these photographs were singled out because they were considered already to be professional criminals or likely to fall into a life of vice and crime.[21] In the "Specials," people wore their own clothes not prison uniforms. They were allowed to keep on hats that hid their hair and parts of their faces, and to sit or stand naturally, often in groups. The intention was that these naturalistic photos would help the police to recognise the subjects easily if they saw them in the street or other public places. Rather than measuring sticks to indicate height, a bentwood chair was included in most shots as a way to judge the size of the subject.

By 1930, the Sydney police had built up a collection of glass negatives for over 2000 of these "Specials" portraits. They were used for some time but eventually were packed away in boxes, ending up in a leaky warehouse and finally being moved to a loft over the Justice and Police Museum near Sydney's Circular Quay. There they were rediscovered in 2004 by researcher Peter Doyle. When he started to pull out the sheets of glass, he realised that he had found not only a crime history resource but a social history treasure trove. Since then, these beautifully composed and atmospheric photos have formed the basis of numerous museum exhibitions, books and even fashion shoots.

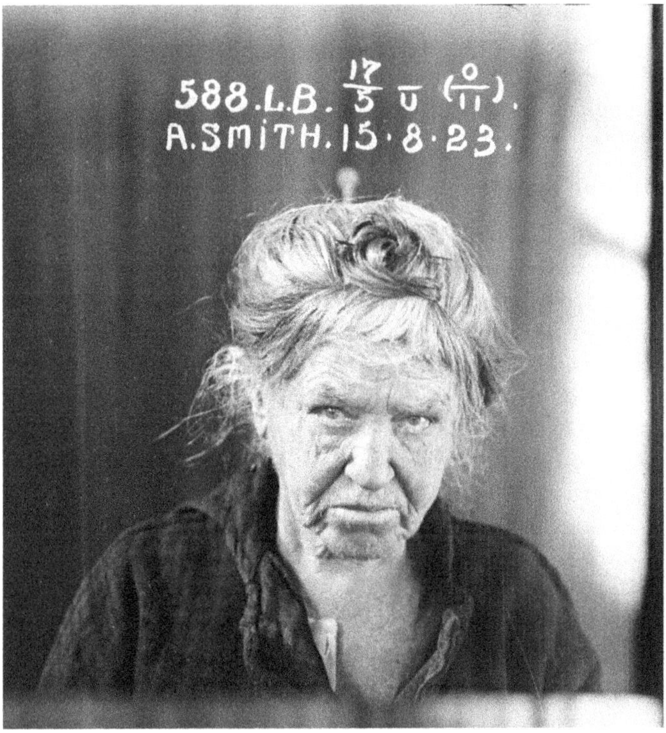

Figure 6.1 A photograph taken of Agnes Smith as part of her admission to Long Bay Women's Reformatory in Sydney in August 1923, for an unknown crime. The process of creating a negative on a glass plate negative produced a very high-resolution image in which fine details of appearance can be seen.

Source: Mug shot of Agnes Smith, 15 August 1923, Long Bay Women's Reformatory. New South Wales. Police Dept. Prisoner identification photograph no. LB 588, held by Justice and Police Museum.

Looking into the faces of these past offenders and people of interest to the police in these photographs, it is tempting to make judgements about them. The camera doesn't lie after all. Or does it? Curator Caleb Williams quoted Susan Sontag who wrote that photographs cannot explain anything but invite endless deduction, speculation and fantasy. Williams deduced that he saw attitudes of "louche defiance, cavalier indifference, disgruntled incomprehension and melancholic resignation" in the photographs.[22] Singling out a few faces from the crowd available online through the Sydney Living Museums' library, E.A.R. Mortimer looks self-assured but perhaps too much so, as if he has something to hide.[23] Agnes Smith, an older woman with a heavily lined face, seems weary while being admitted to Long Bay Women's Reformatory – not for the first time? See Figure 6.1[24] Aiden Feutrill appears thin, poorly dressed, perhaps desperate.[25] Young Isabella Higgs looks sweet, bewildered, about to cry: surely a case of mistaken identity.[26] Francis Flood is steely eyed, no nonsense, with a direct gaze.[27] Based on a set of assumptions which extend from his time to ours, we interpret his photograph and conclude that this one really was a criminal, perhaps part of an underworld.

The Criminal Type

What does a criminal look like? There have always been assumptions about this, based on past experience, prejudices and instinct, but in the nineteenth century, there were several attempts to develop and articulate theories to link actual and potential lawbreakers with specific physical attributes.

The first of these theories was phrenology. Phrenologists believed that the brain was made up of dozens different "organs" or zones, each one relating to a specific aspect of the personality and character.[28] Well-developed attributes created a bump on the skull while flat areas or dips showed that the person was lacking in this trait. Someone who was destructive, for example, would have developed a bump over their right ear, where this character trait was believed to reside, while those who lacked compassion would have a flat section on their upper forehead. For those who believed in phrenology, skulls were seen literally as hard evidence of a person's character and characteristic behaviours, which could predict their future conduct or explain past actions. The founder of phrenology was Austrian physician Franz Gall who published on the topic between 1800 and 1830. His ideas were popularised in Britain by his colleague Johann Spurzheim and were carried to Australia. Phrenology enjoyed long-term popularity in the colonies, with interest divided between encouraging self-improvement amongst settler colonists, demonstrating the assumed inferiority of Aboriginal Australians, with skulls acquired through purchase and the crime of grave robbing, and analysing the skulls of criminals.

Research linking physical traits with behaviour was facilitated in Britain by the Murder Act of 1752 which decreed that the bodies of executed criminals could not be buried in consecrated ground but should be hung in chains in a gibbet to slowly and publicly decompose.[29] As an alternative form of undignified death, the body could be dissected for medical purposes. The awareness that most of the cadavers used in medical training were those of criminals triggered interest in whether they might have features that differed from those of law-abiding people. Back in Australia, the skulls of offenders were used as drawcards to attract audiences to travelling phrenologists' lectures.[30] The reach of these skulls was extended by making plaster casts of the heads of executed murderers and bushrangers which were placed on display to show how deviance was expressed in physical form.[31]

The concept of linking physical traits with criminality was most thoroughly developed by Italian army doctor Cesare Lombroso. Now credited with being the founder of criminal anthropology and its successor, criminology, as a field of study, Lombroso developed his own theory of how moral character could be identified through physical characteristics. Taken together, he designated these features as signalling a criminal type.[32] His core idea was that offenders were evolutionary throwbacks who were inferior to non-criminals and displayed more "primitive" physical and behavioural characteristics. By controlling this group, he reasoned, personal harm and social disorder could be minimised. Lombroso published his theories in the book *L'uomo delinquente (Criminal Man)* in 1876, followed by several revised editions, and *La donna delinquente (Criminal Woman)* in 1893.

While Lombroso made the study of criminal bodies more scientific, his work was clearly informed by long-term prejudices European people had about the hierarchy of races and who was most likely to behave in criminal ways. Lombroso built on these beliefs, developing tools to measure body parts with great precision and tests designed to determine sensitivity to pain and propensity to lie, including a very basic lie detector. Lombroso collected items related to criminals as he conducted his research, extending to death masks, pieces of skin bearing tattoos, prison art and skulls.[33] He opened a museum of these objects in Turin, Italy, in 1896. It was closed in 1948 and reopened in 2009 as the Museum of Criminal Anthropology. Lombroso's own skeleton is on display there, as is the head of the first criminal he examined, thief and arsonist Giuseppe Villella.

Drawing on his examinations of actual criminals and Darwin's theory of evolution published in 1859, Lombroso concluded that those predetermined to break the law had features like those of the apes from which humans had descended. He followed phrenologists in thinking that the head showed the greatest disturbance because the "brain-case" conformed to its distorted contents. In his view, in comparison with the general population, lawbreakers would be expected to have more protruding lower jaws and cheekbones, larger less symmetrical faces, more prominent ridges above the eyes, and ears more closely attached to the head, of unequal size or unevenly placed on the head.[34] The born criminal had eyes which were hard, frequently with drooping eyelids and could be unequal in size or colour, while their teeth tended to be large and well separated. Those who conformed to the criminal type had hair which was more typical of opposite sex, abundant in women and scanty in men, while eyebrows were bushy and could be slanted or meet across the nose. Arms were excessively long and hands might have extra or missing fingers or pronounced webbing. Criminal women, he argued, were likely to have facial anomalies, visible in their teeth, thin lips, hairiness and premature wrinkles. He judged women of the criminal type to have faces with a hard, cruel look.[35] Along with these physical features, according to Lombroso, went other traits including a love of idleness, strong sexual urges and the use of slang language. Tattooing was associated with the criminal type because of their high pain threshold, a preference for visual communication and a need to demonstrate membership in social groups.[36]

According to Lombroso's theory, it was not having these features which made people bad, or that living a life of crime could produce them, but that these physical traits were the expression of an inherent disorder and decline in the individual. He wrote, the criminal "reproduces in his person the ferocious instincts of primitive humanity and the inferior animals." He concluded:

> These anomalies in the limbs, trunk, skull and, above all, in the face, when numerous and marked, constitute what is known to criminal anthropologists as the criminal type, … they are [not] the cause of the anti-social tendencies of the criminal.… They are the outward and visible signs of a mysterious and complicated process of degeneration, which in the case of the criminal evokes evil impulses that are largely of atavistic origin.[37]

For law enforcement agents and the general public at the time, however, being told that criminals had a distinctive appearance and that crime was in the nature of these people added scientific weight to long held suspicions of those who looked different. Ideas like these circulated widely in the Australian colonies. In 1865, a journalist writing for the *Sydney Morning Herald* reported his surprise on viewing the body of bushranger Ben Hall that his face "was free of anything repulsive" as he expected to see visible signs of Hall's lawlessness there. In contrast, bushranger Mad Dan Morgan was described in the same year as having a "villainously low forehead." In 1880, having made a death mask of bushranger Andrew Scott alias Captain Moonlite, phrenologist Walter McGill said Scott's head was formed in such a peculiar way that it was not possible for him to be honest.[38] With older assumptions backed by new theories, it was thought that police work could become more systematised, focusing on those with the telltale signs of criminality. This surveillance would deter those inclined to offend or enable them to be caught in the act of committing crimes, and they could be punished in ways which would keep them away from society.

Theories of criminality like phrenology and Lombroso's criminal type have long since been discredited and discarded. Both were deeply embedded in the racist assumptions of the late 1800s and early 1900s when around the world, people of European origin were finding ways to articulate and institutionalise race as a concept, to their own advantage. Lombroso made this clear in stating that the shapes of lips, noses and even the feet of born criminals were shared with Africans, effectively criminalising the people of an entire continent.

However, when looking through collections of photographs of offender, Lombroso's identified features can be found: asymmetry of eyes and ears, prominent jaws, bushy eyebrows. There are several possible explanations for this. If a large enough group is created, some are likely to have the named characteristics. Another is that police, victims, witnesses and judges shared assumptions about the criminal type and so were more likely to arrest, identify and convict someone who had these characteristics, especially when they fit in with existing biases related to race and class. There are also typical physical traits which accompany some forms of cognitive impairment which are linked with offending because they cause difficulty with self-regulation or interpersonal skills.[39] Finally, some of the features Lombroso identified were acquired rather than inherent, like wrinkles and tattoos, and reflected life experiences of those who were involved with crime rather than expressing an innate tendency to offend.

In the twentieth century, while written and photographic records of offenders continued to be made, managed and shared in increasingly sophisticated way, new means of identification were added to them. Prominent amongst them were fingerprinting, blood typing and DNA testing. These new techniques focused the scale of identification efforts down from the whole person to specific bodily components. While each raised new issues, when used appropriately, they were more objective ways to identify offenders, as has been seen in the instances of guilty verdicts being overturned, even decades after a crime was committed, when evidence from the scene is analysed using such techniques. By taking away some of bias which was present when identification hinged on individual memory and observation, new forensic methods on the whole were an aid to criminal justice processes.

The use of fingerprints for identification began in Bengal in 1858 when a colonial administrator, William Herschel, had the idea of using inked finger and palm prints as a way of authorising documents for people who were not literate in English.[40] He had to establish that fingerprints were distinctiveness and also that they did not change over time. This concept was taken up by Henry Faulds, a Scottish doctor working in Japan in the 1870s. He published his finding about the common patterns in fingerprints, known as loops and whorls, and how they took unique forms which could be used for identification, including in criminal justice. He had the further insight that it was not just the fingertips themselves which could be used to identify an individual, but the prints left behind when they touched non-absorbent surfaces. Francis Galton further developed the concept by developing a system to identify the specific elements of fingerprints. He imagined fingerprints being recorded as people entered prison and held in a register, but also as being of use for identifying dead bodies in wartime and civilian settings, and as a memento of absent friends and relatives.[41] After the use of fingerprint identification was adopted in Great Britain, Argentina and the United States, it was taken on by police forces in Australia from the first decade of the twentieth century. Police used the innovation to build up their reputations as masters of complex technology who were increasingly effective at detecting unobserved crimes and prosecuting unknown offenders.[42] By 1935, the Queensland Police force had 47,000 sets of impressions of individual fingers' prints and there were some 400,000 Australia wide in 1941.[43] Being able to take fingerprints and analyse them and then send that analysis to another jurisdiction made detection of offenders who had moved to different states faster and more reliable.

Forensic investigations became increasingly important through the twentieth century and will be encountered when we explore the Pyjama Girl mystery, the Graeme Thorne case and, notoriously, the Azaria Chamberlain disappearance. In these cases, evidence in dental records, fabric fibres and even dog hair were used to help to identify both offenders and victims. As this work became more specialised, it has continued to create records but ones with less value for historians than the careful written descriptions of the nineteenth century and the naturalistic photographs of the early twentieth century.

Conclusion

Keeping records of the appearance of offenders and potential offenders has been a long-term practice in settler colonial Australia. When they were made, these records were working documents which helped to keep track of mobile populations and to link offenders with crimes. Over time, new means of identification were introduced, including photographs and fingerprints, and new theories were developed with the intention of narrowing the law enforcement focus to those likely to constitute an underworld, based on their physical appearance. There was no substance to the assumptions of the phrenologists or theorists like Lombroso but a belief that they did have some predictive power led to increased suspicion of those who were unfortunate enough to have the designated traits. While having their description written down by convict authorities or their photograph taken by the police was not something most people submitted to willingly, over time these records have become a very valuable archives of ordinary people: their physical dimensions, the scars disease, work or accidents had left on their bodies, and how they chose to present themselves through clothing, hair styles and tattoos. For both historians and descendants, records made to identify offenders are valuable and welcome relics of the criminal justice system.

Suggested Readings

Doyle, Peter and Caleb Williams, eds. *City of Shadows: Sydney Police Photographs*. Sydney: Historic Houses Trust of New South Wales, 2013.

Gilmour, Joanna. *Sideshow Alley: Infamy, the Macabre and the Portrait*. Canberra: National Portrait Gallery, 2015.

Lombroso-Ferrero, Gina. *Criminal Man According to the Classification of Cesare Lombroso*. New York: Knickerbocker Press, 1911.

Stannard, Penny. *Captured Portraits of Crime 1870–1930*. Sydney: State Archives of NSW, 2017.

Wilson, Dean., "Reading Ned's Head: Colonial Phrenology, Popular Science and Entertainment." Craig Cormick, ed. *Ned Kelly: Under the Microscope*. Melbourne: CSIRO Publishing, 2014.

ESSAY: UNDERWORLD FIGURES? DESCRIBING VAGRANTS

Catharine Coleborne

Living without a fixed address and moving freely through streets and between towns without a reason or clear purpose was sometimes defined as the crime of vagrancy in nineteenth and early twentieth century Australia. Vagrants came from many places and different social backgrounds; they were men and women, and were often new immigrants to the colonies, reflecting the composition of society at the time.[44]

In the new colony of Victoria in the 1850s, with a growing population drawn by the gold rush, the need for order became more urgent in the minds of colonists, including the government's lawmakers. The policing of regional towns and districts beyond Melbourne was different to the policing of city streets and urban spaces, where the "discretionary power of the move-on laws" signalled the intention to keep the city free of ill-defined dwellers and lurkers.[45]

Descriptions of vagrants can be found in all newspapers of the period and drew from both court reports and colonial *Police Gazettes*, including the *Victoria Police Gazette* which first appeared in 1853. The *Police Gazettes* were distributed among the police and used to share information about arrests, warrants, missing persons, escaped prisoners, court lists and other matters relating to law and order. These descriptions give us an interesting perspective on what contemporaries – in this case, police – wanted to know about vagrants in order to locate them or identify them in public. Like earlier descriptions of transported convicts, they included physical details such as hair and eye colour, the state of skin, presence of scars or tattoos, deformities and disability.

One reason that these descriptions were useful to police was that it was relatively common for people in this period to "fake" or reinvent their identities. Before passports and identity documents, and other forms of the bureaucratic management of populations around the world, colonial men and women could exercise considerable freedom in the way they chose to use names and tell stories about themselves.[46] This could be harmful: historian Christina Twomey has written about the way police looked for men who had deserted their wives in colonial Victoria, leaving them destitute with children and no means of support. A successfully reinvented identity could mean women and families did not receive maintenance payments.[47] Reinvention may also have been liberating, as in the case of early examples of men passing as women or vice versa through disguising their gender identities.[48]

This concept of identity "passing" was also important to what Dean Wilson defines as "policing poverty."[49] Many vagrants were recidivist offenders, and were arrested multiple times, often in the same places or traversing similar territory. Police came to know and understand the needs these people had and also became aware of their physical identities and capacities, such as forms of disability or compromised health. Vagrants were sometimes arrested for "lunacy" under the legislation governing institutions for the "insane" or people exhibiting signs of mental illness during the period.[50] By describing their bodily differences such as tattoos, deformities and scars, the police could create "identikits" of the people they encountered, rendering them identifiable in daily police work. There is some evidence that policing the cities of colonial Australia also involved moral judgements based on the stereotypes of nineteenth-century gender, sexual, class and ethnic "norms." Policing vagrancy and lunacy also involved the policing of "nonconformity," as historians note.[51]

Details about people arrested as vagrants in newspapers and police communications offered poignant vignettes of men and women who lived rough. One report in the *Record* from Emerald Hill, Victoria, in 1898 is typical. It named an "old man," Edward Heron, who was charged and on remand "with having no lawful visible means of support." Police constable Asker noted that Heron was "semi-imbecile," had been in jail and was covered in vermin.[52] This interesting case adds detail about the reactions of people to his evidently poor state of health: locals were worried about children playing near Heron; he stank of tobacco smoke and slept in stables, with their "owners ... afraid that their property would be burned down."[53]

As this story suggests, vagrants tended to find places to sleep and stay safe and warm that were just out of view but were still deemed inappropriate as places to "stop," such as alleys, hidden doorways, sheds and outhouses. This added to the concern that vagrants were potentially dangerous or threatening to commit crimes such as theft, assault or vandalism. There was a general fear of the vagrant. Historians agree that vagrancy was a circumstance of the flux of colonial life, highlighting a time when people were mobile and often relying on partial systems of support and relief, including seasonal work.

The statistical record of arrests for vagrancy shows that in Victoria, arrests peaked in the late 1880s and again in the early 1890s, both times of economic and social change, as well as greater police capacity.[54] Whether or not vagrancy was "over policed," as some contemporaries claimed, the views about the threat posed by vagrants shifted over time and in relation to the wider social context.

Attitudes towards vagrancy present an opportunity for historians to investigate the fears and preoccupations of colonial society from the 1850s onwards, including responses to social ferment, rapid population growth and economic depression in the late nineteenth century.

PRIMARY SOURCE: FROM THE VICTORIA POLICE GAZETTE, 1901

As well as circulating within the police forces across Australia, the information from *Police Gazettes* was also available to the general public through the newspapers. Here, arrest warrants, notices of stolen horses and thefts reported in the Victoria *Police Gazette* have been reprinted in the *Bendigo Independent* newspaper in 1901, along with descriptions of those wanted by police. As in the convict indents, descriptions include name, age, height, complexion, religion, hair and usual clothing, with additional details if known, like 16-year-old Edward Austin's distinctive second set of teeth.

Police Gazette.

The Police Gazette notifies:—A warrant of commitment has been issued by the Prahran bench against Benjamin Aarons for two months' imprisonment, in default of payment of £13 7s 6d. Description—Jew, 35 to 40 years of age, 5ft 5in or 6in high, thin build, dark complexion, dark moustache only; usually wears a short Beaufort coat, check tweed trousers and vest, and a brown or black boxer hat.—Two men, names unknown, are charged, on warrants, issued at the instance of John Carter, battery owner, Marong, with being rogues and vagabonds, at Marong, on the 20th inst. Descriptions—1st. 24 or 25 years of age, 5ft 7in high, stout build; wore dark clothes. 2nd. 25 to 30 years of age, 5ft 8in or 9in high, stoutish build; wore dark clothes. Offenders, with three others arrested, were found on the battery grounds of Mr. Carter—James Foy, grazier, Crosbie, near Heathcote, reports stolen from his dwelling, between the 6th and 14th inst., two promissory notes, one for £21, signed P. Toohey, and a promissory note for £22, signed D. Richardson; both payable at the Commercial Bank, Heathcote; value £43; and a pocket-book.—Edward Austin is charged, on warrant issued at the instance of Mrs. Milton, farmer, Myers Creek, Bendigo, with vagrancy, at Bendigo, on the 17th inst. Description—16 years of age, 5ft high, medium build, dark complexion, very large brown eyes, double set of teeth in front of top jaw; wore a brown coat, mole trousers, and heavy boots; carried a swag. May go to Melbourne.—Cuthbert Corke, draper, Echuca, reports stolen at Echuca, on the 19th inst., a dark bay mare, 7 years, 16 hands, hollow back, branded S over J over T on near shoulder, buggy stamp.—Value £12.—Martha Waterfield, servant, National Hotel, High street, Bendigo, reports stolen from her room, on the 22nd or 23rd inst., a lady's silver hunting keyless Geneva watch, No. 15370. Value

Figure 6.2 "Police Gazette," *Bendigo Independent*, 3 October 1901, 5.

The very specific descriptions of Benjamin Aarons and Edward Austin show that, they are known in the surrounding communities. The more general descriptions of other suspected vagrants reflect the uncertainty and suspicion directed at those who were unknown.

Notes

1 Caleb Williams, "The Forensic Eye: Photography's Dark Mirror," Peter Doyle and Caleb Williams, eds. *City of Shadows: Sydney Police Photographs, 1912–1948*, Sydney: Historic Houses Trust of New South Wales, 2013, 16.
2 This account of the convict indents draws upon Deborah Oxley, Convict Indents (Ship and Arrival Registers) 1788–1868, Digital Panopticon, https://www.digitalpanopticon.org/Convict_Indents_(Ship_and_Arrival_Registers)_1788-1868 (accessed 4 March 2022).
3 R.W. Byard and H.M. Stewart, "The Potential Forensic Significance of Convict Archives from Van Diemen's Land, 1820–1877," *Forensic Science, Medicine and Pathology* 14 (2018): 129.
4 Lisa Ford and David Roberts, "The Convict Peace: The Imperial Context of the 1833 Convict Revolt at Castle Forbes," *Journal of Imperial and Commonwealth History* 49, no. 1 (2021): 1.
5 Convict Indents (Ship and Arrival Registers) 1788–1868, https://www.digitalpanopticon.org/Convict_Indents_(Ship_and_Arrival_Registers)_1788-1868 (accessed 4 March).
6 Hamish Maxwell Stewart, Kris Inwood and Jim Stankovich, "Prison and the Colonial Family," *History of the Family* 20, no. 2 (2015): 232.
7 Nicholas J. Meinzer, "The Western Australian Convicts," *Australian Economic History Review* 55, no. 2 (2015): 172–73; 181.
8 David Kent, "Decorative Bodies: The Significance of Convicts' Tattoos," *Journal of Australian Studies*, 21, no. 53 (1997): 79.
9 Gary Crockett, "The Convict Tattoo," *Social Alternatives* 17, no. 4 (1998), 15.
10 "The Tattooed Man, Arthur Riley," *Captured, Portraits of Crime 1870–1930*, Sydney: State Archives of NSW, 2017, https://www.paperturn-view.com/nsw-state-archives/captured-portraits-of-crime-1870-1930?pid=MTQ14977&p=39 (accessed 22 June 2022).
11 Alana Piper, "'I Go Out Worse Every Time': Connections and Corruption in a Female Prison," *History Australia* 9, no. 3 (2012): 141.
12 The Registry of Flash Men is held by NSW State Archives and Records as item NRS-3406. One page can be viewed in the Dictionary of Sydney: https://dictionaryofsydney.org/media/58678 (accessed 11 March 2022).
13 "Extracts from Victoria Police Gazette, from Police Gazette, 7th July 1864," *New South Wales Police Gazette and Weekly Record of Crime*, 29 (1864): 226.
14 Joanna Gilmour, *Sideshow Alley: Infamy, the Macabre and the Portrait*, Canberra: National Portrait Gallery, 2015, 52, 56, 65.
15 Anne-Marie Willis, *Picturing Australia: A History of Photography*, Sydney: Angus and Robertson, 1988, 5.
16 Jens Jäger, "Photography: A Means of Surveillance? Judicial Photography, 1850 to 1900," *Crime, Histoire & Sociétés / Crime, History & Societies* 5, no. 1 (2001): 1.
17 Willis, *Picturing Australia*, 20.
18 Louise Steding, *Forensics and Police Through Time, Australia in Context*, Sydney: In Focus Press, 2016, 52.
19 Gilmour, *Sideshow Alley*, 82–84.
20 Jäger, "Photography: A Means of surveillance?", 4.
21 Peter Doyle, *Crooks Like Us*, Sydney: Sydney Living Museums, 2009, 17.
22 Caleb Williams, "The Forensic Eye," 16.
23 Mug shot of E.A.R Cavendish, 31 May 1926. New South Wales. Police Dept. Special photograph no. 131A. Justice & Police Museum, https://library.sydneylivingmuseums.com.au/images_linked/32204/179.jpg (accessed 31 May 2022).
24 Mug shot of Agnes Smith, 15 August 1923, Long Bay Women's Reformatory.

New South Wales. Police Dept. Prisoner identification photograph no. LB 588, Justice and Police Museum, https://library.sydneylivingmuseums.com.au/images_linked/31322/139.jpg (accessed 6 June 2022).

25 Mugshot of Aiden Feutrill, 4 May 1920, location unknown. New South Wales. Police Dept. Prisoner identification photograph no. 17167, Justice and Police Museum, https://library.sydneylivingmuseums.com.au/images_linked/31209/050.jpg (accessed 6 June 2022).

26 Mug shot of Isabella Higgs, 21 February 1924, Central Police Station, Sydney. New South Wales. Police Dept., Special Photograph no. 1091. Record number, 32213, Justice & Police Museum, http://collection.hht.net.au/firsthht/fullRecordPicture.jsp?recnoListAttr=recnoListRI&recno=32213 (accessed 6 June 2022).

27 Mug shot of Francis Flood, Central Police Station, ca. May 1920. New South Wales. Police Dept. Special photograph no. 128. Justice and Police Museum, https://library.sydneylivingmuseums.com.au/images_linked/32205/180.jpg (accessed 6 June 2022).

28 Paul Turnbull, "British Anatomists, Phrenologists and the Construction of the Aboriginal Race, c. 1790–1830," *History Compass* 5, no. 1 (2007): 39–41.

29 Sarah Tarlow, "Curious Afterlives: The Enduring appeal of the Criminal Corpse," *Mortality* 21, no. 3 (2016): 214.

30 Alexandra Roginski, *The Hanged Man and the Body Thief: Finding Lives in a Museum Mystery*, Melbourne: Monash University Publishing, 2015, 43.

31 Dean Wilson, "Reading Ned's Head: Colonial Phrenology, Popular Science and Entertainment," Craig Cormick, ed. *Ned Kelly: Under the Microscope*, Melbourne: CSIRO Publishing, 2014.

32 David Horn, *The Criminal Body: Lombroso and the Anatomy of Deviance*, Taylor & Francis, 2003.

33 Kate West, "Visual Criminology and Lombroso: In memory of Nicole Rafter" (1939–2016), *Theoretical Criminology* 21, no. 3 (2017): 272; 275.

34 These characteristics are set out in the translation of *Criminal Man* published by Lombroso's daughter as "Physical Anomalies of the Born Criminal," with photographic illustrations (Gina Lombroso-Ferrero, *Criminal Man, according to the Classification of Cesare Lombroso*, London: G. P. Putnam's Sons, 1911, 10–21. Read more here: https://www.gutenberg.org/files/29895/29895-h/29895-h.htm

35 Cesare Lombroso, Guglielmo Ferrero, Nicole Hahn Rafter and Mary Gibson, *Criminal Woman, the Prostitute, and the Normal Woman*, Durham, North Carolina: Duke University Press, 2004, 130.

36 Scott Jacques, "What Criminals' Tattoos Symbolize: Drawing on Darwin, Durkheim and Lombroso," *Deviant Behavior*, 38, no. 11 (2017): 1308.

37 Gina Lombroso-Ferrero, *Criminal Man According to the Classification of Cesare Lombroso.* New York: Knickerbocker Press, 1911, https://www.gutenberg.org/files/29895/29895-h/29895-h.htm (accessed 11 March 2022). This was the first English language translation of Lombroso's book but his ideas had been in circulation for several decades. Atavistic means a recurrence of a trait or characteristic from an earlier and in his view, more primitive form; what might be called a throwback.

38 All three descriptions are reprinted in Gilmour, *Sideshow Alley*, 82, 89, 103.

39 "Towards a Just System: Mental Illness and Cognitive Impairment in the Criminal Justice System," *Mental Health Commission of NSW*, July 2017, 8; Harry Blagg and Tamara Tulich, "Diversionary Pathways for Aboriginal Youth with Fetal Alcohol Spectrum Disorder," *Trends and Issues in Crime and Criminal Justice* 557 (August 2018), 2.

40 This section draws upon Louise Steding, *Forensics and Police through Time, Australia in Context*, Sydney: In Focus Press, 2016, 84–88.

41 "Topics of the Week," *The Australasian*, September 19, 1891, 22.

42 Dean Wilson, "Traces and Transmissions: Techno-scientific Symbolism in Early Twentieth-Century Policing," Barry S. Godfrey and Graeme Dunstall, eds. *Crime and Empire 1840–1940: Criminal Justice in Local and Global Context*, London: Routledge, 2012, 115.

43 "Fingerprints," *Maryborough Chronicle, Wide Bay and Burnett Advertiser*, October 31, 1935, 7; "Police Chief Approves Fingerprints," *Examiner* (Launceston), July 29, 1941, 4.
44 For an overview of histories of vagrancy in Australia, see Julie Kimber, "Poor Laws: A Historiography of Vagrancy in Australia," *History Compass*, 11, no. 8 (2013): 538.
45 Andrew May, *Melbourne Street Life: The Itinerary of our Days*, Melbourne: Australian Scholarly Press/Arcadia and Museum Victoria, 1998, 56.
46 Catharine Coleborne, *Insanity, Identity and Empire: Colonial Institutional Confinement in Australia and New Zealand, 1870–1910*, Manchester: Manchester University Press, 2015, 102–04.
47 Christina Twomey, *Deserted and Destitute: Motherhood, Wife Desertion and Colonial Welfare*, Melbourne: Australian Scholarly Publishing, 2002, 5.
48 See Susanne Davies, "Sexuality, Performance, and Spectatorship in Law: The Case of Gordon Lawrence, Melbourne, 1888," *Journal of the History of Sexuality* 7, no. 3 (1997): 395–408.
49 Dean Wilson, "Policing Poverty: Destitution and Police Work in Melbourne, 1880–1910," *Australian Historical Studies* 36, no. 125 (2005): 97–112.
50 Coleborne, *Insanity, Identity and Empire*, 101.
51 Adrien McCrory, "Policing Gender Nonconformity in Victoria, 1900–1940," *Provenance: The Journal of Public Record Office Victoria* 19 (2021): 33–42.
52 "Vagrancy," *Record*, January 29, 1898, 3.
53 *Ibid.*
54 Susanne Davies, "'Ragged, Dirty ... Infamous and Obscene': The 'Vagrant' in Late-Nineteenth-Century Melbourne," David Philips and Susanne Davies, eds. *A Nation of Rogues? Crime, Law and Punishment in Colonial Victoria*, Melbourne: Melbourne University Press, 1994, 163.

7 Race, Class and Sexual Violence

Concern over unruly youth, referred to by the judge in Ned Kelly's trial, grew in the 1880s, as the centenary of colonisation in 1888 approached. As they did during the 1988 bicentenary, settler colonists thought of the centenary as a time to celebrate the progress they had made since the arrival of the First Fleet. They looked around at their large modern cities, huge flocks of sheep, fields of wheat and ships taking their produce to markets overseas and were very proud of what they had achieved from inauspicious beginnings. The Aboriginal people who had been displaced by this activity were little thought of. Crime and its associations with convictism were definitely not welcome.

In particular, crimes involving sexual violence were viewed as a legacy of the past which should be suppressed. Sexual violence includes any sexual act, or attempt to obtain a sexual act, using coercion. This includes the actual use of force, threats or intimidation and sexual acts performed when the person is incapable of giving consent, including because they are too young.[1] Some of the specific crimes in this category are rape, within or outside of existing relationships, sexual abuse of children and forced prostitution. In this period, the word rape was considered too strong to print in some newspapers, with masking terms such as outrage, criminal assault and capital offence used in its place. As has been made clear from the many recent revelations of sexual assaults which occurred decades ago, there tend to be low levels of reporting sexual assault and only a small proportion proceed through the legal system to a prosecution. The current estimate is that only one in ten sexual assaults is reported to the police, in part because survivors do not want to draw attention to their situation, do not want to subject themselves to a legal process or do not trust the system to bring them justice. In cases which are reported, lack of evidence can also mean that cases do not proceed.

In the early colonial period, the society and the legal system provided even less encouragement for survivors to report sexual offences. Without a witness and evidence of the use of physical force and of resistance, a charge of sexual assault was readily dismissed as either having no foundation at all or being motivated by regret or revenge after a consensual

DOI: 10.4324/9781003273561-8

sexual encounter. The result was that sexual assault, was likely to lead to a conviction and that many offenders went unprosecuted. Later in the century, there was greater attention to sexual crimes. This was the high Victorian period (i.e., late in Queen Victoria's long reign, 1837–1901), when the middle class had drawn a veil over sexuality. Although no longer the majority of voters, they still largely controlled the making and administration of the law and, in a quest for order, brought a new focus to policing and punishing sexual offences.

Most of these cases were dealt with quietly and attracted little public attention. A few became highly publicised. For historians, analysing both types of cases can be revealing of attitudes to women and relations between the sexes, and of how ideas about race, class and religion shaped the prosecution of sex crime. The two crimes which form the focus of this chapter are the Mount Rennie outrage which caused a sensation in Sydney in 1887 and a less well-known rape case in Hamilton, Victoria, brought to notice by historian David Philips. Together, these cases bring together many of the trends in the colonial society and the anxieties they fuelled about whether the Australian colonies were as civilised as places elsewhere and how the youth of the colonies were to be controlled.

Sexual Violence in Colonial Australia

Feminist historians of the 1970s led by Anne Summers, the author of *Damned Whores and God's Police*, drew attention to the widespread sexual violence in the early settler colonial history of Australia. Basing the first colonies on convict transportation meant that despite the best efforts of authorities to find women who could be punished in this way, there was a large and persistent sexual imbalance in settler colonial Australia in favour of men. This heightened anxieties around homosexuality and male on male sexual violence amongst the convicts, leading to the threat that anyone found guilty of what was then the crime of sodomy would be sent to New Zealand to be eaten by the Māoris.[2] This was not followed through upon, but men were punished harshly for homosexual acts, whether consensual or not, during and after the convict period.

Summers argued that female convicts were only transported to serve as sexual partners for the men, and that this exposed them to systemic sexual violence. She called the penal authorities "an imperial whoremaster" which forced women to provide sexual services to convict men and then condemned them for moral failings.[3] Later historians have gone more closely into the records to show that this was an exaggeration. Women were not just handed out from the ships to whoever wanted them. Like convict men, they were matched with employers looking for particular skills sets, and while some moved frequently between positions and in and out of the female factories, others held just a few positions until they married or their sentence expired. Sexual violence was still a part of the colonial society but not one which was institutionalised. It was Aboriginal women who were most subject to sexual violence, both on an individual basis and as part of the larger war of occupation, rape being a commonly used tactic to degrade and demonstrate power over a wartime enemy.[4]

In the 1830s, trying to address the low percentage of women in the colonies, governments invested in assisted immigration programs which were specifically directed at single women and families. Caroline Chisholm was a British emigration advocate who became both a lobbyist and a practical helper for these newly arrived single women, ensuring that they had somewhere secure to stay in Sydney and helping them to find work. These poor women were often stigmatised as being as bad as the convicts and moving more or less willingly into prostitution.[5]

The gold rush period which started in 1851 in NSW and then more dramatically in the newly separated colony of Victoria brought in another huge wave of immigration from Europe, North America and China. While young men predominated, it was a more balanced group this time with whole families relocating not only for the gold but for the economic opportunities gold created. Even so, the tendency of women and children to stay in towns while men went out to the goldfields created yet another situation in which men largely lived outside of family settings. Statistics over the next few decades continued to show that while urban areas were starting to have quite equal proportions between the sexes, rural areas continued to be male dominated. That white women were left without natural protectors, in the presence of bushrangers, itinerant bush workers and Aboriginal men, created an anxiety that these women were particularly vulnerable to sexual assault in the bush, despite the reality that sexual violence occurred in a wide range of settings.

Rape was removed from the list of capital crimes in England in 1841, as part of a series of reforms intended to modernise their legal system. The shift was in keeping with that observed by Foucault, from bodily punishments to long-term imprisonment with strict regimes of work and reflection. Only two capital crimes were retained in Britain: murder and treason. In Australia, the colonial legislatures decided to continue with capital punishment for rape because the racial composition of the population, the disproportion of men and women and concerns about the convict presence.[6] Not adopting a reform which was in place in Britain was controversial, as it made it seem that the colonies were less civilised and showed less mercy to offenders than the mother country did. *In their essay accompanying this chapter, Andy Kaladelfos demonstrates that the imposition of the death penalty varied according to region, the race of the offender and the victim, and the perceived innocence of the victim.* While upholders of the law would argue that it is impartial and colour blind, it is clear that race influenced the severity of punishments for rape in nineteenth-century Australia.

The Prosecution Project Database (https://prosecutionproject.griffith.edu.au/) was created by researchers at Griffith University to make historical court records readily available. It can be used to track the prosecution of sex offences in each colony over time. For example, using the "Visualise Records" function to show the number of rape cases heard in the South Australian Supreme Court for the century after it was established in 1844 shows that no more than 12 cases were heard per year. Many years had no cases or very few, with only four at nine or above: 1854, 1859, 1871 and 1947. Limiting the search to cases which led to a conviction reflects the same pattern, with five guilty verdicts in each of six years between 1862 and 1882, and the greatest cluster of convictions during and immediately after the Second World War.

Before drawing conclusions from the changing incidence of these offences, however, we need to recall that only a small proportion of sexual assaults were reported to the police, and an even smaller number advanced to a court hearing. A rise in the number of cases in court can be more related to other factors. One is times when there is greater confidence that an accusation of rape will be taken seriously. Law and order campaigns and active policing during those periods create this confidence, which can have the effect of suggesting there is more crime being committed. In contrast, a lack of attention to an offence can produce a perception that it is not occurring, with low rates of reporting and prosecution. The cases we will now explore both came during a period when victims were given some credibility because of wider social issues. This places them in the minority of rape cases: those in which offenders were found guilty and severely punished for their crimes.

The Mount Rennie Outrage

The Mount Rennie Outrage was the name given to the gang rape of 16-year-old Mary Jane Hicks which took place in Sydney in September 1886.[7] Hicks was an orphan who had attended a convent school in Bathurst and came to Sydney to find work as a servant. As she walked to an employment agency in the central city, the 35-year-old driver a horse-drawn cab offered her a lift. With some misgivings, she accepted this unfamiliar treat and found herself being taken to Moore Park, in the suburb of Waterloo. There, the cabman tried to force himself on her. Her calls for help attracted a young man passing by. He intervened, helping her out of the cab and guiding her further into the park, to an area known as Mount Rennie, while the cabman drove off.

A group of young men gathered around Hicks. They were said to be members of the Waterloo Push, one of the groups of larrikins then active in Australia's inner suburban areas, in this case in the Redfern and Waterloo areas. We will return to the topic of whether they were or were not a youth gang in Chapter 10. The youths were in their teens and early twenties and worked as labourers, general cleaners, plasterers, marble polishers, wool washers, engine cleaners and dealers (selling goods and making deliveries).[8] Several had been in trouble with the law, mainly for petty theft and riotous conduct.

The youths offered to help Hicks return to the city by tram but instead lured her into the scrub and then up to nine of them took it in turns to sexually assault her, while others watched. Shipwright William Stanley and another man were drawn to the scene by Hicks' screams and tried to rescue her but were pelted with stones, sticks and bricks by the offenders. Stanley ran to the Redfern police station to raise the alarm. Eventually, a policeman arrived, freeing Hicks after a 6-hour ordeal, and arranging medical care for her injuries. Investigations were undertaken and charges laid against 16 men, with 11 ultimately facing trial. During the hearing, the reputations of both the attackers and the victim came under scrutiny: Hicks by the defence, the men by the prosecution, and both in the press.

In the courtroom, newspaper coverage and the community much was made of the identity of the accused who were called such names as "lustful fiends" and "social ghouls."[9] Coming just a few years after two gang sexual assaults in the Waterloo area in 1883 which led to the death of the victims but no successful prosecutions, and in the context of ongoing street crime by people characterised as larrikins, the response can be seen as a moral panic. That is, a state of high anxiety in which some elements of a society become so concerned about a particular issue that they start to imagine inflated threats to the social order, and vilify and stigmatise particular locations, individuals, groups or activities with a view to controlling it. In this case, it was members of the urban middle class who became gravely concerned about the behaviour of young working class men. Products of the post gold rush baby boom, there were large numbers of these youths and they were a visible presence in urban areas. Unaware that similar groups of unruly youths were being identified elsewhere, many observers believed that they had developed a "hunting pack" mentality as a unique outcome of Australian conditions. Critics blamed fine weather, the general high standard of living, lax parenting, truancy from school and predispositions to criminality inherited from convict parents and grandparents, which then infected those without a convict heritage, for creating youths who resisted authority and sought to create a disordered society.[10]

On the other side were people who thought the offenders in this case were being unfairly characterised as villains because of who they were and where they lived. These supporters were mainly members of the Catholic Church, which in Australia during this period generally meant being of Irish origin. As we saw in Ned Kelly's community, the tensions between Catholics and Protestants, known as sectarianism, were pronounced in the nineteenth century, with a Catholic school system coexisting with the new public schools and separation in terms of places of residence, employment and marriage. Like race and class, religion was a factor at play in who was criminalised – that is, who in the society was readily accused of crimes and held responsible for them. Immigrants from Ireland (6.6% of the NSW population in 1891) were overrepresented in offences against the person (making up 13.9% of arrests), property (up to 13%) and good order (16.3%), and those with Irish parents similarly had greater than average encounters with the legal system.[11]

Catholic community leaders were willing to speak on behalf of the accused youth, to testify that some were of exceptionally good character and several regularly attended mass. One of those who was praised, George Read did not serve himself well, running away with William Boyce, who had a criminal record including an assault on a female witness during an earlier rape case.[12] The pair were arrested near the Queensland border and forcibly returned to face trial.

Using the only weapon they felt they had at their disposal, defenders of the youths tried to blame Mary Jane Hicks, also a working-class Catholic but with no strong ties in Sydney, for what happened to her. Attempts were made to portray Hicks as a willing participant. A counternarrative was developed that Hicks was a liar and a prostitute who only made her accusations because she was not paid. The cross-examination of Hicks was specifically designed to rake "up any antecedents she might possess" and managed to draw out of her that she had been assaulted by a married man in a boarding house two years earlier and had made no complaint at the time. She rejected suggestions that she had been ejected from a boarding house for misbehaviour or had lived with a man as his wife.[13] This treatment was part of a long pattern in rape cases, that the degree of virtue of the woman was considered to be relevant in judging the guilt of the rapist. One supporter accepted that the youths were ruffians but repeated a popular belief of the time "no respectable woman had ever been outraged."[14] The recently established *Bulletin* journal, with an editorial line that was highly critical of women's rights, repeated the view that Hicks had had sex with the men voluntarily. Editor J.F. Archibald wrote: "one never hears of the forcible defilement of chaste and circumspect women" but only of those who were "lewd."[15]

To counter these beliefs, witnesses for the prosecution were careful to observe that Hicks had mounted a fierce resistance, kicking and biting her assailants. A journalist covering the case wrote that her dress was in tatters and the state of her discarded underclothing, "bore silent but corroborative testimony to the evidence" given, as did the many bruises on her body.[16] The issue of resistance was important because at 16, she was four years beyond the age of consent. Those under twelve were deemed unable to give consent for sexual activity so any acts performed on them were automatically designated as a sexual assault, also known as statutory rape or if under 10, as carnal knowledge.

The judge hearing the case, William Charles Windeyer, was known as a proponent of women's rights. He had been central to making divorce more accessible and agreed that in this case a harsh sentence was needed both to adequately punish the offenders and deter future crime. Windeyer heard the trial of the cabman first. The jury found him guilty of intent to commit a rape and Windeyer sentenced him to 14 years of hard labour with two floggings.[17] A bill to abolish flogging had recently been rejected as most believed it was the one form of punishment dangerous youths understood.

Figure 7.1 The bravado of the accused in the Mount Rennie case is evident in this photograph taken while they were being held in Darlinghurst Gaol awaiting trial

Source: Frederick William Neitenstein papers: pictorial material, ca. 1883–1911, Mitchell Library, State Library of NSW, PXD 1117/5.

The trial of the 11 alleged rapists was conducted over one week (Figure 7.1). The fifth day of the hearing lasted 18 and a half hours in the hot and crowded courtroom, followed by a 9 am start the next day for a summing up by the judge which lasted into the evening. Two of the accused were found not guilty. Each of the nine who were convicted was permitted to protest his innocence before the ceremony for the handing down of a death sentence was performed. Their cases were then referred to the Executive Council. Under pressure from public meetings, petitions, deputations and concerns about the colony's reputation, the decision was made to commute the sentences of three of the offenders to hard labour for life, with the first three years in irons. On the eve of the executions, this mercy was extended to two more of the offenders.[18] For four of those convicted, ranging in age from 17 to 19, there were no last-minute reprieves.

At the time appointed for the executions on 7 January 1887, a crowd of 2000 people gathered outside of Darlinghurst Gaol. Although executions were no longer undertaken in public, there was still a sense of occasion and macabre interest in a crowd said to be mainly supporters of those being executed. Inside, 32 official witnesses and up to 150 spectators gathered to view this first indoor execution in NSW, scuffling and straining for a good view of what turned out to be mismanaged hangings.[19] A large gallows was designed so that they all experienced the drop at the same time, but for one, it took up to ten minutes for breathing to cease.

The Mount Rennie executions were applauded by some. They thought the death penalty was warranted, viewing gang rape in particular as a chilling confirmation of a convict stain still infusing society that would be noticed throughout the empire. After other notorious rapes had gone unpunished, this was seen as an opportunity to demonstrate the severity of the law, to warn those who might otherwise commit the same crime. On the other side were those who felt the executions themselves brought shame to the colony. Capital punishment, rather than gang rape, was viewed as evidence that the people of NSW had not grown in civility since the convict period and that its government was still as violently authoritarian as in convict days. Between them were people who agreed that women should be strongly protected from rape but believed that the death penalty made juries less likely to return a guilty verdict, as they did not want the responsibility of sending an offender to their death. Providing some evidence that this was the case, after the abolition of the death penalty in Queensland in 1899, the rate of convictions for rape there increased.[20]

The youths who attacked Mary Jane Hicks were guilty of a terrible crime but without the contemporary moral panic about dangerous youth, the debate over the role of capital punishment meant they were unlikely to have been executed for it. The last person executed for rape in NSW lost his life in 1897 but the penalty remained in place until 1955.

The Condah Case

The Condah rape case took place 18 months after the Mount Rennie Outrage.[21] The setting was very different from the inner suburbs of Australia's oldest city. The rape was perpetrated in the rural Western District of Victoria. The locality was Lake Condah (Tae Rak), an important place for the Gunditjmara people. Their creator being, Budj Bim, resides in a dormant volcano by that name, known as Mount Eccles by settler colonists. An eruption of the volcano some 30,000 years ago created a large area of wetlands through which the Gunditjmara dug channels linking artificial ponds with stone walls designed to hold eels and other fish. Called by John Newton "one of Australia's first aquaculture ventures," this reliable food source facilitated the establishment of a settled society in the region, with people living in homes made from the local volcanic rock.[22] Its cultural and historical significance has led to the Lake Condah Indigenous Protected Area being included in the World Heritage-listed Budj Bim Cultural Landscape (designated in 2019).

There was limited appreciation of this ancient culture in the 1880s. As elsewhere, the Aboriginal population plummeted after colonisation through disease and killing. The non-Aboriginal population of the district was 83 at the 1891 census. Aboriginal people were not counted in government censuses until after 1967 but they were part of the life of the district, residing both on the Lake Condah Mission and in the wider community. This was an area in which most people knew one another, in contrast with the anonymity of the capital cities. Recently added to the resident population was a contingent of men working on the draining of the Condah swamps, ignoring the rich biodiversity they supported in favour of converting them into agricultural land. These three groups came together at the Condah horse races, creating the opportunity for the crime. Unlike the high-profile Mount Rennie case, this one attracted little attention at the time outside of the region. Brief accounts did circulate in newspapers around the country, generally expressing disgust at the crime, and always noting that the victim was a married Aboriginal woman.

The assault unfolded as three Aboriginal people, Jenny Green, then in her 50s, her husband Tommy and their son, Arthur walked home from the races on 23 March 1888 accompanied by their friend Billy Gorry. The Greens had formerly lived in the Lake Condah Mission Station, set up in 1867 by Victoria's Central Board for Aborigines, later the Board for the Protection of Aborigines. From 1869 in Victoria, Aboriginal people began to be compelled to live on reserves, where they would have some protection from violence but had to accept a web of rules set by the government and the missionaries who ran them. A photograph of a woman named Jenny Green taken at Lake Condah in the 1860s is held by the State Library of Victoria. She is identified as a skilled maker of the baskets used to catch eels and a teacher whose great, great granddaughters keep her memory alive as they continue the tradition of making baskets.[23] The Greens were sent off the mission after being involved in what was labelled a rebellion there in 1878. In 1888, they lived and worked on a local farm, camping on Breakaway Creek.

As people made their way home from the races in the early evening of this autumn day, several passed the Greens. One man walked along with them for a while, chatting as they went. Another gave them some of the cake he had bought for his family. According to several witnesses, they were sober and orderly, while others said they were drunk and fighting amongst themselves. At a certain point, a cart carrying a group back to the drainage works from the races overtook the Greens, and two of the men climbed out to join them. Frederick Wilson and Martin Holly, both labourers, were described as being stupidly and loudly drunk in the case of Wilson and helplessly drunk in the case of Holly.

As in the Mount Rennie case, the offenders initially appeared to be friendly but were using this as a ruse. Having spoken to the Greens, Wilson grabbed Jenny by the hair and tried to force her to drink from a bottle of alcohol he was carrying. He sought Tommy's permission to have sex with Jenny, which was refused. When Tommy and Billy tried to intervene to protect Jenny, they were kicked, hit with a piece of wood and driven away. Wilson raped Jenny while Tommy called for help from a nearby farmer, who came running and saw the assault in progress. The farmer was attacked by Wilson with a bottle, wounding his ear. Wilson threatened that he had a revolver and the farmer retreated to his house, while Holly renewed the sexual assault on Jenny Green. Jenny was dragged along the road and thrown over a fence into a paddock where she was again assaulted, and lay until dawn, stunned and with her clothing torn.

Who were these men? Wilson, aged 26, was the Tasmanian-born son of two convicts. As the studies of height and well-being would lead us to expect, he was short, being referred to as "the little fellow" in court. Because of this background and his own passage from one institution to another, his life can be tracked through the historical record, using his birth name of Thomas Glyde. In 1870, when Glyde was eight, his mother was convicted of larceny and with both parents being judged not capable of raising their children, he was sent with his brother to the Queen's Asylum for Destitute Children in Hobart. He regularly won prizes at the school, including an academic prize in 1872 and one for good conduct in the choir two years later.[24] At the age of fourteen, Glyde was apprenticed out to work as a servant in Evandale, Tasmania. He stayed in service for five years and became a petty thief, described as a larrikin by the local police superintendent. He committed a string of offences and was involved in a fight which led to the death of one of his workmates when he was working a jockey at a Launceston racecourse in 1885.[25] Glyde joined a circus in 1887, travelling as many former convicts and convict offspring did, across Bass Strait to Victoria. There he gave himself a new name in his own personal quest to escape convict origins.

Martin Holly we know less about because he was, until the crime was committed, a law abiding young man. He was born 22 years earlier in Ararat, Victoria, where his family still lived. Regarded as quiet, respectable and industrious, he was said to have been kicked in the face by a horse as a child which his family claimed had left him slightly cognitively impaired and susceptible to alcohol.[26] The contrast in detail is a good reminder of how sources tend to lead us to the troubled and the troublemakers, as they are well covered in newspapers and government documents, while the law abiding generate many fewer records, often limited to birth, marriage and death.

The involvement of the farmer was crucial in the investigation of this case, as the local mounted police had to respond when he reported having been assaulted. Two police constables visited the Greens at their camp to confirm that they had also been attacked. Philips notes that even after the Royal Commission into the Victorian police force which followed the fiasco of the search for the Kelly Gang, the actions of the main investigator in this case, Constable Maurice Crotty, were lax, including not taking formal written statements from the victim and witnesses. This could reflect his usual practice or his assessment that the sexual assault did not have to be taken too seriously.

Nonetheless, the case was pursued. Wilson and Holly were arrested in their tent at the drainage works. After being identified by the Greens and the farmer, the local police magistrate and two justices of the peace committed them for trial in the Supreme Court in its next sitting in Hamilton, in early

May. Like other rape victims, Jenny Green had to undergo a medical examination for evidence of the assault, a procedure often experienced as a second violation. The doctor found that she had wounds on her arm, neck, nose and lip and a black eye although "it was difficult to distinguish bruises on a person of colour," another issue which continues to be problematic as medical standards take a light complexion as the norm.[27]

As the trial began, the judge had all women and children other than Jenny cleared from the courtroom before the 24 witnesses gave evidence. Of course, the jury was all male and all white. They were specifically warned that they could not let matters of race affect their judgement.

Court testimony was one of the few instances in which the actual words of Indigenous Australians were recorded in the colonial period. Billy Gorry stated that when Holly asked Tommy to lend Jenny to him for sex, Tommy had replied: "no, that too much like olden time," referring to past, and indeed continuing, assumptions that Aboriginal women were sexually available to settler colonist men.[28] Further, Tommy said that Holly ought to know that the Bible said such behaviour was wrong. Having been sequestered on a mission run by a religious order, they were well versed in Christianity. It was reasonable that they would expect settler colonists who were part of an ostensibly Christian society to be held to these standards. While some of the witnesses revealed racist assumptions and the defence counsel tried to undermine the reliability of the Aboriginal people's testimony, there was no longer any doubt that they could give sworn testimony in court. The judge was very clear on this and also noted to the jury that there was no evidence to suggest that Jenny was of poor character. Her character, of course, should not have been of any consequence in deciding the guilt of the accused, but as seen in the Mount Rennie case, was a matter routinely raised in investigating sexual assault.

Both men were found guilty after just 20-minute deliberation by the jury. Sentences of death were recorded rather than being stated in court, signalling that the judge did not think the case warranted the death penalty. Philips argues that the decision not to recommend that the men be executed could have been informed by the judge's opinion that the rape of an Aboriginal woman was less serious than the rape of a non-Aboriginal woman. However, as we have seen, it was not usual by this time to carry out a death penalty for rape. The Governor in Council accepted the recommendation for mercy. To allow for a conviction for rape without execution being a possible punishment, a new offence was created in Victoria that same year: "rape with mitigating circumstances."[29]

Although their lives were spared, Holly and Wilson were not let off lightly. Each was sentenced to two floggings of 15 lashes and 18 years imprisonment with hard labour in Melbourne's Pentridge Prison. Prisons were at this time complex institutions with individual cells and strict daily schedules of sleep, hygiene, eating and work to be followed. The requirement that hard labour be undertaken during the sentence was common.

Whereas in earlier periods, prisoners had been made to undertake demeaning and often pointless work, by the late nineteenth century, attempts were made to set more productive tasks which could benefit society as well as help inmates to develop a work ethic and skill set, although this was limited by concern not to compete with free labour and by a continuing intention to achieve reform through suffering.[30] In contrast, the floggings were part of the older ideas about punishing the body which were by the 1880s largely reserved for sex offenders.

Although Aboriginal people were still not equal citizens in late colonial Victoria, in this settled district at least, the promise of protection under the law was honoured in the case of Jenny Green. As Philips demonstrated, legal protection could still not be relied upon by Aboriginal people in other parts of the continent. Indeed, the sexual abuse of Aboriginal women was still taken as a norm in many contexts.[31]

As well as the racial dimension, this case brings out a contrast in the treatment of the two men based on their family histories. Wilson was portrayed as the evil, hardened leader. He had started the incident and was seen by two of the witnesses raping Jenny, while only Jenny herself said that Holly had also raped her. After the verdicts and sentences were heard, a campaign began to have Holly released, as an innocent led astray by someone he thought was his mate. Petitions were drawn up and signed by the leading citizens of Ararat, focusing on his good record and respected family and systematically attacking the character of Jenny Green. It took several years, but Holly was released in 1897, on the promise of his mother that they would move to another colony and make a fresh start.[32] Wilson was deemed insane by 1894 and transferred to the Ararat Asylum, coincidentally in Holly's hometown. Wilson had spent his whole life moving through what Foucault called the carceral archipelago: starting with parents in the convict system; then going from orphanage, to apprenticeship, through lower and higher courts, prison and asylum. Jenny Green, who is not known to have broken any laws, was also trapped with systems of surveillance as an Aboriginal woman in settler society. Although she managed to escape the mission, she remained subject to intense scrutiny. In 1907, aged about 70, she also ended up in Ararat, being committed to the Asylum in a frail state, on the grounds that she was depressed and disturbed, suicidal and overly fearful for the welfare of her son. She died after just four months there, in January 1908, with the causes of death noted as heat exhaustion and senile decay.[33]

The Mount Rennie and Condah cases reveal the concern in the late 1880s that the colonies should be viewed in a favourable light as the centennial of the settler colonisation was marked. They bring together the idea that a convict stain persisted in the colonies, directly in the case of Wilson/Glyde in the Condah case, and indirectly, as a contagion, in the Mount Rennie case. In order to maintain control over this seething mass of potential wrongdoers, more harsh penalties had to be inflicted than were used in Britain, including execution for rape. Holly's origins in what was considered a morally upright pioneer family went in his favour, not sufficiently that he was found not guilty but in his early release. While the authorities sought to deter and punish sex crimes, legislatures rejected more restrictive bills, including in NSW the Seduction Punishment Bill of 1887 and the Vice Suppression Bill of 1892, which would have raised the age of consent to 17.[34]

Presumptions about people's ethnic, religious and racial identities can also be seen to affect the process of the law. In the Mount Rennie case, there was a strong sense that it was prejudice against the Irish Catholic identity of many of the accused which contributed to their initial arrest and to their final execution. In the Condah case, the Aboriginality of the victim and several witnesses was used as a way to try to lessen the gravity of the crime and to undermine their testimony. However, having been educated as Christians, the victims were permitted to give sworn evidence, confirmed by a respectable local settler colonist, and the offenders were convicted. In both cases, women were being offered protection from sex crime that they had not had in the earlier years of the colony, and which Aboriginal women still did not have access to many parts of the continent. The cost for both women was having their own lives and morality closely examined in the process.

Suggested Readings

Bellanta, Melissa. "The Mount Rennie Outrage." *Larrikins: A History*. Brisbane: University of Queensland Press, Chapter 4, 2012.

Douglas, Roger and Kathy Laster. "A Matter of Life and Death: The Victorian Executive and the Decision to Execute, 1842–1967." *Australian and New Zealand Journal of Criminology* 24 (1991): 144–60.

Kaladelfos, Andy. "The Politics of Punishment: Rape and the Death Penalty in Colonial Australia, 1841–1901." *History Australia* 9, no. 1 (2012): 155–75.

Kukulies-Smith, W. and S. Priest, "The Mount Rennie Rape Case of 1886: Politics, Mercy and Justice in Late Nineteenth Century Australia." Patricia Easteal, ed. *Justice Connections*. Newcastle upon Tyne: Cambridge Scholars Publishing, 2013.

Peers, Juliet. "The Tribe of Mary Jane Hicks: Imaging Women through the Mount Rennie Rape Case 1886." *Australian Cultural History* 12 (1993): 127–44.

Philips, David, "Anatomy of a Rape Case, 1888: Sex, Race, Violence and Criminal Law in Victoria." David Philips and Susanne Davies, eds. *A Nation of Rogues?: Crime, Law and Punishment in Colonial Australia*. Melbourne: Penguin, 1994.

ESSAY: SEXUAL VIOLENCE, RACISM, AND THE DEATH PENALTY

Andy Kaladelfos

Maintaining the death sentence for rape until well into the twentieth century was a distinct feature of Australian criminal justice systems. Despite England having removed the death penalty for rape in 1841, Australian criminal justice administrators maintained that the death penalty for rape was necessary because of the historically specific contexts of their colonies.[35] This short essay presents updated historical data on the use of the death penalty for rape in Australia that shows that the critical factors in political decisions about execution were region, the prisoner's racial background, and the victim's race, age, and marital status.[36]

Colonial executions themselves were highly political affairs, each the decision of the Governor as the head of state, taking advice from the Executive Council – a process separate from, and taking place after, a criminal trial.[37] This political decision-making means that patterns in state executions can reveal systemic issues in the administration of justice. After 1841, there were 54 executions for rape in Australia and 1 death in custody from 227 capital convictions.[38] In other words, nearly one in four men sentenced to death for rape was executed. But executions were not equally meted out across all regions (see Table 7.1).[39]

Table 7.1 Prisoners Executed for Rape Since 1841, Australia

		Racial background	*Aboriginal*	*S. S. Islander*	*African American*	*White*	*Total*
State	**NSW**	**Count**	**6**	**0**	**1**	**10**	**17**
		% within NSW	35%	0%	6%	59%	100%
	QLD	**Count**	**13**	**3**	**0**	**1**	**17**
		% within QLD	76%	18%	0%	6%	100%
	TAS	**Count**	**0**	**0**	**0**	**9**	**9**
		% within TAS	0%	0%	0%	100%	100%
	VIC	**Count**	**0**	**0**	**1**	**5**	**6**
		% within VIC	0%	0%	17%	83%	100%
	WA	**Count**	**0**	**0**	**0**	**5**	**5**
		% within WA	0%	0%	0%	100%	100%
Total		Count	**19**	**3**	**2**	**30**	**54**
		% of all states	35%	6%	4%	56%	100%

Men sentenced to death for rape in Queensland were twice as likely to be executed as the national rate. Queensland execution decisions focused on punishing Black men – 16 of the 17 men executed were Aboriginal or South Sea Islander, the highest number of any state in Australia. Tasmania and Western Australia executed no Aboriginal men for rape, while NSW, during the same period, executed six Aboriginal men and one African American man. A prisoner's race was as determinative of execution as the victim's race, age, and marital status. Black men in NSW and Queensland were almost exclusively executed for the rape of white adult married women in regional settings.[40] Nationally 82% of executed Black men were convicted of the rape of white adult women, compared to less than half of white men executed.

Scholars of capital punishment discuss the symbolic utility of the death penalty. A mechanism of extreme state power, executions were displays of the authority of colonial governments, used to punish crimes deemed to threaten settler colonialism – here seen to be embodied in protecting white women's virtue.[41] Racist social views on the sexual danger Black men were purported to pose to white women are a well-known part of structural inequalities in the Jim Crow American South, leading to wrongful convictions and lynching of Black men across the region.[42] In Queensland, such racist social views existed alongside ongoing frontier massacres, theft of Aboriginal land, and exploitative use of South Sea Islander indentured labourers – all conditions that governed the political use of executions.

While these racist views were prevalent across the country, other Australian states operationalised another strain of gendered and racialised discourse. By the mid-nineteenth century, many states had large populations of white ex-convict men and their male children, seen as particularly dangerous due to their convict heritage or the isolation of living in the bush.[43] Political fears about white women's safety narrowed to focus on protecting young white girls at risk from these dangerous white men, including their own fathers. As the nineteenth century continued, white men were more often executed for the rape of young white girls rather than adult women. Protecting the honour of white women centred upon defending the "honour of our virgins," as NSW Colonial Secretary Sir Henry Parkes put it in an 1879 speech about a capital rape case.[44] In the nineteenth century, crimes against respectable young white girls and white married women were deemed so grievous that they regularly attracted state-sanctioned executions.

These execution patterns not only show how discrimination was operationalised by those punished but also in those cases that rarely appeared. Crimes against single white adult women were less often prosecuted, rarely resulted in a conviction, and only once led to execution.[45] Victim-blaming of adult women was pervasive in this period, resulting in adult women being regularly disbelieved, accused of having given sexual consent or making false allegations, and conviction rates for rape remained low (an aggregate nationally of 50%). Likewise, sexual violence against Aboriginal or Black women of any age was rarely prosecuted and rarely led to a conviction.

The execution of white man and ex-convict John Caldwell in Western Australia (1860) is the only instance of execution for the rape of Aboriginal women or girls.[46] Caldwell's case illustrates the dynamics of colonial violence, racism and age explained above. The victim, in this case, was a young Aboriginal girl known as "Neacho," reported to be between 10 and 12 years old. Caldwell has been a hut keeper near Neacho's family's land. In deposed testimony, Neacho's brother told the court that one day Caldwell demanded Neacho be sent to his hut, threatening violence against her and her brother. Her brother said that he tried to protect her by offering to send an older Aboriginal woman – indicating a background of white men's sexual exploitation of Aboriginal women. Evidence was heard from Aboriginal witnesses and a medical officer was that Neacho had been severely injured during the offence. This evidence did not stop Caldwell and another white man from using the defence that Neacho had consented and regularly had sexual relations with white men. Neacho, her brother, and her mother were forced to defend against these allegations during the deposition hearing. Later the injuries to Neacho proved so severe that she died before the criminal trial had occurred. Caldwell was not then charged with felony murder but only with rape despite her death. An aggravating factor in Caldwell's execution was that he was an ex-convict at a time of rapid increase in the convict population in Western Australia, enhancing the severity of his crime in the eyes of the government. His execution shows that white men's violence against Aboriginal women was punished in only the most extreme circumstances. In contrast, white men's routine exploitation of Aboriginal women did not attract state punishment.[47]

This analysis has shown the specific operationalisation of racism and violence in Australia's criminal justice history. Location, historical context, race and age of both prisoners and victims were central to political decisions about executions. Capital punishment served a deliberate function in Australian settler colonies: it was used to maintain the authority of colonial legal institutions, enact exemplary punishment as symbolic illustrations of governmental power, and maintain the appearance of protecting white women and girls, but only those deemed to be of the utmost sexual virtue.

PRIMARY SOURCE: OPPOSING CAPITAL PUNISHMENT, THE *BULLETIN*, 1889

By the late nineteenth century, there were strident debates in Australia over how extensively execution should continue to be used as a punishment, especially after Britain reduced its capital crimes to just two, murder and treason. As seen in the Mount Rennie, Louisa Collins and Frances Knorr cases discussed in Chapter 8, many people were moved to voice their opinions in favour or against the use of capital punishment based on everything from a general stance against "judicial murder" to very specific arguments about the identity of the offender, the morality of the victim, or details of the evidence. In Sydney, the *Bulletin* (established in 1880), led by its editor JF Archibald, was firmly opposed to capital punishment and to corporal punishment more broadly, using both words and images to make its points. This cover from just after the execution of Louisa Collins combines the journal's republicanism and anti-capital punishment stance by showing Governor Lord Carrington disregarding a long petition asking that Collins' life be spared, and exaggerating the youth of the Mount Rennie rapists executed two years earlier.

Figure 7.2 The Yawning Guv'nah and the Yawning Grave, *Bulletin*, 12 January 1889, 9 No. 465, 3.

Notes

1 "Sexual Assault in Australia," Australian Institute of Health and Welfare, August 2020, 2, https://www.aihw.gov.au/getmedia/0375553f-0395-46cc-9574-d54c74fa601a/aihw-fdv-5.pdf.aspx?inline=true (accessed 7 June 2022).

2 Joshua L. Reid, "Makahs, Maori, and the Settler Revolution in Pacific Marine Space," Kate Fullagar and Michael A. McDonnell, eds. *Facing Empire: Indigenous Experiences in a Revolutionary Age*, Baltimore: Johns Hopkins University Press, 2018, 267.

3 Anne Summers, *Damned Whores and Gods Police*, revised edition, Melbourne: Penguin, 1994, 315–16.

4 Libby Connors, "Uncovering the Violence on an Australian Colonial Frontier," Robert Mason, ed. *Legacies of Violence: Rendering the unspeakable past in modern Australia*, Oxford: Berghahn, 2017, 35.

5 Melanie Burkett, *Opposing Australia's First Assisted Immigrants, 1832–42*, Cham, Switzerland: Palgrave Macmillan, 2021, 171–73.

6 Andy Kaladelfos, "The Politics of Punishment: Rape and the Death Penalty in Colonial Australia, 1841–1901," *History Australia* 9, no. 1 (2012), 157.

7 This account draws upon Melissa Bellanta, *Larrikins: A History*, Brisbane: University of Queensland Press, 2012, Chapter 4, "The Mount Rennie Outrage," W. Kukulies-Smith and S. Priest, "The Mount Rennie Rape Case of 1886: Politics, Mercy and Justice in Late Nineteenth Century Australia," Patricia Easteal, ed. *Justice Connections*, Newcastle upon Tyne: Cambridge Scholars Publishing, 2013; and Juliet Peers, "The tribe of Mary Jane Hicks: Imaging Women through the Mount Rennie Rape Case 1886," *Australian Cultural History*, 12 (1993): 127–44.

8 "The Mount Rennie Outrage," *Daily Telegraph*, October 6, 1886, 6.

9 "Mount Rennie Martyrs," *Evening News*, 28 December 1886, 4.

10 Peter Grabosky, *Sydney in Ferment, Crime, Dissent and Official Reaction, 1788–1973*, Canberra: ANU Press, 1977, 88.

11 Grabosky, *Sydney in Ferment*, Table 7.2, 87.

12 "Central Criminal Court," *Daily Telegraph*, November 23, 1886, 3.

13 "The Mount Rennie Outrage," *Evening News*, October 6, 1886, 6.

14 "The Mount Rennie Outrage. Deputation to the Governor," *Sydney Morning Herald*, January 4, 1887, 3.

15 Nina Philadelphoff-Puren, "Reading Rape in Colonial Australia: Barbara Baynton's 'The Tramp', The *Bulletin* and Cultural Criticism," *JASAL* 2009 Special Issue: *Common Readers and Cultural Critics*, 3–5.

16 "The Mount Rennie Outrage," *Evening News* (Sydney), October 6, 1886, 6.

17 "Mount Rennie Outrage, The Cabman Sentenced," *Armidale Express and New England General Advertiser*, November 30, 1886, 5.

18 Kukulies-Smith and Priest, "The Mount Rennie Rape Case of 1886," 232–37.

19 Rachel Franks, *An Uncommon Hangman: The Life and Deaths of Robert "Nosey Bob" Howard*, Sydney: NewSouth, 2022, 139–43.

20 Robyn Lincoln and Shirleene Robinson, "When the Penalty Was Death," R. Lincoln and S. Robinson, eds. *Crime Over Time: Temporal Perspectives on Crime and Punishment in Australia*, 201.

21 This account draws upon David Philips, "Anatomy of a Rape Case, 1888: Sex, Race, Violence and Criminal Law in Victoria," David Philips and Susanne Davies, eds. *A Nation of Rogues?: Crime, Law and Punishment in Colonial Australia*, Melbourne: Penguin, 1994, 97–122.

22 John Newton, *The Oldest Foods on Earth: A History of Australian Native Foods with Recipes*, Sydney: NewSouth, 2016, 16–17.

23 Emily Bissland, "Act of Rebellion as 'naughty girl' Connie Hart Wove against Oppression," ABC South West Victoria, July 8, 2018, https://www.abc.net.au/news/2018-07-07/act-of-rebellion-as-naughty-girl-wove-against-oppression/9943694 (accessed 9 April 2022).

24 "Christmas Examinations," *Mercury*, 28 December 1872, 2; "Christmas Examinations," *Mercury* (Hobart), December 30, 1874, 2.

25 "Inquest at the Hospital," *Launceston Examiner*, February 21, 1885, 3.

26 "News of News," *Hamilton Spectator*, May 8, 1888, 2.

27 Neil Singh, "Decolonising Dermatology: Why Black and Brown Skin Need better Treatment," August 13, 2020, https://www.theguardian.com/society/2020/aug/13/decolonising-dermatology-why-black-and-brown-skin-need-better-treatment (accessed 5 January 2022).

28 Libby Connors, "Uncovering the Shameful: Sexual Violence on an Australian Colonial Frontier," Robert Mason, ed. *Legacies of Violence: Rendering the Unspeakable Past in Modern Australia*, Oxford: Berghahn, 2017, 39–41.

29 R. Douglas and K. Laster, "A Matter of Life and Death: The Victorian Executive and the Decision to Execute, 1842–1967," *Australian and New Zealand Journal of Criminology* 24 (1991), 146.

30 Mark Finnane, *Punishment in Australian Society*, Melbourne: Oxford University Press, 1997, 47–51.

31 See, for example, Liz Conor, "The 'Drover's Boy' and Indigenous Women's Unthinkable Consent," Alana Piper and Ana Stevenson, eds. *Gender Violence in Australia, Historical Perspectives*, Melbourne: Monash University Publishing, 2019, 102.

32 "Released from Gaol," *Herald* (Melbourne), May 3, 1897, 1.

33 Ela Dara, "Jennie Green – Queen of an Ancient Land," 20 February 2019, https://jacsplace.wordpress.com/2019/02/20/jennie-green-the-queen-of-an-ancient-land/ (accessed 9 April 2022).

34 Grabosky, *Sydney in Ferment*, 92–93.

35 The death penalty for rape was repealed in South Australia in 1845; Tasmania 1885; Queensland 1899; Western Australia 1902; Victoria 1949, New South Wales 1954; and federally including Northern Territory, 1968.

36 For earlier analysis see Ross Barber, "Rape and Other Sexual Offences in Queensland," MA Thesis, University of Queensland, 1970.

37 On the history of capital punishment debates in Australia, see Steven Anderson, *A History of Capital Punishment in the Australian Colonies, 1788 to 1900*, Cham: Palgrave Macmillan, 2020.

38 The death in custody case was an Aboriginal man known as Kipper Billy (Queensland, 1862).

39 There was no uniform system or location of recording death penalty decision within or across Australian jurisdictions. Data here have been updated using Finnane, Kaladelfos, Piper, Smaal et al., *The Prosecution Project Database*; Macnab, Castle, Kaladelfos, *NSW Capital Convictions Database*; individually cross-referencing each case in the National Library of Australia's newspaper databases; archival deposition materials from all states, Government and Police Gazettes; and comparing to previously published material cited here. Final dataset in author's possession, available on request.

40 The definition of "adult" here is 18 years old, the highest age of consent nationally. States also maintained a related capital offence of "carnal knowledge of a girl under 10." These cases are not considered here and therefore the ages of "child" in this essay are defined as between 10 and 18.

41 Amanda Nettelbeck and Robert Foster. "Colonial Judiciaries, Aboriginal Protection and South Australia's Policy of Punishing 'with Exemplary Severity.'" *Australian Historical Studies* 41, no. 3 (September 1, 2010): 319–36.

42 Estelle Freedman. *Redefining Rape: Sexual Violence in the Era of Suffrage and Segregation*, Cambridge, MA: Harvard University Press, 2013.
43 Andy Kaladelfos, "The Politics of Punishment: Rape and the Death Penalty in Colonial Australia, 1841–1901," *History Australia* 9, no. 1 (2012): 155–75.
44 *The Sydney Mail*, "The Premier's Deliverances," May 24, 1879.
45 *The Prosecution Project Database*, Trial ID #454884, Tasmanian Australian Supreme Court, Samuel Haines, 1852.
46 *The Prosecution Project Database*, Trial ID #8175, Western Australian Supreme Court, John Caldwell, 1860.
47 Libby Connors, "Uncovering the Shameful: Sexual Violence on an Australian Colonial Frontier" in Robert Mason, ed. *Legacies of Violence: Rendering the Unspeakable Past in Modern Australia*, New York, NY: Berghahn Books, 2017.

8 Husband Poisoners and Baby Killers

Women Criminals

Throughout the history of settler colonial Australia, women have been much less likely than men to break the law or to be convicted for an offence. In Australia in 2019–20, three-quarters of the offenders proceeded against by police were male. For every 100,000 males in the country, there were 2559 offenders, while for every 100,000 females, there were just 813.[1] Shifting the focus back in time, there was an even more pronounced difference between the numbers of men and women transported as convicts, with only one in six being a woman.[2] Despite the best efforts of authorities to avoid a large gender imbalance in the colonies, too few women were appearing before the British courts. In this chapter, we will explore why this has consistently been the case and how women's tendency not to break the law affected the treatment of the small minority who did offend. The focus will be on the late nineteenth century, when a movement to improve the status of women was unsettling Australian society. As concern grew that women would move into public life and abandon their domestic roles, capital punishment was applied to a cluster of women found guilty of crimes against those in their care. We will look closely at the cases of two of these women: Louisa Collins, the last woman to be executed in New South Wales, and Frances Knorr, one of Melbourne's infamous baby farmers. That both Collins and Knorr failed to live up to contemporary expectations of femininity contributed to making them 2 of only 19 women ever judicially executed in settler colonial Australia.

An Opening Question

Before launching into accounts of these two women, let's begin with a consideration of why men were more likely than women to be law breakers in late nineteenth-century Australia. Were women more virtuous than men? This was certainly the assumption which underpinned the role allotted to women of being "God's police." It assumed that women were not only naturally more moral than men and more likely to be law abiding themselves, but that they could also serve as the Christian God's representatives on earth, exerting their positive influence to produce a more orderly society. According to Anne Summers, with the establishment of more middle-class families in

DOI: 10.4324/9781003273561-9

Australia from the 1850s, women were increasingly expected to influence others to be good through their roles as mothers, sisters and wives within the family, voluntary helpers for the aged, the sick and those in need, and professional teachers, social workers and nuns.[3] Women earned respect and status for playing this role and most sought to cultivate the image by following both social expectations and the law.

As well as wanting to be seen to be law abiding, many women had limited opportunities to break laws even if they wanted to. The criminal law was mainly concerned with occurrences in the public world which caused harm to people or property. In the nineteenth century, public life was a male domain. By regulation and according to social practice, men dominated paid work, the streets, pubs, politics and the law, while women's sphere was the domestic world of the home.[4] Even there, women did not have autonomy, but were dependent on their fathers and husbands, with married couples not considered separate legal persons under the common law.[5] As in some systems of Aboriginal Law, within which brothers and husbands had the responsibility of identifying and punishing transgressions by sisters and wives, the colonial state delegated control of women's behaviour to men. Intimate partner violence was often understood and explained as men punishing women for poor behaviour and was generally tolerated. As we shall see, when women turned the tables, there was no such acceptance.

Despite the factors limiting their illegal activity, there were female offenders in the late nineteenth century. *The essay in this chapter by leading historian of women's crime Alana Piper discusses the offences for which women were most commonly convicted in this period, showing that the murderers focused upon in this chapter were far from typical.* Instead, most women who offended were found guilty of minor theft such as shoplifting and pickpocketing and offences against good order, like public drunkenness. Amongst them were many repeat offenders who accumulated large numbers of convictions.

Even in terms of these lesser offences, women were often treated more leniently than men firstly by the police and then by the courts, adding to the perception that they offended less. This might seem surprising when we consider that the making and administration of the law at this time was an all-male endeavour. There were no female voters or members of the colonial parliaments; no women judges or jurors; no female lawyers or police officers. The only women involved in the legal system were at the highest level: Queen Victoria who was the reigning monarch over the United Kingdom and its colonies from 1837 to 1901 and at the lowest: the female warders who supervised women in prison. With no say in legal processes, it would be easy to imagine that the criminal justice system would be heavily biased against women, and that they would be harshly victimised within it.

Instead, when women were tried and evidence was presented that they had committed crimes, they were often treated with sympathy and either acquitted or found guilty of lesser charges.[6] In part, this was because women's actions were generally seem as being less important than those of men. Some of the acts committed by women which might have been criminalised were not, or even if what they did was against the law, they were not punished. For example, physical assaults between women were generally not prosecuted as long as they did not involve anyone else. Consider Ned Kelly's mother Ellen who we met in Chapter 5. She regularly sold alcohol without a licence, joined in disputes with other family members and neighbours and aided in the theft of livestock. When she struck Constable Fitzpatrick on the head with a spade, she was found guilty of aiding and abetting and attempted murder but received a sentence half the length of that awarded to her two male co-accused.[7] Kathy Laster called this preferential treatment of women by the courts an "arbitrary chivalry."[8]

Perhaps the most serious crime for which women were regularly treated with leniency was the killing of their own infants. With only rudimentary forms of contraception available, young single women found themselves pregnant, sometimes after experiencing coercive sexual relations, and without any means of supporting a child. Confused and afraid, some single women hid their pregnancy from those around them, gave birth alone and brought about the death of their child, either actively, by abandonment, or through neglect. The only woman to be executed in Van Diemen's Land, convict Mary McLaughlin in 1830, was likely in this situation when she killed her baby, thought to be the child of the man to whom she had been assigned.[9]

Recognising the difficult situations these women were in, the incidence of postpartum psychiatric disorders (then considered "derangements of the mind") and the role of a man who had not behaved honourably in creating the situation, coupled with the high rate of unexplained infant death from natural causes, McLaughlin's fate was rare. Few of these women were charged with murder. Instead, they often faced the lesser charge of concealment of birth. Formal recognition of the complicating factors in these cases came in the early twentieth century when a new crime of infanticide was created in Victoria and NSW. Infanticide is grouped with manslaughter as forms of unintentional killing and applies only to mothers who caused the death of their own infants. Even for married women and those who killed older children, there could be sympathy. When, in 1885, Victorian mother of six Sarah Williams threw her 1-year-old daughter into the Yarra River in 1885 during a confrontation with her drunken and neglectful husband, the judge hearing the case thought she deserved understanding:

> I felt that she was not a murderess in the ordinary sense of the term and that the act she committed was an act of the moment, perpetrated when the woman was worried in mind and worn out in body, and one quite foreign to her nature and disposition as exhibited during the eleven or twelve years of her status as wife and mother.[10]

Williams was found guilty of murder and sentenced to death with recommendations from both the jury and the judge to mercy. The execution was replaced with 2 years of imprisonment.[11]

When they were represented by lawyers who could make claims about their clients' "natural" frailty, irrationality and vulnerability, women were much more likely than represented men to be acquitted.[12] Countering this evidence, however, is new research by Victoria Nagy who cautions that the impact of this chivalry should not be overstated. Her careful review of conviction rates in Victoria in the final four decades of the nineteenth century shows that if charged with murder, women were actually *more* likely than men to be found guilty, even if less likely to be executed.[13] We will examine some factors determining who benefitted from this chivalry in the Collins and Knorr cases.

Going back to our opening proposition about men offending more than women, this stands up but it is complicated. As we have seen, women tended to lead more circumscribed lives which limited their opportunities for crime, and their anti-social acts were considered less threatening than those of men. Women were able to engage in low-profile crime which was never detected, and if it was, they benefitted from leniency within the justice system.

In the late nineteenth century, this favourable position for female offenders came under increased scrutiny. After rising pressure from women's rights groups, some of the ways in which women were disadvantaged were being addressed in the Australian colonies. Married Women's Property Acts were passed between 1879 and 1897 which enabled women to hold property, enter into contracts and to sue for damages in their own right; women gained the right to custody of their children after the breakdown of a marriage; the age of consent for sexual activity was raised from 12 to 14 or 16 (1883–99) and perhaps most momentous of all, women were given the right to vote in South Australia (1894) and Western Australia (1899). Steps like these towards social, economic and political equality for women in this period made some think women no longer deserved special treatment. If women wanted to be equal to men in public life, it was argued, they would also have to face equal consequences for their actions. Chivalry was not dead but it was going to be contested.

This chapter will now closely examine two women who were convicted of very serious crimes in the late nineteenth century and who faced the punishment reserved for the worst offenders. When women committed crimes like murder, society took notice because it was exceptional. In such cases, one of the points of fascination was how a *woman* could do such a thing. It was often asserted that the offender was not a womanly woman but had unsexed herself, having by nature or through her own actions developed what were seen as masculine traits: thinking strategically, having a strong sexual appetite and, as Lombroso would predict, presenting a manly appearance. Just as men were punished for crimes which could upset the social order and were either deviations from or gross exaggerations of what were considered their natural roles, women were most heavily punished for what were seen as betrayals of their appointed roles as wife, mother, nurturer and carer.

The highly publicised crimes, prosecutions and punishments of Louisa Collins and Frances Knorr show how contemporary understandings of femininity and criminality influenced their experience of the criminal justice system.

Louisa Collins

Louisa Collins has attracted attention not only for the nature of the crime for which she was convicted, but because she was the last woman to be executed in NSW. Journalist Caroline Overington wrote *Last Woman Hanged* about her in 2014 and a true crime book on Collins entitled *Black Widow* was published by Carole Baxter in 2015.[14] She has also been the subject of a play and features in many collections about Australian crime.

Collins was originally from the Hunter Valley of NSW, now best known for its wineries and coal mines. She was born in 1847 to an ex-convict father and free settler mother then living on a sheep property called Belltrees near the town of Scone. As Louisa Hall, she worked as a domestic servant before marrying at age 18 and had a typically large family with her husband, butcher Charles Andrews, 14 years her senior. After their fifth child, May, was born in 1877, financial pressure forced the family to move from the Hunter Valley to Sydney, settling at Botany, now adjacent to Sydney's Kingsford Smith Airport, where Charlie was able to find work in the wool-washing industry. In keeping with the expectation that women would remain at home but still needing to contribute to the family economy, Louisa took paying boarders into their four-roomed-rented terrace house in an area called Popple's Paddock, while also bearing another three children. Charlie had a good reputation as a sober and honest man at work, while Louisa became known as a drinker and for keeping a boisterous household.

In December 1886, Charlie Andrews discovered that 39-year-old Louisa was having an affair with one of the boarders, a carter and wool washer in his mid-20s named Michael Collins. Evidently after two decades of marriage, she was not happy in the relationship. Following the passing of the Matrimonial Causes Act in Britain in 1857, the Australian colonies had been invited to adopt their own divorce legislation, which was done in South Australia in 1858 and 1860 in Victoria, amongst the surge in desertion of spouses related to the goldrushes.[15] In NSW, under the Matrimonial Causes Act of 1873, wives like Louisa could petition for divorce on the grounds of bigamy, cruelty, adultery (after 1881), drunkenness and desertion and assault (after 1892). No fault divorce only became available in 1975. In the 1880s, this formal legal process was expensive and not a realistic option for working-class couples like the Andrews. In some cases, couples informally separated, but in this instance, it seemed that Louisa opted for another solution.

Charlie Andrews threw Michael out of the house, assuming that would be the end of the matter. Some 6 weeks after the confrontation, Charlie became unwell, suffering from intense stomach pains and vomiting. Louisa called in a doctor who diagnosed gastritis and prescribed medicine. Charlie was nursed by Louisa but within a week, he died in early February 1887. As soon as Charlie passed, Louisa, who was described by friends and neighbours as unnervingly calm, caught a tram into the city to inform their bank and life insurance company, having taken the precaution of having a will prepared and signed a few days earlier. She chose not to wear mourning clothes as was the custom and, later that week, attended a dance with Michael. Within three months, she was pregnant and they had married, their finances boosted by a £200 life insurance payout, which was used to clear Michael's gambling debts and buy furniture and alcohol. Louisa was said to have become neglectful of her other young children. Sadly, their son, John Collins, born in November 1887, died of natural causes in April 1888 and, the insurance money already gone, was buried in a pauper's grave.

So far, this might just have been a local scandal about a widow disrespecting her deceased husband, except that the following June, Michael Collins experienced pains in his stomach, with vomiting and diarrhoea. He had several visits with doctors who prescribed various remedies. Michael was nursed by Louisa for several weeks before he died in July. The physicians who saw him on his last days, including the same doctor who had attended Charles Andrews, developed concerns that Michael was being poisoned. They reported their suspicions to the police, who interviewed him before he passed away. At the coronial inquest into his death, it was reported that a post-mortem had found inflamed internal organs consistent with exposure to an irritant poison. The government analyst detected arsenic present both in Michael's stomach and in a glass of milk provided for him by Louisa. The Coroner's Court finding was that Louisa had administered fatal poison to her husband and should be tried for wilful murder. A second inquest, into the deaths of Charlie Andrews and little John, found no evidence of foul play in the case of the baby, but that Charlie had died of poisoning administered by Louisa. The jury's decision was based almost completely on testimony from physicians, the police and neighbours about Louisa's behaviour during and after his final illness.

Poisoning was considered a particularly dreadful crime in this society. Unlike more visible violence, poisoning was viewed as a coward's or a woman's crime: sneaky, sinister and stealthy. With domestic arrangements left to women, men were vulnerable to tampering with their food and the poisoning of husbands by wives was perceived as not only wrong but treacherous, a betrayal of the person to whom they should have been most loyal. Indeed, the murder of a husband by a wife, like the murder of an employer by a servant, could be prosecuted as petty or low treason earlier in the century, a more intimate parallel of high treason against the state.[16] Poisoning cases had already been in the news, both those occurring in Australia and in Great Britain, building up the interest in this case.[17]

There followed a huge public spectacle as Louisa faced four separate trials starting from 6 August 1888 in Sydney's Central Criminal Court. The first was for the murder of Michael Collins. During this trial, Louisa and Charlie's 11-year-old daughter, May, testified that they kept the pesticide Rough on Rats in the house. Almost 100% arsenic, Rough on Rats was a popular poison used in the home, and a ramshackle terrace near the shoreline like theirs would have been likely to be visited by rodents. The issue was that May had noticed it on their kitchen shelf only twice: once before the death of her father and again before Michael Collins became ill.

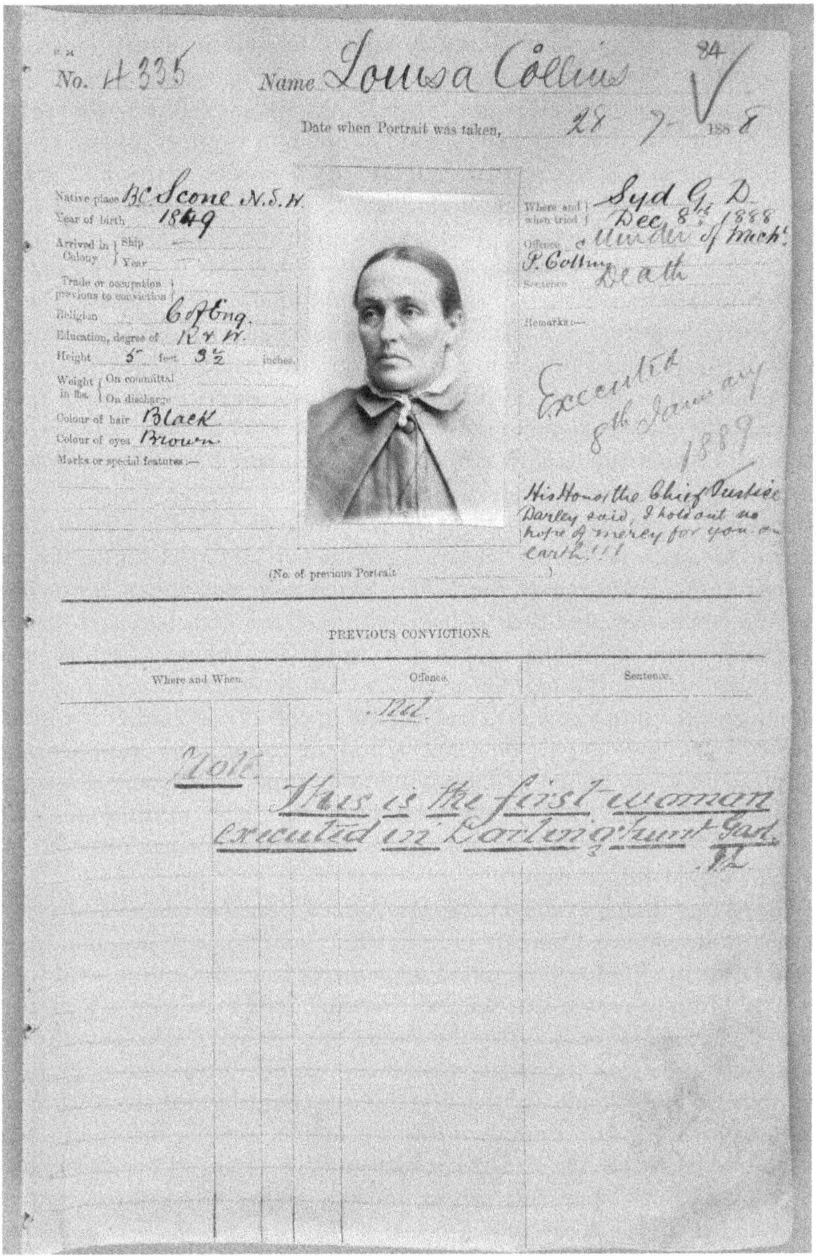

No. 4335 Name Louisa Collins 84

Date when Portrait was taken, 28 7 1888

Native place Scone N.S.W.
Year of birth 1849
Arrived in Colony Ship Year
Trade or occupation previous to conviction
Religion C of Eng.
Education, degree of R & W.
Height 5 feet 3½ inches.
Weight in lbs. On committal On discharge
Colour of hair Black
Colour of eyes Brown
Marks or special features:—

Where and when tried Syd C. D. Dec 8th 1888
Offence Murder of Mich. P. Collins
Sentence Death
Remarks:—

Executed 8th January 1889

His Honor the Chief Justice Darley said, I hold out no hope of mercy for you on earth!!!

(No. of previous Portrait)

PREVIOUS CONVICTIONS.

Where and When.	Offence.	Sentence.
	Nil	

Note. This is the first woman executed in Darlinghurst Gaol.

Figure 8.1 The photograph of Louisa Collins on her Darlinghurst Gaol record showed her as a plain housewife and mother rather than as the woman of fashion portrayed in many newspaper accounts.

Source: NSW State Archives: Darlinghurst Gaol, NRS 2138, Gaol Inmates/Prisoners Photos Index 1870 – 1930. 3/6050, p 84, Photo No: 188, Louisa Collins.

Having heard the evidence, the jury were equally divided amongst those who found Louisa Collins guilty beyond a reasonable doubt and those who did not. The judge noted that it was a case in which men of conscience could reasonably disagree.[18] It is likely that some jurors were influenced by the idea that leniency should be shown to women, particularly to one like Louisa Collins, a petite, middle-aged mother of many children, modestly dressed in grey prison clothing (Figure 8.1). They would have expected a wilful poisoner to have a masculine appearance. On the other hand, those who concluded she was guilty may have been more persuaded by the descriptions of her as calculating and cool under pressure. These were qualities generally considered to be associated with female criminals as Lombroso would confirm in his book on criminal women when it was first published in 1893. In it, he argued that women criminals were "psychologically and anthropologically" more male than female, with a weak maternal instinct and a selfish love of dissipation which could be expressed in excessive drinking or sexual activity.[19]

Because the first jury could not agree, they were dismissed and the case was referred for a new trial at the next sitting of the Circuit Court, taking place at the beginning of November. Here, May added more detail: that her mother had said Michael wasted their money and she drank both beer and brandy. That jury ended up divided as well. Changing tack, the next trial, from 19 November, was for the murder of Louisa's first husband, Charlie Andrews. Although interest in a new man and a desire to collect on Charlie's life insurance policy seemed to provide a motive and the opportunity was offered by the presence of rat poison in their house, the jurors again could not agree. A guilty verdict was finally delivered in December, after a third trial for the murder of Michael Collins. A sentence of death was not just recorded but passed with the full ceremony.

The process then moved on to the Executive Council to consider a reprieve of the death sentence. Ordinary citizens tried to influence its decision. Many asked Governor Lord Carrington to show mercy towards Collins, while others urged him to ensure that she was executed. The main line of argument taken by her supporters was that she should be reprieved not because she was innocent but because she was a woman and women were a lesser sex ruled by emotion who should not be held fully accountable for their actions.[20] Sydney phrenologist P. Besomo wrote a pamphlet arguing that the breadth of Collins' forehead, the size of her eyes and the height of her cheekbones all pointed to her being determined, innately crafty, cold hearted, morally blind and of a type to become a poisoner. In his view, she was guilty but had no control over her actions, and her life should be spared.[21] Those conscious of women's inferior legal status asserted that with women not equal in terms of law making or administration, they should not have to face equal consequences for breaking the law, making execution a legislative homicide. Others said she should be spared for the sake of her children, especially poor May whose evidence had helped to secure the conviction.

No mercy was forthcoming, and while still asserting her innocence, Collins was hanged on 8 January 1889, a punishment delayed just long enough that it did not besmirch the 1888 centennial of colonisation. The view that she should be executed comes through strongly in newspaper articles printed that day, including "The Botany Murder Case" printed in the *Evening News*, which included a gruesome account of her hanging, one of several where miscalculations by hangman "Nosey Bob" Howard made the end even more awful.[22] In over two pages of coverage, Louisa Collins was disparaged as showing a "callousness almost unprecedented in the annals of crime."[23] As an illiterate drunkard, a neglectful mother and a poor housekeeper she was not just a murderer but a bad woman with no prospect of reform. Her calmness after the deaths of her husbands and through her trials, sometimes described as indifference, was counted against her. The assumption was that a more feminine woman would have been distraught when her husbands died and that since she was not, she must be guilty. Countering this view, there were many who believed that there was insufficient evidence to convict Louisa and that she had been pursued relentlessly through the four trials as a warning for all women who were contemplating escape from their marriages. Uncertainty around her conviction remains. When a new courthouse was being built in Newcastle in 2015 to serve the Hunter Region, relatives of Collins lobbied to have a statue of her placed outside it as a reminder of the consequences of decisions made by judges and juries. Their request was denied.

Frances Knorr

Our next case, focusing on Frances Knorr, takes us to Melbourne, the capital city of the colony of Victoria. The setting was not the buoyant economy of Sydney in the centennial year, or the Marvellous Melbourne of the long boom which followed the 1850s goldrushes. A deep economic depression had settled over much of the continent in the early 1890s, and Melbourne was particularly severely affected by a series of strikes and bank collapses. Unemployment was high, and with little government assistance available, many people had to rely on charities to survive. In such circumstances, the lives of single women were even more difficult than usual. They were low paid, had few forms of employment open to them and childcare was largely informal. An unplanned pregnancy could mean disaster. Some turned to abortionists, while others killed their babies at birth.[24]

There is no doubt that many women were in a terrible position but there were alternatives. They could place their babies in charitable or privately run institutions which in Melbourne included the Maternity Aid Society and the Victorian Infant Asylum, from which they could be adopted into new families. Those not prepared to give up their child permanently could leave the baby with one of the many women who took in infants for a small weekly fee, as a means of earning an income from home. Placing a child out freed the mother to continue working to support both herself and the child and opened the possibility of reclaiming the child in the future. A variation on this practice was that the mother paid a higher one-off fee to have the carer adopt the child. In either case, many of these babies did not survive. Infant deaths could be readily explained at a time when infant mortality rates were generally high, especially for babies that were exposed to impure water and cow's milk through bottle feeding. However, in some instances, they were due to deliberate actions.

While outsourcing infant care had been practised for decades, there was rising concern about all deaths of infants in the 1890s. This followed on from a decline in what had been a very high birth rate in the preceding decades, when settler colonist women were having seven children on average.[25] At the same time, there was a push to increase the European-derived population of Australia both to secure the claim to the continent and to expand the economy. Along with immigration from Great Britain, encouraging the birth of more children within marriage and ensuring infants grew into citizens became government priorities. Reproductive crimes like abortion, infanticide and neglect of babies in care were increasingly heavily policed. Between 1891 and 1893, there were 99 inquests into the deaths of infants at the Melbourne Morgue, with 62 findings of wilful murder.[26] Some of these children had been in care.

The term "baby farming," first used in Britain in the 1860s, began to be applied in Australia for the practice of taking in babies in exchange for a payment but then not treating them with the care they deserved, and the mothers expected. Several pieces of legislation were passed in Victoria to try to regulate the industry, including amendments to the Public Health Act in 1883 which set up local boards to oversee children placed in care, and the Infant Life Protection Act of 1890 which required carers to be registered and created the new offence of wilful neglect of a child. A Children's Protection act followed in NSW in 1892, requiring adoptions to be registered and the reporting of all infant deaths. This was all positive but without proper enforcement and without giving women alternatives to placing their babies out – such as free refuges, public financial support, forcing men to take equal responsibility for their children or greater acceptance of single parenthood – they had limited effect. Measures which would make it easier to raise children born outside of marriage were resisted on the grounds not only of cost but because they might encourage illicit sexual activity. Both well-intentioned mothers and carers were vilified for being part of the very flawed system.

Instead of support, governments used the power of the law to try to deter the worst instances of baby farming. In Sydney, the show trial was that of John and Sarah Makin.[27] The couple had charged mothers up to £5 to permanently adopt their babies, but instead of seeking long-term homes for them or raising the infants themselves, they were killed. Thirteen infant corpses were found buried in their inner-city backyard. John was seen as the mastermind and was executed in 1893 while Sarah was also found guilty but had her capital punishment commuted to a 14-year prison sentence.

Melbourne's demonstration case was that of Frances Knorr.[28] She had emigrated from the United Kingdom to Sydney in 1887 as Minny Thwaites, working as a domestic servant and a waitress, but also spending a month in jail after stealing a dress. Her crimes continued: stealing money, false pretences and theft of a sewing machine. She married an immigrant from Germany, Rudolph Knorr, who had his own reputation as a swindler. The couple moved to Melbourne and had a baby there in 1892. When Rudolph was sent to jail for fraud, Frances struggled to support herself and their child by dressmaking. She supplemented her income by taking in other women's babies, moving from one rented house to another around the inner Melbourne suburbs of Brunswick, South Yarra, Brighton and St Kilda. When released, Rudolph assisted in this business and the couple also paid girls as young as 12 to care for up to 10 babies at any given time. Some of the babies were passed on to other carers, with the Knorr's retaining a cut of the money from the mothers. Frances developed a poor reputation as a carer and appeared in the *Victorian Police Gazette* in August 1893, wanted for unlawfully abandoning one of the children. She was described in the *Gazette* as 5 feet 3 or 4 inches tall, with a stout build, brown hair and a heavy lower jaw, and usually dressed in a black dress, jacket and gem hat. Wanting to avoid arrest, the family decided it was time to move on.

In the suburb of Brunswick, a new tenant moved into one of the houses Knorr had briefly occupied and made a gruesome discovery in the back garden: the decomposing body of an infant. Other properties were inspected, and two more bodies found, including one with a cord around his neck which showed that he had not died of natural causes. Knorr was traced to Sydney, where she had recently delivered her second child, and was brought back to Melbourne for trial, leaving her elder daughter in the Sydney Benevolent Asylum (Figure 8.2). Inquests held into the deaths of each of the three babies led to both Frances and Rudolph being committed to be tried for murder.

In the proceedings, Knorr was characterised not only as deceitful and ruthless but also as promiscuous – one of the characteristics contemporaries expected to see in a bad woman. She made herself look worse when a letter was produced that she had written to a former partner during the inquest asking him to find people to lie on her behalf. A girl who had worked in the Brunswick house gave evidence that one of her tasks was to borrow a spade so Knorr could work in the garden. A mother testified that Knorr had refused to let her see her child, and when she was reunited with the baby, it died within a fortnight.

In December 1893, Knorr was found guilty of killing one female child and sentenced to be hanged. As in the case of Louisa Collins, there were petitions for mercy, on the grounds that she was not fully responsible for her own actions. "The Women of Victoria," including prominent feminist Ida Goldstein, made the claims that the men of the legal system deciding to kill a woman was against the moral sense of the community and would bring the law into disrepute; her execution was un-Christian and out of step with legal practice in the United Kingdom, that Knorr deserved a chance of reform and that to kill her would bring shame to Victoria in the eyes of the world.

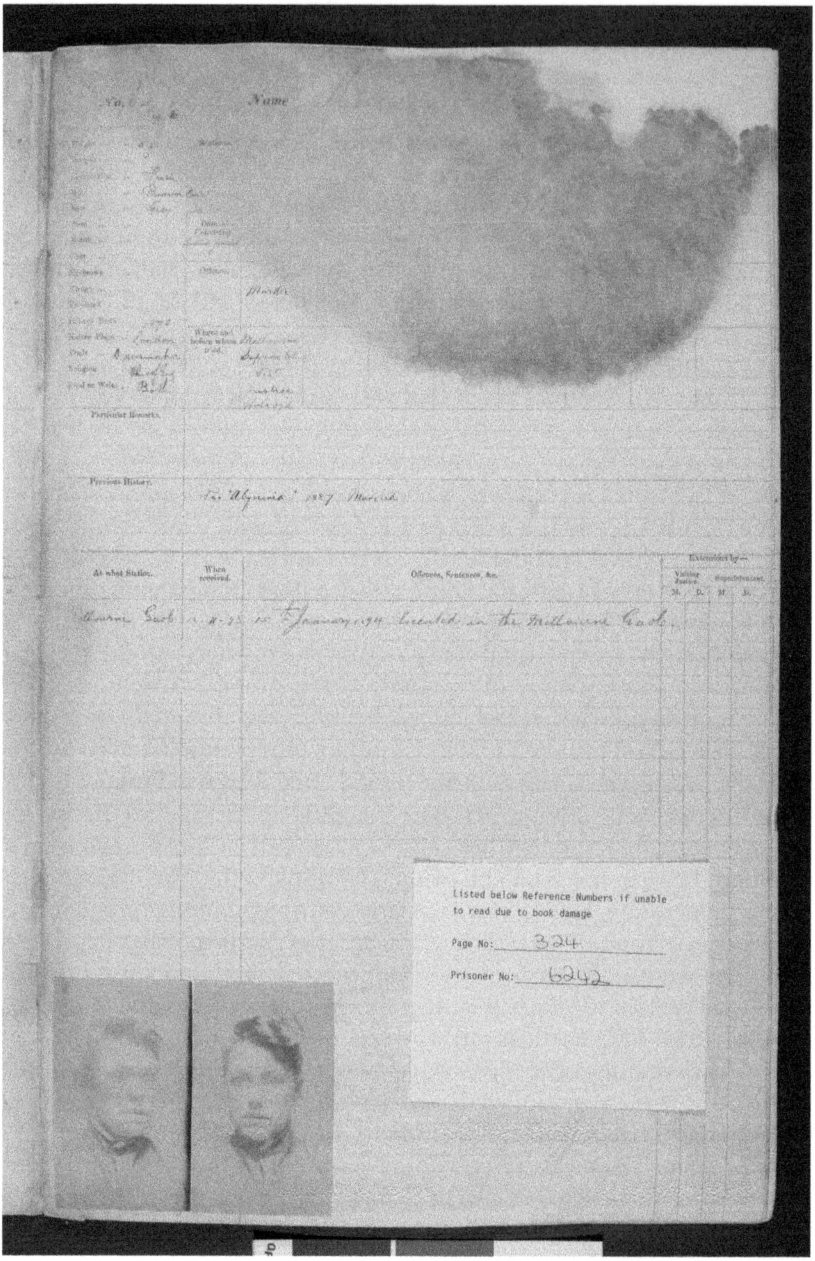

Figure 8.2 Frances Knorr's damaged prison record provides a few details about her appearance and her past life, as well as a now faded photograph and the date of her execution.

Source: Public Records Office Victoria. Central Register of Female Prisoners. VPRS 516/P0000, 5926–6415 (1891–1896), pg. 324, Prisoner 6242, Frances Knorr.

Others felt there could be no worse case and that Knorr showed no glimpses of a better nature, and so should be executed. Thousands took to the streets shouting "Hang Mrs Knorr. Death to the baby killer."[29] Knorr signed a statement acknowledging her guilt for killing two of the babies, noting a hope that her fate would be a warning to others, although the extent to which this was done of her own free will was disputed.[30] The Melbourne hangman, known only as Jones, was so distressed by repercussions which would flow from executing a woman that he took his own life. Nonetheless, the authorities were committed to showing that infants would be protected, and Frances Knorr was hanged in January 1894, aged 24. A death mask was made and her skull was put on display at Old Melbourne Gaol before being passed to the National Trust Australia (Victoria) and, in 2006, to the Melbourne Dental School.[31] In a sad coda, Knorr's own child died in care after her execution.

Two years later, a Society for the Prevention of Cruelty to Children was formed in Melbourne. They recognised that most out-of-home carers were not monsters but poor women themselves who were trying to make a respectable living. The Society helped to secure the passage of a new Infant Life Protection Act in 1907 but it was not until after the First World War, in 1919, that the Maintenance of Children Act provided for an allowance to be paid to mothers in need, relieving the terrible financial strain which had contributed to the deaths of so many infants.

Conclusion

Of the 95 women convicted of murder or manslaughter in Victoria between 1860 and 1920, only four were considered so callous and irredeemable, or timed their crimes so poorly in terms of contemporary concerns, that they were executed. The others, if considered bad, served long prison sentences; or if deemed mad, lived out their lives in asylums.[32] The first to be executed was Elizabeth Scott in 1863, for persuading her lover and another man to kill her husband. Three women were executed in the 1890s. Knorr was followed later the same year by Martha Needle who was hanged for poisoning her brother-in-law, with the assumption that she had also killed her husband and two children. The following year, Emma Williams was found guilty of drowning her 2-year-old in Melbourne's Yarra River and hanged. Over half a century later, Jean Lee became the last woman executed in Victoria and all of Australia, in 1950, for a murder committed with two male accomplices. In NSW, executions of women were equally rare at six, half of whom were convicted of having killed their husbands. Husband murder was also the crime committed by the women executed in South Australia (Elizabeth Woolcock in 1873) and Queensland (Ellen Thompson in 1887), in both cases after having endured intimate partner violence.

Reflecting on the notorious cases of Collins and Knorr, both hinge on women who subverted the usual, expected and required role set for women in the late nineteenth century. When sentencing, Martha Needle, the judge said that she had killed those who "by the law of God and of man are confided to her for comfort and support," making her crime more heinous because it was a very serious betrayal of trust. The same logic was applied to Collins, who, Judge Darley said, was "day by day giving poison to the man whom above all others [she was] bound to cherish and attend."[33] Knorr's crimes also turned on assumptions about a woman's role. By taking in infants that mothers could not look after, and fathers in some cases knew nothing about, carers were supposed to be helping both the economy and the production of the next generation. At a time when there was concern about increasing Australia's settler colonist population, any waste of infant life, even that of the poorest and most marginal members of society, was not acceptable. Mothers needed to have safe places they could leave their babies and those who betrayed this trust had to face the ultimate sanction. As the political and economic rights of women were increased, so were they to be held more fully responsible for their actions.

All women found guilty of murder in the late nineteenth century were punished, and rightfully so, but execution was reserved for just a few. The clerk who wrote on Louisa Collin's jail record that she was the first woman to be executed in the new Darlinghurst Gaol did not add what he could not have known: that she would also be the last woman to be executed in New South Wales.[34] This small group were not members of extensive criminal networks, consistently earning a living from the proceeds of crime. Instead, they were members of the working class who undertook a variety of activities to earn the typically low incomes available to women in this period. Not all of their crimes had an economic motive, with love and passion also playing a role. The category into which they were placed was of unfeminine women who had rejected what was seen as their naturally appointed role and interfered with the status quo with which men were well satisfied, where they could dominate public life and have their domestic needs for food, homes and childcare reliably looked after by women.

Suggested Readings

Cushing, Nancy. "Woman as Murderer." *Journal of Interdisciplinary Gender Studies* 1, no. 2 (1996): 146–57.

Laster, Kathy. "Arbitrary Chivalry: Women and Capital Punishment in Victoria, Australia, 1842–1967." *Women and Criminal Justice* 6 (1994): 67–95.

Nagy, Victoria. "Homicide in Victoria: Female Perpetrators of Murder and Manslaughter, 1860–1920." *Journal of Interdisciplinary History* LI, no. 3 (2021): 405–28.

Piper, Alana and Victoria Nagy, "Versatile Offending: Criminal Careers of Female Prisoners in Australia, 1860–1920," *Journal of Interdisciplinary History* 48, No. 2 (2017): 187–210.

Piper, Alana and Lisa Durnian. "Theft on Trial: Prosecution, Conviction and Sentencing Patterns in Colonial Victoria and Western Australia." *Australian and New Zealand Journal of Criminology* 50, no. 1 (2017): 5–22.

Sussex, Lucy. "Portrait of a Murderer in Mixed Media: Cultural Attitudes, Infanticide and the Representation of Frances Knorr." *Australian Feminist Law Journal* 4 (1995): 39–54.

ESSAY: THE ORDINARY CRIMES OF FEMALE OFFENDERS

Alana Piper

In 1887, an inquiry into Queensland's prison system reflected on the difference between the prevailing conception of crime as the province of a distinct criminal class and the ordinariness of most of the offenders that entered the colony's jails, observing that:

> Criminal population is here used in its widest signification as embracing all persons who have brought themselves within the grasp of the police or prison authorities. These may not, and very probably do not, all come within the category of persons making a profession of crime; the majority, in all likelihood, are the victims of a sudden accession of passion, a momentary succumbing to strong temptation, a temporary lapse from an honest and upright course of life.[35]

Of Queensland's women prisoners, it was stated that while repeat offending among them was especially high, most of these recidivists could be classed as "confirmed drunkards rather than professional criminals."[36]

Popular constructions of criminality often do not match its more prosaic realities, perhaps especially when it comes to female offenders. The violent crimes of women still notorious today – like husband-poisoner Louisa Collins and baby-farmer Frances Knorr – were the exception, not the rule. Of the 1,351 female arrests in Queensland in 1887 (around a tenth of the number of male arrests), less than 10% were for serious offences involving violence or property (compared to just over 20% among men). The bulk of arrests were for offences against public order, such as drunkenness (45% of women's arrests, 40% of men's).[37] This reflects a more general trend repeated across other jurisdictions and time periods: violent crimes typically constitute a minute proportion of charges against women and a small one of those against men, with property offences constituting the majority of serious charges against both, and petty offences (particularly drunkenness offences in the nineteenth and early twentieth century, and traffic offences from the mid-twentieth century onwards) forming the vast bulk of "criminal" activity dealt with by the state.

However, such statistics provide only a single snapshot of female offending, telling us little about women's participation in criminal underworlds, which can more accurately be assessed by examining women's offences across their entire life course. An example is provided by the lives of 33 female inmates interviewed by the 1887 prisons inquiry at Toowoomba Gaol (the colony's jail for women serving sentences of longer than a fortnight) on 29 June 1887. Looking only at the offences for which they were imprisoned on that day, the picture of female offending is similar to that disclosed above: only two were jailed for offences against the person, one for murder, the other for concealment of birth after being acquitted of the more serious charge of infanticide; six were imprisoned for property offences; and the remainder for public order offences such as vagrancy, drunkenness, obscene language or indecent exposure. However, a slightly different image of the degree of these women's "criminality" emerges when looking at their entire conviction histories, with 27 out of the 33 being repeat offenders, many amassing dozens of convictions. The bulk of these convictions also consisted of petty offences, but 14 women were convicted at some point in their lives of violent offences (mostly minor assaults) and 17 of property offences (predominantly pickpocketing from men in the course of prostitution).[38] Individual convictions thus do not always disclose the extent to which an individual may be considered a serious offender or part of a criminal underworld.

Examining the women's entire life histories is also revealing of the role that gender played in the policing of women and the contexts of female offending. Violence had a larger role in the lives of many inmates than the figures above disclose. Several were victims of gender violence, assaulted by intimate partners, pimps, "johns" or random strangers; at least one interviewee's conviction for violence resulted from provocation by an abusive partner. Violence between women themselves also appears commonplace, but was seldom dealt with seriously by police, who instead often charged both parties of such assaults with offences like disorderly conduct. Some property crimes also point to a police tendency to minimise the seriousness of female offending, charging women with larceny from the person in cases that could have merited a conviction for robbery with violence. This provides potential support for the "chivalry" interpretation of why crime figures generated by police suggest women offend less, and less seriously, than men.[39]

Inmates' theft convictions also point to the limited economic opportunities of women in this period. Poorly paid domestic service was the largest legitimate employer of women, including one interviewee who, following coercion from the man courting her, stole from the house where she worked. That many women were charged with stealing within the context of soliciting prostitution underscores how sex work was one of the few viable options women had to support themselves.

Although prostitution was not illegal in Queensland at the time, police used public order charges against sex workers in an expression of community double standards over sexuality (male clients facing no such policing). More generally, women who contravened the gender norms, from using obscene language to white women engaging in sexual relationships with men of colour, became targets for petty charges. Some inmates claimed they had been doing absolutely nothing when arrested by police for riotous behaviour, perhaps victims of officers eager to increase their arrest rates with easy convictions of known offenders whose own evidence was seldom believed by magistrates. This cycling in and out of jail – sometimes with less than 24 hours in between – also meant many of the women struggled with homelessness as it became harder to secure or maintain employment or lodgings. With no alternatives, a return to prison became their only means of support, with some women even requesting police arrest them for this reason. Many women also struggled with substance abuse, with 26 out of the 33 female interviewees in the Toowoomba Gaol amassing at least 1 conviction for drunkenness, while 5 were convicted of opium use. Such addiction was perhaps symptomatic of the other struggles in the women's lives that left them vulnerable to criminalisation. Police, magistrates and prison officials frequently expressed the uselessness of repeatedly returning such troubled women to jail but continued to do so due to the perceived lack of alternatives.

While their conviction records consisted overwhelmingly of minor offences, many of the 33 inmates interviewed in the 1887 inquiry thus belonged to a female criminal subculture centred around the sex trade in Brisbane. A loose network existed among them, with 18 of the women having had documented connections to each other (such as joint arrests) prior to 1887 and 14 having such connections afterwards. This led to a companionable subculture within the prison, with the board of inquiry horrified by inmates' disclosures of women in the cells at night singing, dancing, discussing lewd topics, sharing smuggled goods including tobacco and alcohol, and even engaging in sexual intimacy together. Not all the women interviewed were part of this subversive subculture; according to the testimony of prison officials and the women themselves, those excluded were usually the long-sentence prisoners arrested for more serious but typically one-off offences. It was the women who passed in and out of jail frequently for petty offences who were portrayed as the greater nuisance both to the prison and broader community.

While it is sensationalist offences that have received the greatest attention in popular culture and even academic studies, ordinary offences thus also provide significant insights into how gender and legal history mutually shaped each other.

PRIMARY SOURCE: VICTORIA GAOL BY JANET DIBBEN, 1904

In the title of this collection of her poetry, Scottish-born Janet Dibben is referred to as a lady who has travelled, but the subjects of several of the verses reflect her experience of periods without much mobility, when serving a long prison sentence. As the client of a baby farmer, Dibben was convicted of the manslaughter of her infant son in 1888 and served four years in Melbourne Gaol.[40] This poem "Victoria Gaol" gives an insider's view of the bodily experience of imprisonment, from the recording taking of descriptions and photographs to the hard work, low-grade food and weight loss. In contrast with Dibben's own experience, the narrator of the poem remains upbeat, suggesting the fun that led to imprisonment was worth the cost.

8

The day will come when the clock strikes ten ;
Then you can say good-bye to all your dear friends.
Up to your cell then you must be ;
Half-past six next morning before you are let free.
When you go—it is your first time—
You will get three bob ; you can do that in wine.

XII.

Victoria Gaol.

This is the building once I was in—
It's saved your lives both out and in :
There you can learn everything.
I'm sure it is well-kept and clean,
In the morning we must rise,
The bell rings at half-past five.

At the door the Matron stands
The slate and pencil it's in her hand.
We were in there a day or so,
We want the nurse called Nelson, you know.
Put my name down if you can,
I'm that bad I can't walk nor stand.

Up to the cells we had to go
To see old docter Shields, you know.
He would view you then from top to toe—
It's to the hospital we must go.
You lose your temper and find your tongue—
Into solitary you had to run.

Up to the workroom we did go,
You were like the soldiers, all in a row.
Rachel counts us one by one,
We got the oakum, and down we run.
We're in the yard all day long
Telling yarns and singing a song.

We work from eight till half-past three,
We teased a pound of oakum, you see.
If we were short of our weight,
The officer would book you, that's telling you straight.
Down the corridor we did go
To get the hominy, you know.

It's in the yard we walk about,
Wishing our time was up, that we could get out.
The glass-house officer rung the bell,
It's up we went to our virtuous cell.
The Matron met us at the door,
She said three and walked on before.

9

The officers they bolt the door,
We're all locked up at half-past four;
Saturday it's half-past three,
The officers want to have a spree;
Sunday it is the same time—
Don't you think I'm right in my mind.

CHORUS—

Never mind now what they say
You are sober there both night and day;
Never mind now what they say
You are chucked in there both night and day.

XIII.

The cottage is built with a very good wall.
But the devils that are in it are the worst of it all;
They work from Monday morning till Saturday night.
But they can't drink the beer out of the pint.
When you go in your head it does ache,
You are not long in when you lose your weight.

Once you were fat, and then you were thin,
There's nothing but hominy, that's a good thing.
When you go in your heart it is broke,
You lose your sweetheart, and that is no joke.
You write him a letter to tell him to come in,
He says: "No, my dear, it's a very bad thing."

They will take your height before you are free;
It's into the office, for the Matron to see.
There is the books and the desk, and then there is the chair;
The Matron is fat, she has a fine head of hair.

This is the way she does now begin
She will take your description the very first thing;
The pen and ink is at her command—
The Matron is the one that can write it down grand—
That if you are dark or if you are fair,
The colour of your eyes, not forgetting your hair.

When the visitors they come in,
It's into the cage you are popped in.
There's two of the officers standing by,
"Ten minutes is up"—that is the cry.
The worst of it is over, the best is to come;
Jail is the place to make you pay for your fun.

It's when you drink beer you're sure to go there,
There's nothing but brown bread and cold spuds there, my dear.
It's out of the pawnshop, down goes the beer,
It will bring you to gaol, to do oakum, my dear.
Down the yard there is a small house,
Your photo. is taken, for the detectives, of course.
It's when you come in and when you go out.

Figure 8.3 Victoria Gaol by Janet Dibben, 1904

Source: "XII. Victoria Gaol," Janet Dibben, *Songs and Recitations Written and Composed from Experience by the Lady That Has Travelled*, St Kilda: Hubbard & McMichael, 1904, 8–9. Held by the State Library of Victoria.

Notes

1 Recorded Crime – Offenders. Statistics about offenders proceeded against by police including age, sex, Indigenous status and most serious offence for financial year 2019–20. Australian Bureau of Statistics, https://www.abs.gov.au/statistics/people/crime-and-justice/recorded-crime-offenders/2019-20 (accessed 3 August 2021).

2 Even to attain this proportion, women offenders were transported at a much higher rate than men offenders, who more frequently had sentences of transportation reduced or set aside. See Deborah Oxley, *Convict Maids: The Forced Migration of Women to Australia*, Cambridge: Cambridge University Press, 1996. Also note that the final phase of transportation, to Western Australia between 1850 and 1868, was exclusively for men.

3 Anne Summers, *Damned Whores and God's Police: The Colonisation of women in Australia*, Sydney: NewSouth Publishing, 2016, 256.

4 Patricia Grimshaw, Marilyn Lake, Ann McGrath and Marian Quarterly, *Creating a Nation, 1788–1900*, Melbourne: McPhee Gribble, 1994, Ch. 5 "Men's Space, Women's Place," esp. 117–19.

5 David Lusty, "Is There a Common Law Privilege against Spouse-Incrimination?" *UNSW Law Journal* 27, no. 1 (2004), http://www.austlii.edu.au/au/journals/UNSWLJ/2004/1.html (accessed 11 August 2021). There was an exception for testimony in criminal matters related to harm done by one spouse to the other.

6 Alana Piper and Lisa Durnian, "Theft on Trial: Prosecution, conviction and sentencing patterns in colonial Victoria and Western Australia," *Australian and New Zealand Journal of Criminology* 50, 1 (2017): 16.

7 Jacqueline Zara Wilson, "Kelly, Ellen (1832–1923)," *Australian Dictionary of Biography*, National Centre of Biography, Australian National University, https://adb.anu.edu.au/biography/kelly-ellen-13021/text23543, published first in hardcopy 2005 (accessed 3 September 2021).

8 Kathy Laster, "Arbitrary Chivalry: Women and Capital Punishment in Victoria, Australia, 1842–1967," *Women and Criminal Justice* 6 (1994): 67–95.

9 Robyn Lincoln and Shirleene Robinson, "When the Penalty was Death," *Crime over Time: Temporal Perspectives on Crime and Punishment in Australia*, Robyn Lincoln and Shirleene Robinson, eds. Newcastle upon Tyne: Cambridge Scholars, 2010, 196.

10 Justice Williams, quoted by R. Douglas and K. Laster in "A Matter of Life and Death: The Victorian Executive and the Decision to Execute, 1842–1967," *Australian and New Zealand Journal of Criminology* 24 (1991), 151.

11 "Town News," *Australasian*, January 16, 1886, 27.

12 Alana Piper and Mark Finnane, "Defending the Accused: The Impact of Legal Representation on Criminal Trial Outcomes in Victoria, Australia, 1861–1961," *Journal of Legal History* 38, no. 1 (2017), 37–38.

13 Victoria Nagy, "Homicide in Victoria: Female Perpetrators of Murder and Manslaughter, 1860–1920," *Journal of Interdisciplinary History* LI, no. 3 (2021): 413.

14 Caroline Overington, *Last Woman Hanged, The Terrible True Story of Louisa Collins*, Sydney: Harper Collins, 2014; Carole Baxter, *Black Widow: The True Story of Australia's First Female Serial Killer*, Sydney: Allen and Unwin, 2015. This account draws upon Overington's book and Nancy Cushing, "Woman as Murderer," *Journal of Interdisciplinary Gender Studies* 1, no. 2 (1996): 146–157.

15 Bruce Kercher, *An Unruly Child, A History of Law in Australia*, Sydney: Allen and Unwin, 1995, 137–41.

16 In a case heard in Sydney in 1825, five servants were tried for petty treason and murder for having killed their employer, John Brackfield. They were all sentenced to execution, although not to burning at the stake which had been the former punishment for this offence ("Supreme Court of Criminal Jurisdiction," *Sydney Gazette and NSW Advertiser*, 27 January 1825, 2).

17 George Robb, "Circe in Crinoline: Domestic Poisonings in Victorian England," *Journal of Family History* 22, No. 2 (1997): 176–190.
18 "The Botany Mystery," *Australian Star*, 9 August 1888, 5.
19 This from the English translation: Caesar Lombroso and William Ferrero, *The Female Offender*, New York: D. Appleton and Co., 1915, 153.
20 These arguments are canvased in Cushing, "Woman as Murderer" 146–57.
21 P. Besomo, "The Botany Poisoning Case: A Brief History of the Most Famous Female Poisoners, Borgia Family, etc. … with Phrenological and Physiognomical Sketch of Mrs. Louisa Collins, the Botany Murderess," Sydney: P. Besomo and Co, 1889.
22 Rachel Franks, *An Uncommon Hangman, The Life and Deaths of Robert "Nosey Bob" Howard*, Sydney: NewSouth, 2022, 157–59.
23 "The Botany Murder Case." *Evening News,* January 8, 1889, 3.
24 See Jan Kociumbas, "Azaria's Antecedents: Stereotyping Infanticide in Late Nineteenth-Century Australia," *Gender & History* 13, no. 1 (2001): 138–60.
25 Gordon A. Carmichael, "So Many Children: Colonial and Post-Colonial Demographic Patterns", Kay Saunders and Raymond Evans, eds. *Gender Relations in Australia, Domination and Negotiation*, Sydney: Harcourt Brace Jovanovich, 1992, 106–07.
26 "Infant Mortality," *Ballarat Star*, 6 January 1894, 3. Other causes claimed were sudden deliveries leading to injury to the baby, wasting from improper feeding or overlaying, which was accidentally smothering an infant when sharing a bed.
27 Annie Cossins, *The Baby Farmers: A Chilling Tale of Missing Babies, Shameful Secrets and Murder in 19th Century Australia*, Sydney: Allen and Unwin, 2013.
28 This account draws upon Lucy Sussex, "Portrait of a Murderer in Mixed Media: Cultural Attitudes, Infanticide and the Representation of Frances Knorr," *Australian Feminist Law Journal* 4 (1995): 39–54.
29 R. Douglas and K. Laster, "A Matter of Life and Death: The Victorian Executive and the Decision to Execute (1842–1967)," *Australia and New Zealand Journal of Criminology* 24 (1991): 152.
30 Franks, *An Uncommon Hangman*, 309.
31 Rita Hardiman, "Martha Needle and Frances Knorr," Jacqueline Healy, ed. *Dentistry: Innovation and Education*, Melbourne: Henry Forman Atkinson Dental Museum, University of Melbourne, 2020, 76.
32 Nagy, "Homicide in Victoria," 441.
33 "The Botany Murder," *Sydney Morning Herald*, December 10, 1888, 11.
34 Louisa Collins, Gaol Inmates/Prisoners Photos Index 1870–1930, NSW State Records and Archives, Series NRS2138, Item No. 3/6050, 84.
35 "Report with Minutes of Evidence Taken Before the Board of Inquiry Appointed to Inquire into the General Management of the Gaols, Penal Establishments, and Lockups of the Colony of Queensland," *Queensland Votes and Proceedings (QV&P)*, vol. 1, Brisbane: Government Printer, 1887, x.
36 *Ibid.*, xi.
37 "Report of the Commissioner of Police for the year 1887," *QV&P,* 1888, 938.
38 Alana Piper, "'I go out Worse Every Time': Connections and Corruption in a Female Prison," *History Australia* 9, no. 3 (2012): 132–53.
39 Alana Piper, "Victimization Narratives and Courtroom Sexual Politics: Prosecuting Male Burglars and Female Pickpockets in Melbourne, 1860–1921," *Journal of Social History* 51, no. 4 (2018): 760–83.
40 Alana Piper provides a broader account of Dibben's poetry and what it reveals about criminal women in "'I'll have no man': Female Families in Melbourne's Criminal Subcultures, 1860–1920," *Journal of Australian Studies* 39, no. 4 (2015): 444–60.

9 Popular Crimes

Underworlds by their nature are subversive, anti-social and even frightening. And yet, as demonstrated in the recent burgeoning of true crime series and podcasts, as well as the steady readership for crime fiction and media stories about crime, some aspects of criminal activity are also strangely attractive. Crimes can have features that are so unexpected, intriguing or puzzling that they capture widespread attention, creating a sensation which simultaneously attracts and repels. Several cases from the middle decades of the twentieth century rose to this status within Australia. This chapter will focus on three: the Pyjama Girl, the Shark Arm murder and the Graeme Thorne kidnapping, while also referring to other notorious crimes of the period. Particular attention will be paid to how these crimes appealed to contemporary anxieties around the family and the role played by the media in heightening interest in them.

Historical Context of Mid-Twentieth Century Popular Crimes

To understand why particular crimes captured the public imagination in the mid-twentieth century, it is useful to consider three aspects of Australian history at that time: continuing anxiety about race and ethnicity, an economic cycle of boom and bust, and growth in media consumption.

Race and Ethnicity

Australia was a prosperous and in some ways progressive place in the early decades of the twentieth century, but one where racism was institutionalised. The six separate colonies united as the Commonwealth of Australia in 1901, and in 1902, Australia became the second nation after New Zealand to enfranchise female voters, although only those of European descent. Proud claims were made that the Australian population was 98% British in ancestry, with the rest composed of small numbers of Aboriginal people and Chinese and continental Europeans who had arrived during and since the goldrushes. Aboriginal and Torres Strait Islander people were increasingly being forced out of the general society through state-level protection acts which required

DOI: 10.4324/9781003273561-10

them to live on missions and reserves and were neither counted in the census of the Commonwealth nor permitted to vote in elections.

In keeping with this discrimination against Aboriginal people, one of the first pieces of legislation passed by the federal parliament was the Immigration Restriction Act of 1902 which excluded certain categories of people from entering Australia. It did not name people of colour as the target, but as in Natal in South Africa, used the device of a dictation test, initially in English, and later in any language, to exclude anyone who was not of European ancestry.[1] Anyone attempting to enter Australia who was identified by customs officials as a member of what was then referred to as a "coloured race" was made to write down a passage of 50 words read out by the official. If they were able to do so, they were subjected to another test, in another language, until they failed. The act also targeted those with recent criminal convictions, prostitutes and persons who lived on the prostitution of others, amongst others not wanted in Australia.[2] Not even those inside the country were safe from the dictation test. If convicted of a violent crime in Australia, anyone who was not a British subject by birth or naturalisation had to sit the test after they had served their sentence and was deported when they inevitably failed. The dictation test for immigrants of colour remained in place until 1958 and the White Australia policy until the late 1960s. Although it was primarily designed to limit immigration, and there were some exceptions for tourists, business people and students from places like India and China, even visitors who were not European were rare.

Not all of the Europeans who were permitted to come to Australia were fully accepted, with those from the southern parts of the continent viewed with particular suspicion. Revisions to the Immigration Act in 1925 created a quota system limiting the entry of people from selected countries, including Italy from 1928. When Italy entered World War II on the side of the Germans in June 1940, Italians in Australia were placed in internments camps and some Italian prisoners of war were also sent to Australia.[3] After World War II, the drive to "populate or perish" meant former restrictions were lifted and large numbers of Italians and refugees from the parts of eastern Europe which became communist were welcomed into Australia as part of a mass immigration program. Although they were helping to meet government aims of increasing the national population and strengthening both defence and the economy, people from southern and eastern Europe continued to be viewed with mistrust by some of the resident population while those from Asia and Africa were still entirely excluded. Immigrants from places other than Britain were considered to be outsiders and readily associated with criminality.

War and Depression

Another relevant element of historical context for the mid-twentieth century is the cycle of war, prosperity and economic depression through this period. Australia entered World War I in 1914 not in its own right but because

Britain's declaration of war on Germany committed Australia to the conflict as well. Australia sent 300,000 men overseas to fight in Turkey, North Africa, Europe and German New Guinea. After the First World War, there was a great ambition to modernise Australia, to try to shift its economy away from its heavy dependence on primary production and to increase the population by bringing out more British immigrants. Money was borrowed abroad by state and federal governments, as well as individuals, to fund nation building projects. When the money market tightened up at the end of the 1920s, Australia was pushed into the Great Depression. Officially the dates of the Depression in Australia are 1929–1932, so the crimes from 1934 and 1935 which are examined here occurred after the worst of the downturn. In terms of people's lived experience, however, times were still hard and it was not until the Second World War began in 1939 that many long-term unemployed and underemployed found full-time work, in the armed forces and war production.

Once again, troops were sent off to Europe. Japan entered the war at the end of 1941 with its coordinated attacks across the Asia Pacific, including on Pearl Harbor and Singapore, leaving Australia also expecting invasion. The arrival of a large contingent of American servicemen during the war was greeted with relief, although they were primarily interested in using Australia as a base for operations against Japan. The war continued until 1945, after which the huge program of immigration was commenced. The population of Australia rose from 7.5 million in 1947 to 12.7 million in 1971.[4] As after the First World War, the decade following the war was prosperous and there was an increasing American inflection in the society and economy.

Each of these phases – war, prosperity and economic depression – was accompanied by opportunities for crime, whether motivated by desperation or encouraged by greater mobility and social mixing.

Media

The expansion and differentiation of the media during this 30-year period was an important background to how crime was understood. Australia had a vibrant print media going into the twentieth century. There were a variety of newspapers: morning, afternoon and evening; at least one for most small towns and some suburbs; and catering to specific audiences, such as workers or those interested in sport. We have already seen in the cases of Ned Kelly, Louisa Collins and the baby farmers that the print media was active in reporting on crime and encouraging readers to think about investigations and trials as stories unfolding like mystery novels. Wanting to know the latest news about a celebrated case was a good reason to buy a newspaper on a daily basis, or even twice a day.

The introduction of film provided an opportunity to expand the paying audience. The technology of film arrived early in Australia, from the mid-1890s. Initially, short moving pictures were integrated into variety shows, toured around to multi-purpose halls or shown outside at night, but by the 1920s, there were dedicated cinemas in most towns and suburbs and many people attended a screening each week. A 1928 Royal Commission found that there were 1250 cinemas and 110 million admissions in Australia the previous year, making film going the most popular commercial entertainment.[5] As part of the bill, newsreels were screened before the feature film. They combined serious news with more light-hearted pieces, presented with a humorous voice over. When treating crime, the newsreels took the sensational approach also adopted by some newspapers, led by the *Truth*, which had editions in Sydney, Brisbane and Melbourne. Newsreels continued to be made long after the introduction of television.

The next new communications technology was radio. Both private broadcasters and the public ABC offered varied programming from the 1920s, with news bulletins, children's shows, serial dramas and classical concerts. Television was developed in the Soviet Union and Great Britain and introduced into Australian capital cities relatively late, in 1956, timed to ensure that Australians who could not attend the Melbourne Olympics could at least watch them on a small, grainy, black-and-white screen. Since it was cheaper to buy shows from the United States than to make them, television became another vehicle for Americanisation, but some Australian content was created. When drama series began to be made in Australia, crime was a natural focus. A great success was the police drama *Homicide*, set in Melbourne.[6] It ran on the Seven Network for 12 years from 1964. The series was made in cooperation with the Victorian Police, who supplied actual police cars and police officers as extras, with cases based on real files.

These three aspects of Australian society in the first half of the twentieth century – suspicion of those from other races or ethnicities; a cycle of war, prosperity and depression; and a rising reliance on the media for information and amusement – provide important context for understanding how some crimes went from secretive acts to the talk of the nation.

Pyjama Girl

The Pyjama Girl mystery started on 1 September 1934 when the body of a woman was discovered in a stormwater drain on the outskirts of the town of Albury near the border between New South Wales and Victoria.[7] Her pyjama-clad remains had been placed inside a hessian sack. When examined, the body was found to have head injuries, gunshot wounds and to have been partially burned on the site, in an apparent attempt to disguise or dispose of it.

The press realised this could be a case that would attract great interest, with Melbourne's *Sun* making space on its 3 September front page for a crime scene photograph, with the headline: "Murdered Girl Still Unidentified: Public May See Body."[8] The murder took place after the depths of the Great Depression but there were still people on the move looking for work or cheap places to live, and there were many young women (and men) the whereabouts of whom friends and family had lost track. Although several people claimed to know who the victim was, no positive identification could be made. Police in Victoria and New South Wales took her fingerprints and combed through missing persons files trying to find a match. When it became obvious that this would be a drawn-out process, the body was placed in a solution of the preserving fluid formalin, used in embalming and to preserve scientific specimens. The body was held at Sydney University's medical school, where it could be safely stored over a long period of time. By the middle of the month, the name "Pyjama Girl," which had been used over previous years to describe young women in beach cover-ups, risqué characters in plays and some women in real-life sex scandals, was firmly associated with the case and as her identity proved elusive, the term "mystery" was added to it.[9]

Police investigations narrowed the search to a small number of women who were unaccounted for and who fit the general description of the body. They honed in further using the modern technique of matching teeth and fillings to dental records. Eventually, although the match to her dental records was imperfect, they tentatively identified the Pyjama Girl as 28-year-old Linda Platt Agostini, a British immigrant first to New Zealand and then Australia. According to her friends, Linda was an independent woman, a trained hairdresser who worked on cruise ships and also held unskilled jobs such as being a cinema usherette. She liked to drink and had a stormy relationship with her husband, Antonio Agostini, whom she had married in 1930. Having arrived from Italy in 1927, Agostini was an educated man, with a degree in wool and textile engineering. He wrote for the main Italian language newspaper in Australia *Il Giornale Italiano* but at that time operated the cloakroom in the popular Sydney restaurant Romano's. The couple had moved to Melbourne in 1933 to advance Agostini's career in journalism but also, according to some of their friends, so they could make a fresh start on what was a troubled marriage. When questioned, Agostini said his wife had left him and he did not know where she was. People who knew Linda were shown the body but could not positively identify it.

A coroner's inquest into the death was conducted in 1938 finding only that the woman was murdered but offering no new insights. Keeping the case in the public eye, in 1939 Australia Today made a newsreel with the assistance of the NSW police.[10] Re-enactments, reconstruction and voice-over narration were used to tell the story of the investigation as a crime thriller, mixing fact and fiction. Only scorched fragments of the victim's clothing survived but the newsreel shows an almost intact panel from what is presented as the by-then famous pyjamas, with a prominent Chinese dragon design adding to the air of exotic mystery to what had earlier been described only as white pyjamas with yellow trim. Having raised the intriguing elements of the case, viewers were addressed directly to ask for their help in solving the crime.

In 1944, errors in the recording of the victim's dental work were discovered, and when the various missing teeth and fillings were replotted, they were found to be an exact match of the records for Linda Agostini. Her family in the United Kingdom were contacted and reported that they had not heard from her since 1934, the year the Pyjama Girl's body was found. People who had known Linda Agostini were asked again and were able to give very detailed accounts of her appearance, including her distinctive ears, freckles on her upper arm, brown eyes, a long nose, even teeth and light brown hair. One of the few female police officers of the time (the first having been appointed in 1915) was asked to put make-up on the face of the corpse and style the hair, and friends were again invited to try to identify the body. This time some concluded it was Linda.

This breakthrough came while Australia was still embroiled in the Second World War, in which Italy was one of the enemy nations, with Germany and Japan. Antonio Agostini, like other men of Italian origin, had been forced to spend most of the war in internment camps in Orange, Hay and Loveday. He had only recently been permitted to return to Sydney, where he again found work at Romano's, this time as a waiter. The identifying of the Pyjama Girl as Linda Agostini made Antonio the prime suspect in the murder. He was arrested, and provided a confession, claiming that a fight had taken place in their Melbourne home, during which Linda had threatened him with a gun and in the struggle over it, she was shot.

Antonio's statement was that he had panicked and drove to the NSW border, thinking that he could escape detection if he dumped the body in another state, and to make identification more difficult, had set it alight. In his study of the case, Richard Evans concluded that there were a large number of anomalies and inconsistencies in the case overall, including in the confession.[11] His theory was that senior police who frequented Romano's knew Agostini and might have just used him as a convenient person to blame for this notorious unsolved murder.

Whatever the circumstances, Agostini was charged with the murder, extradited to Victoria and put on trial in Melbourne's Supreme Court. In keeping with the leniency often extended to perpetrators of intimate partner violence, his explanation of an accidental killing was accepted. He was found guilty of manslaughter rather than murder, despite his treatment of the corpse and his long period of denying any involvement. The sentence was 6 years in prison with hard labour. Linda Agostini's body was finally buried, in a Melbourne cemetery. Antonio Agostini was released after serving 4 years of his 6-year sentence. In 1948, as the Immigration Act dictated, he was deported to his native country of Italy, where he remarried in 1952 and lived until 1969.

Shark Arm Case

The Shark Arm case is one of those instances in which truth is stranger than fiction. Having captured public attention at the time, it later became the subject of a 1960 film, and at least three books, in 1963, 1995 and 2020, the last of which, by Phillip Roope and Kevin Meagher, has been drawn upon for this account.[12]

Events began in April 1935 when Bert Hobson, one of the owners of the Coogee Aquarium in Sydney, caught a 4.4-metre tiger shark. Knowing there was a great interest in large sharks – a fascination linked with revulsion much like that felt for compelling crimes – he and his brother often put them on display in the Coogee Aquarium Baths (now Coogee Pavilion), which was an indoor swimming pool used as an aquarium in the cooler months.[13] There was a particularly heightened appeal in 1935 because three young men had recently been taken by sharks and a woman had suffered terrible injuries, events later covered in newsreels.[14]

The shark was in poor condition after having been caught and carried to the aquarium. It swam a little around the pool but appeared to be ill. After about a week, as a dozen or so people looked on, it began to violently regurgitate, before ejecting into the water a human arm with a length of rope attached. The immediate reaction was that this was proof that this shark was a maneater, although some were of the opinion that the arm could be medical waste dumped in the ocean and scavenged by the shark. The Hobsons called the police.

Things became even more interesting when the arm was retrieved and examined. It was found not to have been bitten off, but to have been non-surgically severed, and to feature a roughly executed tattoo of two boxers in a fighting stance. As for the convicts a century earlier, the tattoo was used to make a positive identification, as were fingerprints which were able to be taken from the hand. Hoping for more evidence, the shark was killed and its stomach contents examined, but no additional human remains were found.

News of the arm produced by the shark quickly spread under headlines like "Aquarium Horror" and "Shark's Grim Meal." Having read about the case in *Truth*, a man named Edwin Smith contacted police to say that his brother had such a tattoo and had not been seen for a few weeks. The tattoo and the fingerprints confirmed that the arm belonged to Jim Smith, a small-time criminal, sometime builder, bookmaker, boxer and allegedly a police informer.

As we have seen in other cases, when there is a death from suspicious causes, a coronial inquest is held to decide whether a criminal investigation is warranted. There was some discussion about whether a coronial inquest should be held with only an arm instead of a whole body, as Smith could still be alive. In the end, the inquest went ahead, and medical experts confirmed that the arm had been cut from the body. Like the Pyjama Girl, the arm was stored in formalin at the University of Sydney, while the tattooed skin was removed and separately preserved.

Although the first explanation was that Smith might have been swept off rocks while fishing, slowly a different story emerged. He had last been seen drinking with an old friend named Patrick Brady at a hotel in Cronulla and had gone to Brady's home that night. Brady was a known offender who had charges pending against him. The day after he was seen with Smith, Brady had taken a taxi to the house of Reginald Holmes, who had a successful boatbuilding business at McMahon's Point – almost under the new Sydney

Harbour Bridge, opened just 3 years earlier. This location and his access to boats had enabled Holmes to run a smuggling ring, carrying cocaine, cigarettes and other items from ships passing Sydney Heads into the city. Smith had been part of these operations but the men had had a falling out and it was speculated that he had been trying to blackmail Holmes, threatening to reveal what he knew to the police. Both Holmes and Brady would have been relieved to have Smith out of the way.

Brady and Holmes were taken in for questioning but no charges were laid. When the police decided to arrest Holmes, he did all he could to avoid them, embarking on a 4-hour boat chase around the harbour and out past the heads before surrendering. Holmes agreed to give evidence against Brady for having murdered Smith but was found shot dead in his car before he could do so.

In court, witnesses gave evidence about the relationship between Brady and Smith, and Brady's trips in cabs around the time of Smith's disappearance. Smith's wife was presented with tattooed skin from her husband's arm and was able to identify it as his. However, without Holmes' testimony, there was insufficient evidence against Brady. The judge directed that the jury should find him not guilty and he was acquitted. Brady maintained his innocence in this crime, although he had other convictions for uttering and fraud. Almost 30 years later, he was still plagued by the case, seeking an injunction to stop the screening of an American made-for-television movie about the Shark Arm case in 1960.[15]

The Graeme Thorne Case

The Graeme Thorne case in July 1960 is remembered as a kidnapping but it became a murder. The sensationalising of the disappearance and murder of an 8-year-old demonstrates how distanced from the reality of a crime the public can become.[16]

Graeme Thorne lived with his family in a flat in Bondi. His father was a commercial traveller, and his mother looked after Graeme and his younger brother. They came to public attention in June 1960 when Bazil Thorne won the tenth drawing of the Opera House lottery. While Australians had a well-established reputation as gamblers, official lotteries were still a relatively new phenomenon at that time. The use of a lottery to fund the construction of the Opera House was novel and the winners of the £100,000 pound prize received a great deal of media attention.[17]

Amongst the people interested in the Thorne's good fortune was Stephen Bradley, who had immigrated to Australia as a political refugee from Hungary in 1950. He had married, twice, changed his name from Istvan Baranyay and had a blended family of three children. He had entered into a series of schemes to build his fortunes but with only limited success. His decision to kidnap Graeme and demand a ransom payment seems to have been driven by this search for instant wealth. He began to make preparations, visiting the Thorne's flat in the guise of being a private investigator to extract their unlisted phone number and watching Graeme's movements on his daily trip to school.

On 7 July, Bradley waited in his car, a metallic blue Ford Customline, for Graeme to start his walk to the street corner, where he was usually picked up by a friend's mother who drove them both to school. He enticed Graeme into his car and drove with him to Centennial Park where he sedated him with chloroform. Wrapping the boy in a travel blanket, he placed Graeme in the boot, before binding his arms and legs and tying a scarf around his mouth as a gag. Bradley then drove towards his rented home in Clontarf, already having sent his family on a holiday trip. Stopping at a phone booth, he called the Thorne's flat saying that he had Graeme and wanted a payment of £25,000 that day, or he would "feed him to the sharks." Exactly what happened next is unclear, but the later coronial examination found the causes of death to be asphyxiation and a blow to the head.

The police mounted a major operation to try to find Graeme, using helicopters, sniffer dogs and the army. Many of those who heard about the case wanted to become involved. Some genuinely tried to be helpful, joining in mass search efforts organised by the police, but the flood of tips and alleged sightings was overwhelming. Bradley's car had been noticed in the Thorne's neighbourhood and the police began to trace all 4000 owners of that model.[18] For a small minority, involvement took a dark turn, with people contacting the police or the Thornes purporting to have information with the intention of extorting money or causing more pain to the family.[19] More constructively, members of the public located evidence, such as Graeme's school bag which was found on a roadside in the northern suburb of French's Forest, helping police to track his movements.

The big break in the case came in mid-August when children playing on a vacant block in Seaforth found Graeme's body still wrapped in the plaid travel blanket. They did not immediately tell their parents, instead incorporating the corpse into their game of cowboys and Indians, but eventually it was reported to the police.[20] From this stage, forensic work by the police Scientific Investigation Bureau came into play. Death was dated to within a day of the abduction based on the maturity of fungi growing on Graeme's shoes. Bradley was identified as the owner of the car sighted at the time of the abduction and when his house was searched, they found a tassel that was missing from the travel blanket and that dog hairs on the blanket matched those of the Bradley's Pekinese dog, Cherry. The dog was taken as evidence and in another unlikely turn of events, it was accidentally run over, and then preserved by a taxidermist so it could be used as evidence in court.[21] Small pieces of foliage and pink lime mortar found on Graeme's clothes were also linked to Bradley's house.

Bradley was conscious of the increasing likelihood that he would be caught and made arrangements to leave the country with his family at the end of September. He journeyed as far as Ceylon (now Sri Lanka) where he was intercepted by police in October and flown back to Australia in November.

After initially signing a confession, Bradley then said he had been forced to do so. A coronial inquest in December found that he should stand trial for murder. During his March 1961 trial, he denied any knowledge of Graeme Thorne or having been in Bondi on the date of the abduction. The courtroom filled each day with people wanting to see the spectacle of a successful prosecution. They cheered and clapped when he was found guilty, in a carnivalesque display reminiscent of the crowd behaviour at executions in the previous century. Given a life sentence, and with an appeal rejected, Bradley died in 1968 in Goulburn Gaol while playing in a paddle tennis competition.[22]

Why These Crimes?

These crimes and their investigation were based in Sydney and Melbourne but were followed by people around the country, as well as being reported overseas. As the nation's most populous city, Sydney had the cultural position and infrastructure that helped to catapult its crime news to national status. Any connection to other localities was capitalised upon in local newspapers, as when sniffer dogs were sent from Adelaide to join the search for Graeme Thorne and it was revealed that the travel rug he was wrapped in had been manufactured in South Australia. Alleged sightings of Graeme were reported from all over Australia for four months after he died.[23] Crimes in other cities did also become objects of fascination. During the Second World War, there were the Brownout murders committed by American serviceman Eddie Leonski in Melbourne. In Perth, in 1964, Eric Cooke murdered eight people, earning the title of the Nedlands Monster. Two years later, the disappearance of the three Beaumont children from Glenelg Beach in Adelaide on Australia Day captured public attention, and being unsolved, investigations into this assumed crime continue into the present, as will be treated in Chapter 12.

Reflecting on the three crimes treated in this chapter, it is possible to offer an explanation for why they, of all of the thousands of offences committed and reported upon in the period, were not only of immediate interest but have continued to be remembered and written about. As Garton pointed out about the Graeme Thorne case, there were other violent crimes against children in the same month as the Thorne kidnapping, but they did not attract more than local attention. He concluded that the cases which become well known relate to cultural codes and tensions in their historical periods.[24] That is why they appealed at the time and continue to do so.

To start with, these crimes were able to be presented as stories. In the hands of the media, they unrolled like detective thrillers, from the original crime, through the collection of elusive evidence, false leads, double-checking, breakthroughs and then a long-awaited resolution, at least a partial one. The value of such stories was recognised by the media as shown in the Thorne case when the publishers of the *Sydney Morning Herald* posted a £10,000 reward for information leading to Graeme's return, which was soon matched by Australian Consolidated Press, making it many times the amount offered by the state government. The Thorne case was on the front page of Sydney newspapers for 38 days between July 1960 and March 1961, with up to five additional pages allocated to it elsewhere the papers, and ongoing features on radio and television news bulletins.[25] The people involved could be portrayed as characters in these stories, simplistically good like the Thornes, monstrous villains who deserved what they received from the justice system like Bradley or cultural stereotypes like Antonio Agostini.

Contributing to the narrative quality in each case either while the crime itself was being committed, during its reportage or in some cases, forever, there are elements of these crimes which are not fully understood or entirely resolved. If the Pyjama Girl had matched a police report of a missing person on the first check, her murder would have been much less intriguing. If Graeme's body had been found the day he was kidnapped and Bradley made a full confession, there would have been little room for speculation and the intensity of the interest which emerged. If Smith's body had washed up, intact, on a beach, it would have been much less of a sensation than the mystery of whose arm appeared in the baths and how it had found its way inside a shark.

Following on from the element of mystery, these cases also shared the slow revealing of important aspects over time. This meant people were able to become involved by creating their own theories about what had happened, participating in debates about who might be guilty and offering their own tips to the police. Seeing the shark, viewing the Pyjama Girl's body, reporting a car sighting and attending a trial were all things that ordinary people could do, giving them a sense that they were part of the case. The media directly encouraged this as did the police in their calls for information from the public.

The characters in these crimes fit with people's pre-existing beliefs, especially those connected with race, ethnicity and national origin. Both Antonio Agostini and Stephen Bradley could be placed in the category of outsider based on their places of origin. As immigrants from Europe rather than Britain (as Linda Agostini was), they were viewed with suspicion and their crimes played into anxieties that more diverse immigration would undermine established Australian values. Although Graeme Thorne was murdered, the crime is remembered as a kidnapping because holding someone for ransom was a new crime in Australia, known mainly from the United States and Italy. That the kidnapper was reported to have spoken accented English when making his ransom demand on the telephone would have confirmed fears that "New Australians" might bring new crimes to Australia. Kidnapping defined as "detention for ransom or any other advantage" was added to the NSW Crimes Act in December 1961. Of course, this overlooked the reality that kidnapping as a practice had been part of settler colonial Australia from the beginning, when Aboriginal people including Bennelong were held against their will to extract their cultural knowledge.

In addition to fitting with expectations about the potential criminality of non-British immigrants, the crimes also resonated with other issues and anxieties of the time. The Pyjama Girl played on concerns about mobility and the growing independence of women in the 1930s. Playing up her vulnerability, she was referred to as a girl although she was in her late 20s when she was killed. She was also portrayed as a modern woman, with bleached blonde hair and nail polish, much like the others described somewhat disparagingly as pyjama girls in that period: young women out for a good time in immodest attire. That she could have disappeared and no one had really noticed seemed to signal a distressing breakdown in social bonds. The Shark Arm case started by playing on the anxieties about shark attacks and ended up revealing the presence of an alarming gangland subculture which will be further explored in the following chapter. The Opera House lottery win which drew attention to the Thorne family raised issues around materialism and upward mobility, and how sudden wealth that was not earned through hard work was morally suspect, and might bring some form of retribution.[26]

Finally, to become a popular crime, it is helpful to have central or even minor aspects that capture attention because they are just very strange, gruesome or implausible. The Shark Arm is the winner here, starting with the almost unbelievable coincidence of a shark being caught and put on display just as it was unsuccessfully digesting the severed, tattooed arm of a murder victim. Future unexpected twists and additional crimes as the investigation unfolded made it absolutely compelling. In the Linda Agostini case, the early labelling of the victim as the Pyjama Girl gave it an exotic appeal, onto which was layered a macabre element with the preservation and display of the body. In the Graeme Thorne case, the early declaration that this was a ransom case gave it a novelty which raised interest.

Given the existence of these popular crimes, consideration can also be given to other crimes which did not win such attention. They lacked the excitement associated with high-profile crimes and instead were low key, ordinary or so far outside of people's concerns that they held no appeal, even as a cause of revulsion. *In the accompanying essay, Yorick Smaal writes about crimes which during the Second World War were considered not only unpopular but unnatural: sexual relations between consenting adult males.* On the cusp of the surge in anxiety and attention to such relationships in the 1950s, during wartime while still being prosecuted, they drew little attention.

Is there any harm in popularising crime? Criminologist Xanthe Mallett argues that there is. She warns that in some cases "the salacious details of the crimes overshadow the pain and suffering of victims."[27] As was the case when people cheered the verdict in the Thorne case, while Graeme's parents wept, some forget that real people have been hurt by these crimes. They start to delight in the macabre details and confusing complexities of claim and counter-claim, without regard for the pain, loss and absence triggered by serious crimes like these. In these cases, there is the further concern that the focus on them diverts attention from where the real dangers lie. The long mystery around the identity of the Pyjama Girl distracted attention from the fact that this was an instance of intimate partner violence, which, while it has come to be less socially acceptable, still results in the murder of one woman a week in Australia. Bradley luring Graeme Thorne into his car became an example parents pointed to when warning their children about stranger danger although most crimes against children are committed by people they know, often in the family home. The Shark Arm case offered a window into the world of organised crime in Sydney, allowing people to feel safe because they were not part of that underworld.

Conclusion

A final concern raised by Mallett is that in many notorious cases, the perpetrators of crimes are remembered, and become of almost obsessive interest to some, while their victims are forgotten. In the cases examined here, the reverse is true. Each remains known by some aspect of its victim. With the focus on the period of uncertainty while the crime was being investigated, the identity of the perpetrators is a detail of lesser interest, needed only to wrap up the extended narrative.

These three cases show that although crime should by its nature be something from which most people want to distance themselves, some crimes can have a contradictory attractive power. Undoubtedly media attention is important, keeping cases in the public mind, but unless the crimes hold an inherent appeal, it is difficult for the media to "sell" them. In these cases, that appeal was centred on their victims. Popular crimes take people out of their own lives into other worlds which are more glamorous, dangerous or exciting, but they also need to have points of intersection with those they care about and the things that they worry about.

Suggested Readings

Evans, Richard. *The Pyjama Girl Mystery: A True Story of Murder, Obsession and Lies.* Melbourne: Scribe, 2004.

Garton, Stephen. "'Feed Him to the Sharks': The Graeme Thorne Kidnapping." *Australian Cultural History* 12 (1993): 29–42.

Pascoe, Carla. "Be Home by Dark: Childhood Freedoms and Adult Fears in 1950s Victoria." *Australian Historical Studies* 40, no. 12 (2009): 215–31.

Pierce, Peter. *The Country of Lost Children: An Australian Anxiety.* Melbourne: Cambridge University Press, 1999.

Sanders, Noel. "TV Family 1960: TV, Gambling and the Graeme Thorne Case." *Australian Cultural History* 12 (1993): 43–51.

ESSAY: "UNNATURAL" AND UNPOPULAR CRIMES

Yorick Smaal

Vernon, 25, was dressed in his Australian militia uniform when he met Jack, an American army technician a few years his senior and one of the millions of GIs who passed through Queensland in the Second World War.[1] They first "became friends" at the end of 1943 after crossing paths at Brisbane's Belle Vue Hotel, a popular watering hole bustling with allied troops. Another round of drinks, tea and an evening stroll followed a week later. As the night ended, Vernon and Jack found an out-of-the-way laneway, embraced passionately and enjoyed oral sex.[2] Weeks became months. The couple continued keeping company, drinking, dining out and taking in the occasional show. Jack found himself sleeping at Vernon's four or five nights a week.[3] One morning, the Queensland police knocked on the door arresting the soldiers for suspected practices of "carnal knowledge against the order of nature".[4] Vernon spent the final years of the war behind bars.[5] Jack disappeared from the records after the American provost took him into custody.[6] Vernon's police statement, a doctor's note, Jack's version of events, police testimony, and a few oblique newspaper reports are all that remain of their illicit love.

Vernon and Jack's affections were neither isolated nor uncommon. Like other young men, they discovered the war's queer delights in the hotels and streets swollen with servicemen or on deployment abroad, free from the normative expectations of work, marriage, and family.[7] Recovering these experiences is challenging, despite war's potential for "unnatural" forms of male togetherness. The illegality of homosex demanded discretion. Men who found their privacy in public usually left no evidence unless the state intervened. Journalists remained tight-lipped about the prosecution of consensual cases, avoiding any elevation of Australian men deliberately seeking male-only intimacy. They focused, instead, on "hypersexual" women, who supposedly spread venereal disease, and threatened marriage and the family.[8] Even the salacious Brisbane newspaper *Truth*, never one to miss an opportunity for muckraking, could only mutter a few words of astonishment about Jack and Vernon's romance when the matter appeared in the police court.[9] The armed forces kept equally silent, eager to protect the myth linking "square" male soldiers with national identity. Sexually assaulted males often refused to disclose their experiences, given failings to distinguish sexual violence and pleasure.

Newspapers provided greater coverage when "unnatural" crimes reinforced dominant beliefs—that queer men were mentally ill, sexually voracious, predatory, weak, and effeminate. One individual arrested in female attire and an auburn wig after a pickup gone wrong became the subject of both print and photograph.[10] Their crossdressing made the case newsworthy and reinforced stereotypes, but the courts resolved it summarily without sensational fanfare, as they did with other matters of public indecency.[11] Male-only lewdness was for magistrates, an otherwise unremarkable element of law-and-order policing that hauled a rabble of miscreants before them daily.

Popular assumptions about the weak character or predatory behaviour of queer men, Australian manhood, a general disdain for homosex, and the alleged infectiousness of same-sex activity, informed other types of silence. Adult males grossly underreported their experiences of sexual violence based on the assumption that "real" men easily resisted unwanted advances. Publicity of any kind called into question their masculinity and sexuality. The failure of the *Criminal Code Act 1899* to differentiate mutual encounters from coercive crimes exacerbated the problem. Many potential complainants remained mute given the stigma of published court proceedings, no matter how obscure.

Other beliefs that male-only sex, consensual or otherwise, potentially derailed "normal" (hetero)sexual development prompted adolescent males and their parents to remain silent about offences. According to one prominent Brisbane psychiatrist in 1944, sexual offences against boys potentially caused them to "become somewhat homosexual".[12] Crimes involving young males constituted the most significant proportion of indictable same-sex offences during the war. Most were coercive, although some adolescents sought male intimacy. One 14-year-old Townsville lad practised hero worship of a different kind when he cycled to the local army camp to frolic with the troops.[13] Experts and commentators were unable or unwilling to recognise these sexual practices and invariably cast male teenagers as vulnerable, misled, or victimised by predatory men, even if they were not as "square" or innocent as the authorities believed.[14]

If Australia's wartime identity erased queer teenagers and soldiers from the national story, they became vital public antiheroes in the conservative post-war era as soldiers returned from the frontline and women retreated from traditionally male roles. The "unnatural" vice replaced "hypersexual" women as gender norms and sexual boundaries stabilised with 1950s cultural narratives framing queer men as Australia's "greatest menace" and a major public threat to the nuclear family.[15]

PRIMARY SOURCE: THE "PYJAMA GIRL CONUNDRUM," 1944

Ten years after her body was found near Albury on the New South Wales – Victoria border, *Truth* in Brisbane was confident that its readers would be interested in reading more about the owner of the "most famous pyjamas in the history of crime." In their usual breathless style, they reported the evidence to a coronial inquest being conducted in Melbourne, with verbatim testimony from witnesses, including Linda Agostini's dentist. Evidence was also heard at the inquest that the body was not that of Linda, maintaining the uncertainty over identity which had helped to sustain interest in the case.

PYJAMA GIRL CONUNDRUM

A FEW pieces of tattered, yellow rags, dirty and almost disintegrated, scorched and blackened, with a band of what might once have been a white facing along one edge, now serrated by burns. As rags, completely worthless, but as part of vital identification, these rags have cost £50,000 in one way and another. These rags are all that is left of pyjamas which were found clinging to the dead and partly burnt body of a young woman thrust into a culvert on the Howlong Road, a few miles from Albury, in September, 1934. Since then they have become the most famous pyjamas in the history of crime. Police all over the world have known of them; they have flown for 10 years at the masthead of Australia's most mysterious death, and their latest appearance was as a pitiful exhibit in Melbourne's Coroner's Court during the week, brought there because, at last, the police declare, they have solved that decade old question—the identity of the Pyjama Girl!

SENSATIONAL INQUEST FIGHT TO ESTABLISH HER IDENTITY

Dentist's Story

Saw The Body

Eyes Still Blue

HAD TWO LOOKS

Figure 9.1 "Pyjama Girl Conundrum," Truth (Brisbane), 26 March 1944, 10.

Notes

1 Raymond Evans, *A History of Queensland*, Cambridge: Cambridge University Press, 2007, 187.
2 Queensland State Archives (QSA), Criminal Depositions, Brisbane, R v VO, 6 November 1944, ITM96037.
3 QSA, R v VO, ITM96037.
4 *Criminal Code Act 1899* (63 Vic. No. 9), s208 Unnatural Offences (Sodomy).
5 "Four Years' Gaol for Ex-Soldier," *Telegraph* (Brisbane), December 4, 1944, 2.
6 The Commonwealth recognised the jurisdiction of American military law over troops in Australia; *National Security (Allied Forces) Regulations,* Statutory Rules 1941, No. 302, s3; *National Security (Allied Forces) Regulations*, Statutory Rules 1942, No. 241
7 Yorick Smaal, *Sex, Soldiers and the South Pacific, 1939-45: Queer Identities in Australia in the Second World War*, Basingstoke: Palgrave Macmillan, 2015.
8 Estelle Freedman, "'Uncontrolled Desires': The Response to the Sexual Psychopath," *Journal of American History* 74, no. 1 (1987): 96.
9 "Remarkable Story Told in Court," *Truth* (Brisbane), October 29, 1944, 18.
10 "Man-Women Sent to Gaol for 6 Months," *Truth* (Brisbane), June 11, 1943, 20.
11 Yorick Smaal and Mark Finnane, "Flappers and Felons: Rethinking the Criminal Law and Homosex in interwar Australia, 1920-1939," in *Same-Sex Relationships in History: International Perspectives since 1789*, eds Sean Brady and Mark Seymour, London: Bloomsbury, 2019, 83-93.
12 "Report", 14.
13 Clive Moore, *Sunshine and Rainbows: The Development of Gay and Lesbian Culture in Queensland*, St Lucia: University of Queensland Press, 2001, 96.
14 *Notwithstanding exceptional judicial comments on boys' sexual capacity.*
15 Lisa Featherstone and Amanda Kaladelfos, *Sex Crimes in the Fifties*, Melbourne: Melbourne University Press, 2016, 160.

10 The Long History of Australian Gangs

If the media are to be believed, criminal gangs emerged in Australia in the late twentieth century and were made up exclusively of young men from Asian, Middle Eastern and central African backgrounds.[1] Historians tell a different story. These gangs are just the latest manifestations of a long-term element of Australian society. That is, not gangs themselves, but anxiety that unruly members of society are banding together into criminal organisations which prey on law-abiding citizens. In this chapter, we will explore some of these groups and assess whether they did indeed fit into the category of gangs, starting with the Cabbage Tree Hat mob of the convict period, moving on to the larrikins of the later nineteenth century who we met in the Mount Rennie case, then the infamous razor gangs of the interwar period and finally the motorcycle gangs which were formed after World War II.

Taking this approach does not suggest that criminal gangs do not exist. They do, in many different times, places and forms. Sociologists identify criminal gangs as having a cluster of shared characteristics. They have a coherent, self-formed organisation, including a leadership structure and rules around conduct and loyalty.[2] They operate in public, often trying to dominate specific localities and exclude potential rivals. Gang members share characteristics, which may be inherent such as being born in the same place or having the same ethnicity, or purposefully acquired to demonstrate group membership, such as styles of dress, hair or tattoos.[3] Importantly, ongoing criminal activity is a shared focus and there may be particular types of crime in which the gang specialises.[4]

The problem arises in recognising the differences between criminal gangs and other types of associations or collectives. Anxiety surrounding social disorder has made Australians (and others) far too ready to assume any unruly presence of young people in public constitutes a gang. Associations made for social connection, peer support and self-esteem, especially by those who are for various reasons excluded from ready acceptance in the broader society, are particularly vulnerable to this type of misinterpretation. Ironically, being stigmatised as gangs, harassed by police and excluded from public spaces, often results in more, rather than less, criminality.[5] Although their number, influence and membership have been overestimated in the past as in the

DOI: 10.4324/9781003273561-11

present, a limited number of criminal gangs have had a presence in settler Australia.

Gangs in the Nineteenth Century

The use of the term gangs started in the convict period and these certainly had criminal associations but were not conventional criminal gangs. These were work gangs into which convicts were organised by the penal authorities rather than groups people joined voluntarily. Adopted in the 1790s, by the mid-1820s, the term was being applied to work groups including the Agriculture Gang at Parramatta, the Town Gang in Sydney, the Gaol Gang of those who had reoffended and were being held in custody and the Shell Gang involved with burning shells to produce lime. These gangs contained a mix of skilled and unskilled workers and varied in size from 40 to 60 men.[6] Ganging was considered an efficient way to organise convicts to complete their daily tasks.

When describing what they imagined to be criminal gangs in the nineteenth century, settler colonists tended to use different names, such as mob or push. James Hardy Vaux's 1812 *A New and Comprehensive Vocabulary of the Flash Language* did not include gang or mob but defined a "push" as a crowd of people in the streets or a public place of amusement. See Table 10.1 for other examples of Vaux's Vocabulary. The later use of push as a synonym for gang suggests how what could look innocent from one perspective could be criminalised from another.

The first group to be characterised as a criminal gang in Australia was the Cabbage Tree Hat mob. The name refers to a popular colonial style of hat made of braided fibre from the leaves of the cabbage tree palm (*Livistona Australis*). Wide brimmed and light coloured with a flat or domed crown, the hats were often worn tied around with a long black ribbon.[7] The association of the hat with anti-social behaviour is thought to have originated amongst sawyers and shingle splitters working near the Cooks and Georges Rivers to the south of Sydney. By the 1840s, it was reported that boys and young men wearing these hats were making a nuisance of themselves in the town itself. They frequented theatres and other public places, insulted and assaulted people in the streets at night, including pulling off men's hats and throwing them at ladies and fighting with soldiers. The Cabbage Tree Hat Mob were said to be connected with the "fraternity of thieves," especially the seafaring class and to set up such disturbances as a cover for theft.[8]

A poem of the time portrayed cabbage tree hat wearers as eager to engage in street fighting:

> Twas the midnight, or near it; the theatre done,
> All orderly folks to their suppers were gone,
> And the streets were all silent and quiet;
> Save the boisterous mirth, and the jovial chat,
> Which came from the boys of the Cabbage-tree hat,
> Who were waiting to kick up a riot.[9]

In the poem, they manufacture a premise for a "raging fight" with two passing men before the night watchmen intervene and take the leader of the cabbage tree hat wearers to jail. When using creative writing as a source, historians need to be careful not to assume that the ideas or observations within it are accurate reflections of the topic being treated. Instead, evidence like this reveals something of the worldview of the writer and their intended audience. That the offenders were described as boys in the poem is significant. Concern about youth crime in Britain grew from the first years of the nineteenth century, with urbanisation and population growth. The first British report identifying the issue of juvenile offending was tabled in 1816, with measures to address the issue slow in coming but appearing by the 1840s.[10] These concerns were carried to Australia, where anxiety about inadequate parental control and youths with too much free time created periodic panics over street crime, like that voiced around the Cabbage Tree Hat mob.

There *were* young men in the streets, many of them wearing cabbage tree hats. Some did engage in anti-social behaviour to assert their presence and annoy the respectable. But they did not constitute a gang according to formal definitions, lacking any coherent structure and not having crime as a central intention of their association. Instead, they were a loose social grouping of native-born youths, many of them with convict parents. They banded together for mutual support in a colony they felt was rightfully theirs, but was being run by the more recently arrived immigrants, who were set up in power over them. Being part of a group which was known and to some extent feared gave them a sense of importance. The violence and disorderly behaviour associated with the mob left its mark in popular culture, with a Rockhampton newspaper in 1863 calling the abusive NSW fans of an intercolonial cricket match in Sydney "the Cabbage Tree hat mob." Even another four decades on, a fight amongst wharfies in 1904 was described as being conducted according to the Cabbage Tree hat mob rules.[11]

The term gang was used professionally by Sydney police commissioner William Miles in his *Registry of Flashmen* kept in the 1840s. Miles wrote:

> I have a great number of thieves under my eye in the town, who occasionally do a day's work, and idle, gamble, and thieve the rest of the time.... I have taken great pains to inform myself how these men form themselves into gangs, and I keep a book relative to their movements, the parties who are their companions, and such other information as I may obtain respecting them.

He called one of these gangs the Flash Mob, a name which had earlier been adopted by a group of convict women in Hobart's Female Factory in the 1830s.[12] In both cases, it was a description of their style and presentation, with the term "flash" defined by Vaux as someone who was part of the criminal underworld and wise to its ways.[13] A flash person could by definition understand the flash language of slang words useful in the conduct and concealment

Table 10.1 Some terms from James Hardy Vaux's 1819 Vocabulary of the Flash Language.

Bolt	To run away from or leave any place suddenly, is called bolting, or making a bolt
Cadge	To beg. The cadge is the game or profession of begging
Crap	The gallows. Crap'd – hanged
Fake	To fake a person can mean to rob, shoot, wound or cut them. To fake a man out and out is to kill him
Gammon	Flattery; deceit; pretence; any assertion which is not strictly true: "that's all gammon"
Kid	A child of either sex but particularly applied to a boy who commences thief at an early age
Lag	To transport for 7 years or upwards; a convict under sentence of transportation
Oliver	The moon. Oliver is in town – a phrase signifying that the nights are moonlight and consequently unfavourable to depredation
Pinch	Purloin small articles of value in the shops of jewellers, etc. while pretending to purchase or bespeak some trinket
Ruffles	Hand cuffs
Shutter-racket	The practice of robbing houses, or shops, by boring a hole in the window shutter, and taking out a pane of glass

Source: James Hardy Vaux, A New and Comprehensive Vocabulary of the Flash Language [1819] https://gutenberg.net.au/ebooks06/0600111h.html (accessed 2 June 2022)

of crimes. The presence of this language in Australia hints at an underworld which used slang to build community and allow members to discuss their illegal and other activities in front of uncomprehending outsiders. In the dedication to his book, Vaux claimed he had learned the flash language by associating with the "most dissolute and unprincipled characters" during his eventful life and hoped that it would both amuse the commandant of the Newcastle secondary penal settlement where he was then serving a colonial sentence and help magistrates understand what those who appeared before them were saying. Looking at Vaux's *Vocabulary* two centuries later, some words have crossed over in general usage, while others remained known only to those inside the flash world.

Another group accused of being members of a criminal gang were the larrikins of the later nineteenth century who we discussed when treating the Mount Rennie Outrage. Melissa Bellanta suggests that the name larrikin was brought to Australia as an English dialect word for mischievous youths, although it also resembles Vaux's "leary" meaning fly, vigilant, suspicious, cunning and not easily robbed or duped. The term was first used by urban youths themselves as a proud self-description but by the 1880s had become generally used as a handy "term of abuse … a synonym for 'hoodlum' or 'young scoundrel.'"[14] *Bellanta dismisses the understanding of larrikin pushes as criminal gangs in her essay accompanying this chapter.* She argues that while there were some loose street gangs known as pushes or forties based in the inner ring of crowded working-class suburbs at this time, including the Rocks Push in Sydney and the Woolpacks in Melbourne's Carlton, they were fluid groupings of no more than a few dozen individuals who saw themselves as an elite of street toughs.[15] Many hundreds of young men and women were also subject to being called larrikins, or used the name for themselves, without having any association with the pushes.

Like the Cabbage Tree Hat mob, most of those labelled larrikins were born in the colonies in their case to parents who had arrived as free immigrants during the gold rush period. In the 1990s, research into the problems young people from ethnic minorities faced when trying to establish themselves in Australia found a range of factors: conflicts between their parents' expectations and their own aspirations, unemployment, low self-esteem and the stress of settling into a new environment.[16] These factors were also in play historically, particularly affecting the Irish in Australia who were considered by many in the Anglo-dominated society as inferior in terms of intellectual capacity, work ethic and morality. As we saw in the Mount Rennie case, although the offenders were not immigrants, they were stigmatised because of their Irish origins and Roman Catholic faith. Youths from minority national and religious backgrounds have received negative attention from the police, the media and the public since the colonial period.

The first of the post gold rush generation were adolescents when the term larrikin came into use in Melbourne in 1870. Brisbane discovered the same problem with unruly youth in the 1890s. These young people were increasingly independent and outspoken, emboldened by their large numbers and, not finding places in trades or other steady workplaces, earned their livings through casual work like hawking (selling goods in the streets) and making deliveries. Their demeanour and behaviour troubled both the middle class and the respectable working class, who supported the more vigorous policing of minor offences including vagrancy, drunkenness, obscene language and riotous behaviour.[17] Practices which had previously been tolerated were more often prosecuted, creating an impression that crime and disorder were on the rise, and that larrikinism was the cause. Overall, larrikins had no coherent organisation, leadership structure, single area of operations or shared criminal purpose and so cannot be considered to have been criminal gangs.

The other groups referred to as gangs in the mid-to-late nineteenth century were the bushrangers. Although gangs have come to be associated with urban settings, the bushranger gangs are a better fit with the definition of a criminal gang. They were formed specifically for the purpose of committing crimes, were associated with specific geographical areas, had names and acknowledged leaders and deployed violence to intimidate those who did not support them. Many bushrangers shared the showy and disruptive ethos of other criminal gangs, drawing the attention of other outsiders like the larrikins, who sang songs about the exploits of the Kelly gang. In the Jerilderie letter, Ned Kelly referred to larrikins as fellow victims of police harassment while also demonstrating his disdain for city dwellers by saying that the police in Melbourne were such bullies that it took eight of them to remove "one poor half starved larrikin" to the watchhouse.[18] Bushranger gangs were very small in size compared with many other gangs, befitting their need for secrecy and mobility. This made it difficult for them to have the ongoing life which is associated with successful criminal gangs, with few outlasting their founding members.

Cabbage tree hat wearers, flash men, larrikins and bushrangers were all part of the history of the idea of gangs in Australia and contradict the impression that gangs, both real and imagined, were a development of the twentieth century. Most of them shared an identity as native born rather than immigrants, in societies in which immigrants often held official and economic power and authority. Grouping together allowed individuals who otherwise felt alienated from society to find companionship and establish a sense of identity, through shared activities, language, dress and, in some cases, criminal activity.

Razor Gangs

Moving into the twentieth century, the same inner-city suburbs which had been the home of the larrikins became the turf of razor gangs. At the turn of the millennium, when the true crime book *Razor: Tilly Devine, Kate Leigh and the Razor Gangs* by Larry Writer was published, stories about these razor gangs came back into circulation and the book became the foundation for the very successful *Underbelly Razor* series in 2011. Part of the appeal was an unexpected feature of these gangs in interwar Sydney: they were headed by women. Gangs, and groups assumed to be gangs, generally consist of men and are characterised by behaviours coded masculine: fighting, overt sexuality and crime itself. Women gang leaders came out of specific features of the interwar period, but also signalled a new generation of criminals who were not just involved with small-scale, opportunistic acts but applied more sophisticated business models based on profiting from controlling the supply of illegal goods and services. If bushrangers were the first of Australia's criminal gangs, razor gangs were the second.

These gangs approached the status of organised crime, or what is sometimes called criminal business organisations, which were also being established in Australia in the interwar period. Chief amongst them was the Calabrian criminal secret society known variously as the 'Ndrangheta, Camorra or Black Hand, which made its earliest presence felt in the Queensland sugar towns of Innisfail and Ingham in the early 1920s, and became active in Brisbane, Melbourne, Griffith and Sydney later that decade. In the NSW capital, Giuseppe Mammone, Filippo Pignataro and Domenico Belle headed local operations, using greengrocer and hairdressing businesses as fronts for illegal sales of alcohol and drugs, blackmail, insurance fraud, extortion, arson and prostitution, wielding pistols, knives and fists to ensure that illegal arrangements were honoured.[19] Like other mafia organisations, they were not flamboyant but deliberately low key.

This enabled them to get on with their large-scale and long-term criminal activities, which expanded as the immigrant Italian population rose in the post–Second World War decades.[20] As reported about Victoria in 1964 by an FBI investigator, "In order to further their legitimate endeavours and cloak their illicit operations, Society [mafia] members ... lead an ostensibly quiet and respectable family life and are ever ready to entertain and do favours for the right people."[21]

Razor gangs did not have the international connections or longevity of the 'Ndrangheta. The opportunity on which these gangs were founded was early twentieth-century efforts to clamp down on many of Australians' favourite vices. Pub closing times were changed in most states to 6 pm in 1916, ostensibly as part of the war effort, but fulfilling a long-held wish of many reformers.[22] As part of the same efforts to stamp out disorderly behaviour, prostitutes were banned from working in the streets. Most forms of gambling were outlawed, except on site at licensed racecourses. Heroin and cocaine, which had been sold by chemists as pain relievers, were made illegal.

Of course, prostitution, gambling, drinking and drug taking did not stop because of these legal changes. Instead, they were pushed underground, providing opportunities for criminals to take advantage of the new profits to be made by supplying sex, betting, out-of-hours liquor and drugs. There was an opportunity for gangs to operate as government retrenchment and a tight labour market meant that police numbers in proportion to the population were at an historically low point across Australia as were rates of prosecution.[23]

In Sydney, the centre of this activity was East Sydney and Darlinghurst, areas which had once been well-regarded residential areas, but were becoming run down as the more prosperous people moved out to the new suburbs. There were three main gangs or syndicates working this area in the interwar period (1919–1938), run by Phil "the Jew" Jeffs, Kate Leigh and Tilly Devine. The leading role of the two women was in part because it was illegal for a man, but not a woman, to live off the proceeds of prostitution. This allowed women to take on the role of managing the sex industry more publicly, and from there to become involved with other types of crime. There were frequent fights between these gangs as they sought to protect and expand their elements of the illegal trades. The straight razor became a weapon of choice because another change in the law made the possession of an unlicensed pistol at night a serious offence punishable by six months in jail, while possession of a razor was not regulated.[24]

One notorious gangster of the period was Guido Calletti, a pimp, thief and thug for hire convicted several times of assaulting police, who was shot dead in 1939, aged 37. Another was John "Chow "Hayes, who became well known as a contract killer. Hayes grew up in inner Sydney and began his criminal career as a child, serving time in the Gosford Boys home, which he called a" breeding ground for crims," where he first met Calletti.[25] Hayes had dozens of convictions ranging from riotous behaviour, to assault, stealing and consorting with known criminals from the age of 17 in 1928 until he was found guilty of shooting dead boxer Bobby Lee in a nightclub in 1951. He referred to his criminal associates as mobs rather than gangs, recalling that he had graduated from the Little Railway Mob to the Big Mob, and once been badly beaten by the Surry Hills Mob.

Assuming leadership roles amongst largely male associates, Tilly Devine and Kate Leigh have become what are called celebrified criminals. Criminologist Ruth Penfold-Mounce has developed a typology of this group, including the categories of social bandit (this describes Ned Kelly), the greed-driven criminal (who we met in the Graeme Thorne case), the loathed perpetrator of horrific crimes (Frances Knorr) and the underworld exhibitionist (Devine and Leigh).[26] Like other celebrities, the duration of criminal infamy can be quite brief or very long, extending well beyond the person's own lifespan. It is also evident that the approach taken by the offender plays an important role in this, with social bandits and underworld exhibitionists in particular seeking to draw attention to themselves by performing their criminal roles in public, and with style. Devine and Leigh have been kept alive as criminal characters through numerous portrayals in books and on screens, in which they are generally cast as young and sexually alluring. The evidence suggests a less glamorous reality.

Tilly Devine was the former Matilda Twiss of London, where she was born in 1900.[27] Twiss was working as a prostitute when she met Australian serviceman Jim Devine in 1916. They married the next year and Tilly arrived in Sydney on a ship with other war brides in 1920. The Devines set up business in Sydney, with Tilly working as a prostitute and Jim as the driver taking her and others to meet their clients. A 1925 police report detailed convictions Tilly Devine had acquired for offensive behaviour, indecent language, assault and being a common prostitute, and the fines and short stays in prison she had accumulated. It stated, "She is a prostitute of the worst type and an associate of the worst type of prostitute, vagrants and criminals."[28] That year, Devine attacked a man in the street with a razor and was sentenced to 2 years in Long Bay Women's penitentiary. On her release, she did not return to active prostitution, but set up a series of brothels, focused around Palmer Street in Woolloomooloo. She employed men to protect the brothels including Frank Green, the Little Gunman and Sid McDonald. These men took part in street clashes and a gunfight at Devine's home in Maroubra in July 1929 when some of Kate Leigh's gang attacked. Jim Devine shot one of the assailants dead but was found not guilty of murder because he was protecting his property. The Devines' work and life partnership lasted until 1943, which was a busy time in the brothel business with thousands of American and Australian servicemen passing through Sydney. They divorced and Tilly remarried in 1945, enjoying a life of wealth including a visit back home to London for the coronation of Queen Elizabeth II in 1953. She kept her brothel empire running until the late 1950s when she had to sell off all but one establishment to pay a tax bill of £20,000. Tilly Devine died aged 70 in 1970.

Tilly's great rival was best known as Kate Leigh, later Kate Barry.[29] She was born into the Beahan family in the NSW Central West town of Dubbo in 1887. The first charge on her prison record was being a neglected child, for which she was sent to the Parramatta Industrial School at the age of ten. Industrial schools were one of several measures put in place from the late nineteenth century to try to save vulnerable children from situations of neglect which could lead to them being at first victims and then perpetrators of crime. For many, including Leigh, early institutionalisation did not lay the groundwork for a law-abiding life, and by the 1920s, she was involved with illegal liquor sales and receiving stolen goods in Sydney. While she was serving time in jail in August 1929, Tilly Devine order an attack on Leigh's sly grog shops, an event which became known as the Battle of Kellett Street. The following year, Leigh shot a man who had broken into her Surry Hills house. She never faced charges for this, although she did go to jail for possessing cocaine and consorting with known criminals. Like Devine, Leigh became wealthy from her illegal businesses and went about in public in furs and diamond rings. She was also brought down by unpaid taxes in the 1950s but remained a well-known figure in Sydney for the rest of her life. Asked to comment on the Graeme Thorne kidnapping in 1960, she said it was a type of offence that good Australian criminals would never commit and offered to try to find the offender through her own networks, warning that their punishment would be worse than that of the justice system.[30] Kate Leigh died in 1964.

Just as changes to the laws had created the business opportunities which motivated members of the razor gangs, laws were changed to try to break them up. In 1929, the NSW Vagrancy Act was amended to bring in an anti-consorting clause. This made it illegal "to habitually consort with reputed thieves or prostitutes or persons who have no visible or lawful means of support." From that time, just being in the company of people with reputations as thieves or prostitutes or without regular jobs, which was the case for most gang members, became an offence. Police applied this stringently and sent many gangsters to jail, breaking up the razor gangs by the end of the 1930s. In Melbourne, where similar gangs had emerged, the police responded in the 1920s with a squad known as the terrible ten, who broke up street gangs by brutal means, leaving them unable to function and opening the way for new types of organised crime to flourish in the 1950s.

Motorcycle Gangs

Australia's post–Second World War outlaw motorcycle or bikie gangs were not only an organic outgrowth of local social conditions like the Razor Gangs had been but were inspired by and modelled themselves on American motorcycle gangs. In the United States, outlaw motorcycle gangs (in contrast with older motorcycle clubs) started with returned servicemen who were having trouble fitting back into civilian life after the Second World War. Reproducing the structures experienced in the armed forces, these gangs were hierarchical, with elected presidents and officials, probation periods, written bylaws, formal meetings, weekly dues and payments owed by local chapters to a national headquarters. Following rules such as attending meetings and not fraternising with members of other clubs was important to these gangs, despite the apparent tension with the rebelliousness and freedom-seeking also associated with them.

References to local motorcycle gangs begin to appear in Australian newspapers from 1952, with groups stealing parts from parked motorcycles in Sydney and complaints about vandalism, assault and drinking in Brisbane parks by teenage motorcycle riders, who were still being referred to as larrikins.[31] As the NSW state government began to require the registration of motorcycles and the police tried to force high powered bikes off the roads, riders in that state formed groups to oppose what they saw as harassment.[32] While some of these groups were purely interested in sharing their common love for motorcycles, others, who took the title of "one percenters" from an American description, embraced the idea of being outlaws, seeing themselves as rebels and willing outcasts from respectable society. The Gladiators from the Hunter Valley became Australia's first outlaw motorcycle gang in 1960.[33]

Outlaw motorcycle gangs grew through the 1960s and 1970s. Although now remembered as a time of peace and love, there were significant increases in serious assaults, rape and attempted rape, armed robbery and break and enter offences in the 1960s.[34] As with the baby boom that led to the larrikin gang fears of the late nineteenth century, this was a time when immigration and reproduction were quickly increasing Australia's youth demographic. In NSW, between 1959 and 1969, the number of 18–24-year-old males increased by 58%.[35] Even if rates of offending remained steady, with more young males the number of crimes committed would rise. Motorcycle gangs made up of some of these young men provided a natural focus for concern.

By the late 1960s, in Sydney, bikies who worked by day as mechanics and truck drivers were hanging out at the Royal George Hotel, near the Pyrmont Docks, and holding often violent "kegs" or drinking sessions at the Manly Reservoir on Sundays. [36] As in the United States, men returning from the Vietnam war invigorated the bikie gangs and American films portraying motorcycle gangs including *Hell's Angels on Wheels* (1967), *Hells Angels '69* (1969) and *Easy Rider* (1969) added to their reputations.[37] The Rebels, established in Brisbane in 1969, founded chapters in regional cities like Dubbo and Rockhampton in the 1970s, and then went into other capitals, becoming the largest Australian motorcycle gang under the leadership of Maltese immigrant Alessio Vella.[38] In parallel, American gangs like the

Hells Angels set themselves up in Australia in the late 1960s, after having become an incorporated company and registered their death's head logo in the United States.[39]

American motorcycle gangs brought with them involvement in manufacturing and selling illicit drugs and the violence which accompanied this trade. In 1972, a member of the Hell's Angels gang was found shot dead in Rosebery in Sydney after violence between them and the Adelaide-based Finks gang. The dead man was reported as being Steven Celovic, signalling that this was a likely a recent immigrant from communist Yugoslavia, playing on local anxieties about diversifying immigration.[40]

As their profile rose, motorcycle gangs became perceived as the new menace from which young people should be saved. In 1974, five young motorcyclists from Lake Macquarie were found guilty of damaging a vehicle while "dressed in the uniform of a motorcycle gang," including wearing chains.[41] The youths were told not to associate with one another or any member of a motorcycle gang or face 12 months in jail and were congratulated when they kept to these terms.

Not all were so compliant. Bikies were active in 1977, rampaging through a camp at the Bathurst motorcycle races breaking car windows and crashing into tents; and at Braidwood, where 30 riders on an excursion staged a fight at the Araluen Hotel, drove while drunk, used "unseemly words," (defined until 1970 as obscene, indecent or profane), and were found to be in possession of marijuana, then known as Indian hemp. More serious crimes were committed, including murder and aggravated rape in Morwell, Victoria in a dispute between the Perth-based Coffin Cheaters and Resurrected Bikie Clubs. One of Australia's best-known bikie gang battles was the Milperra Massacre on Father's Day 1984. One thousand members of the Bandidos (one of the big four motorcycle gangs in the US, with its origins in Texas) and Comancheros (a NSW-based gang with a name from a John Wayne film), met by agreement and conducted a gun battle in which seven were killed and twenty injured.[42] Thirty of the participants were found guilty of various offences.

Interviews with former members of outlaw motorcycle gangs in Queensland in 2020 revealed motivations for joining such gangs.[43] The informants talked about their shared enjoyment of riding motorbikes and the camaraderie of socialising with others outside of the usual social constraints, although within their own internal, democratically-run hierarchical structure. They accepted that being club members would involve them in fighting, traffic offences and drug possession but distanced themselves from more recent developments in the gangs, which they found had moved from committing casual criminal acts to being centred on making money from the business of drug manufacturing and sales. They were particularly scathing about the admission of people who had no affinity with other club members or in some cases, even with motorbikes, disparaging them with the label "Nike bikies."

Changes like these have led Australian state governments to step up the policing of outlaw motorcycle gangs, treating them as organised crime groups. According to this definition, they undertake serious crime as structured and long-lasting groups of offenders, with some participants linked by racial, linguistic or ethnic bonds. As in the interwar period, anti-association legislation has been passed to break up the outlaw motorcycle gangs.[44]

Conclusion

The groups introduced in this chapter spanned two centuries and varied in many respects, but they also had some points of commonality, including that the term gang was applied to them, with greater or lesser accuracy. In many cases, the groups were formed based upon an existing sense of shared identity as outsiders in their societies because of where they were born, their religion, their social class or their poverty. Most signalled their identity by shared language, dress and conduct. They used public displays of disorderly behaviour to establish and maintain their common identity and reputation, creating space for themselves in societies where they otherwise felt marginal. This visibility in each case created social panics about disorder, decline and public safety and assumptions that all who acted or dressed in a particular way were members of a criminal gang. With the exception of bushranger gangs, the evidence for the nineteenth century does not bear this out. In the twentieth century, however, razor gangs and outlaw motorcycle gangs, amongst whom violent crime became central to the group's functioning, can be considered genuine criminal gangs. Returning to the concerns over the emergence of youth gangs amongst recent immigrant groups in the twenty-first century, that they might be forming a criminal underworld rather than integrating into society, these fears are the contemporary parallels of those expressed about larrikins and the Cabbage Tree Hat mob, and the early forms of motorcycle gangs. They are a disproportionate response to ongoing efforts of youths to find their place in Australia.

Suggested Readings

Bellanta, Melissa. *Larrikins: A History*. Brisbane: University of Queensland Press, 2012.

Collins, Jock and Carol Reid. "Minority Youth, Crime, Conflict, and Belonging in Australia." *International Migration and Integration* 10 (2009): 377–91.

Cunneen, Chris and Rob White. *Juvenile Justice: Youth and Crime in Australia*, fourth ed. Melbourne: Oxford University Press, 2011.

Dowling, Christopher, Dominic Boland, Anthony Morgan, Julianne Webster, Yi-Ning Chiu and Roger Lowe. "The Changing Culture of Outlaw Motorcycle Gangs in Australia." *Trends and Issues in Crime and Criminal Justice* 615 (2021): 1–16.

White, R.D. "Taking It to the Streets: The Larrikins and the Lebanese." Scott Poynting and George Morgan, eds. *Outrageous!*. Hobart: ACYS Publishing, 2007.

ESSAY: WHATEVER HAPPENED TO THE LARRIKIN PUSHES?

Melissa Bellanta

At intervals across the twentieth century, commentators in the Australian press reminisced about the good bad old days when "larrikin pushes" roamed the districts close to the centre of Australian cities: the Rocks or Redfern in Sydney, Fitzroy or Richmond in Melbourne, Fortitude Valley in Brisbane and so forth.[45] These commentators used "larrikin" in the nineteenth-century sense of the term. They did not mean "laid-back joker," the connotation now attached to this Australian colloquialism. When they spoke of larrikins, they meant something closer to hooligans or hoodlums: adolescents or twenty-somethings given to disorderliness and delinquency. Most of the commentators also used "push" in a sense common in and around the late 1800s, meaning mean "street mob or gang." Much of what they said about the larrikin pushes was unreliable, however – in some cases, outrageously so. No larrikin push was ever a well-organised entity that ruled tyrannically over a particular neighbourhood, led by captains or kings who extracted unquestioning obedience from their underlings. Unfortunately, however, this claim has been made repeatedly in the press and even in academic literature over the years.[46]

While popular commentaries about larrikin pushes are shot through with lurid fantasies about the frightening "lower orders" or criminal underworlds, some contain grains of truth. While there were no organised larrikin gangs ruling their neighbourhoods with an iron fist between the 1870s and 1920s, there *were* groups of young people living in the districts surrounding the centres of Australian cities – mostly young men, but also some women – a good many of whom called themselves "larrikins." The push subculture of this period was characterised by volatile eruptions of violence towards others: attacks on police, assaults on Chinese street-sellers, shoving strangers at harbour-side dance pavilions, and in some terrible cases, gang-raping women in parks.[47] Back in the 1870s, stray records also suggest that there were Melbourne youth claiming that they were "king of the Richmond larrikins" or "king of the Collingwood larrikins."[48] These youth were skiting about how daring they were, however – most likely, too, about their success in bare-knuckle fighting – rather than claiming anything more sinister or grand.

In an excellent summary of the global history of youth gangs, historians Simon Sleight and Jasper Heeks note that the appearance of "juvenile street gangs" such as the larrikin pushes was a widespread phenomenon in the late nineteenth century, by no means confined to the Australian colonies.[49] The key reason was rapid urbanisation combined with rampant inequity, sharpened by the lack of what we would now call a social safety net. The over-policing of particular neighbourhoods also played a role. This over-policing formed the backdrop to incidents such as Sydney's Bondi and Chowder Bay riots of 1884 and 1890, both involving fighting between police and the members of larrikin pushes on public holidays, not to mention countless smaller skirmishes.[50] It is perhaps thus only to be expected that the larrikin push subculture shifted in the early 1900s. The beginnings of a juvenile justice system were taking place at this time, sparking efforts to reduce the degree to which police brought young people before criminal courts. There were also efforts to enforce compulsory education and reduce the amount of insecure unskilled work performed by young people outside factories.[51]

The key effect of these developments was that the culture of youthful pushes became more insular and less animated by violence towards others after the turn of the twentieth century. Fighting over territory or for local status became a stronger, more persistent focus. The members of rival youth mobs regularly set upon each other with fence palings, bicycle chains and fists but ignored others outside the scene. The rivalry was heightened by a proliferation of football clubs and the intensification of local football matches as a spectator sport. Some larrikin pushes such as the White Roses in South Melbourne even bore the names of local football clubs. Many engaged in what would now be called football hooliganism after matches on Saturday afternoons.[52]

When I researched my book *Larrikins: A History*, I focused only on the period between 1870 and 1930, finishing at a time when the terms "larrikin" and "push" were coming to be used airily, even romantically, rather than attached to concrete identities among youth. The elaboration of an actual criminal underworld in Australian cities after the First World War played its own role in this development. The emergence of rackets relating to sly grog and prostitution made it possible for the members of larrikin pushes to graduate into organised criminal circles. This was a path followed in Sydney by John "Chow" Hayes. He belonged to the "railway mob" gravitating around Central Station when in his teens in the early-to-mid 1920s, but later became a gun-toting gangster.[53] Yet Hayes' trajectory was the exception rather than the rule. Most "pushites" of his youth simply grew up: too focused on making do than cutting a swathe on the street scene. The rise of organised crime also drained what was left of the popular animus once directed at larrikin pushes, leaving the memory of what they had once been to fade into myth.

PRIMARY SOURCE: KATE LEIGH PRISON RECORD, 1915

The first entry on Kate Leigh's prison record is "being a neglected child." For her presence in the streets of her hometown of Dubbo, Leigh (then Beahan) was sent to Parramatta Industrial School. By 1915, when this photograph was taken, she had stepped up from charges of vagrancy and abusive words to perjury, lying to provide an alibi for her partner in a case of armed robbery. Leigh was awarded a sentence of 5-year penal servitude. Although she served her time in the new purpose-built State Reformatory for Women at Long Bay, she did not reform. Instead, she began a successful business illegally selling alcohol and became one of the leaders of the notorious razor gangs of Sydney in the 1920s and 1930s.

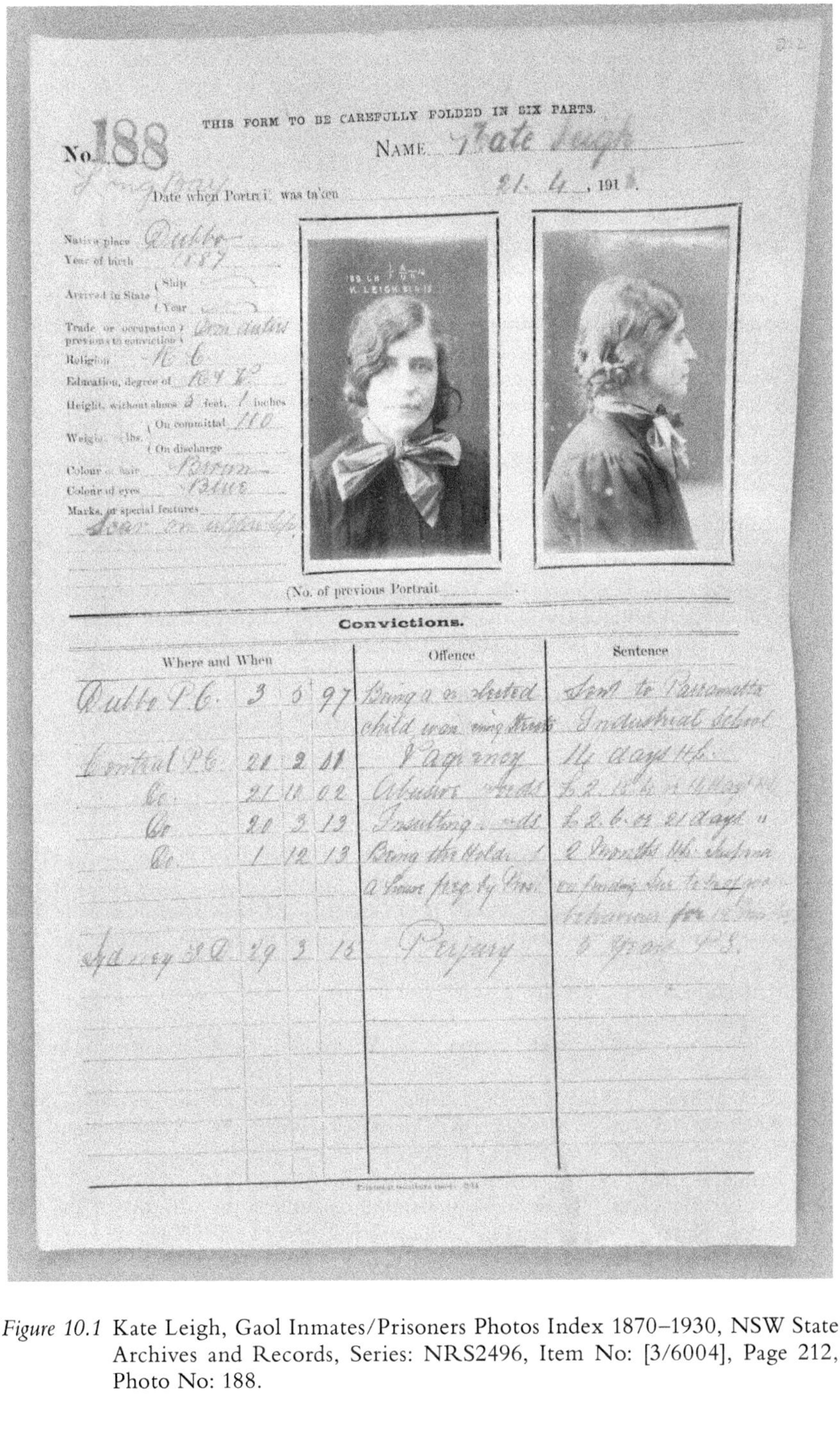

No. 188

THIS FORM TO BE CAREFULLY FOLDED IN SIX PARTS.

NAME Kate Leigh

Date when Portrait was taken 21. 4. 191

Native place Dubbo

Year of birth 1887

Arrived in State { Ship / Year

Trade or occupation previous to conviction

Religion R C

Education, degree of

Height, without shoes 5 feet 1 inches

Weight, lbs. { On committal 110 / On discharge

Colour of hair Brown

Colour of eyes Blue

Marks, or special features

(No. of previous Portrait

Convictions.

Where and When				Offence	Sentence
Dubbo P.C.	3	5	97	Being a neglected child wandering streets	Sent to Parramatta Industrial School
Central P.C.	21	2	01	Vagrancy	14 days H.L.
Do.	21	11	02	[illegible]	[illegible]
Do.	20	3	13	Insulting words	[illegible]
Do.	1	12	13	[illegible]	[illegible]
Sydney Q.S.	29	3	15	Perjury	5 years P.S.

Figure 10.1 Kate Leigh, Gaol Inmates/Prisoners Photos Index 1870–1930, NSW State Archives and Records, Series: NRS2496, Item No: [3/6004], Page 212, Photo No: 188.

Notes

1 For a critical review of this media construction, see Jock Collins and Carol Reid, "Minority Youth, Crime, Conflict, and Belonging in Australia," *International Migration and Integration* 10 (2009): 380.

2 Celinda Franco, "Youth Gangs: Background, Legislation and Issues," John G. Cooper, ed. *Youth Gangs: Causes, Violence and Interventions*, New York: Nova Science Publishers, 2009, 3–4.

3 Santina Perrone and Rob White, "Young People and Gangs," *Trends and Issues in Crime and Criminal Justice*, Australian Institute of Criminology, No. 167, September 2000, 2.

4 Rob White, Santina Perrone, Carmel Guerra and Rosario Lampugnani, *Ethnic Youth Gangs in Australia: Do they exist?* Report. No. 3, *Pacific Islander Young People*, Melbourne: Australian Multicultural Foundation, 1999, 9.

5 White, Perrone, Guerra and Lampugnani, *Ethnic Youth Gangs in Australia*, 11–3.

6 William Robbins, "Management and Resistance in the Convict Work Gangs, 1788–1830," *Journal of Industrial Relations*, 45, no. 3 (2003): 366.

7 For a demonstration of how these hats were made, view this video of a Cockatoo Island DigiTalk on Convicts and Cabbage Tree Hats: https://www.youtube.com/watch?v=EpH-ETLclos

8 "Cricket", *Sydney Herald*, January 2, 1841, 2.

9 "The Battle of the Cabbage-Tree," *Sydney Monitor and Commercial Advertiser*, January 6, 1841, 2.

10 "Report of the Committee for Investigating the Causes of the Alarming Increase of Juvenile Delinquency in the Metropolis" [1816] cited in Chris Cunneen and Rob White, *Juvenile Justice: Youth and Crime in Australia*, fourth edition, Melbourne: Oxford University Press, 2011, 3. This paragraph is informed by Ch 1 "The Development of Juvenile Justice" from that book.

11 "New South Wales, from our own correspondents," *Rockhampton Bulletin and Central Queensland Advertiser*, 18 February 1863: 1; "A Fierce Fight," *Sydney Sportsman*, 2 November 1904, 3.

12 Melissa Bellanta, *Larrikins: A History*, Brisbane: University of Queensland Press, 2012, 119.

13 James Hardy Vaux, *A New and Comprehensive Vocabulary of the Flash Language* [1819] https://gutenberg.net.au/ebooks06/0600111h.html (accessed 2 June 2022) and see Simon Barnard, *James Hardy Vaux's 1819 Dictionary of Criminal Slang and other impolite terms as used by the Convicts of the British Colonies of Australia*, Melbourne: Text Publishing, 2019.

14 Bellanta, *Larrikins*, xix, xiv, 2.

15 Bellanta, *Larrikins*, 69.

16 White, Perrone, Guerra and Lampugnani, *Ethnic Youth Gangs in Australia: Do They Exist?*, 3.

17 R.D. White, "Taking It to the Streets: The Larrikins and the Lebanese," Scott Poynting and George Morgan, eds. *Outrageous!*, Hobart: ACYS Publishing, 2007, 44–45.

18 Jerilderie letter.

19 Stephen Bennetts, "'Undesirable Italians': prolegomena for a history of the Calabrian 'Ndrangheta in Australia," *Modern Italy* 21, No. 1 (2016): 88.

20 Anna Sergi, "The 'Ndrangheta Down Under: Constructing the Italian Mafia in Australia," *European Review of Organised Crime* 5, no. 1 (2019), 7.

21 Bennetts, "Undesirable Italians," 90.

22 In Western Australia, closing was later at 9 pm while Queensland adopted an 8 pm closing time in 1923.

23 Mark Finnane, *Police and Government, Histories of Policing in Australia*, Melbourne: Oxford University Press, 1994, 22.

24 "Pistol License Act of 1927," *Daily Examiner (Grafton)*, September 5, 1927, 6.
25 David Hickie, *Chow Hayes, Gunman*, Sydney: Angus and Robertson, 1990, 32.
26 Ruth Penfold-Mounce, *Celebrity Culture and Crime: The Joy of Trangression* (2009) cited by Belinda Middleweek in "Deviant Divas: Lindy Chamberlain and Schapelle Corby and the Case for a New Category of Celebrity for Criminally Implicated Women," *Crime, Media, Culture* 13, no. 1 (2017), 87.
27 Judith Allen and Baiba Irving, "Devine, Matilda Mary (Tilly) (1900–1970)," *Australian Dictionary of Biography*, National Centre of Biography, Australian National University, https://adb.anu.edu.au/biography/devine-matilda-mary-tilly-5970/text10185 (accessed 5 May 2022).
28 NSW Police Report on Matilda Devine, 4 May 1925, State Archives NSW, NRS 855-19-7289-49, part of online exhibition, Tilly Devine and the Razor Gang Wars, https://www.records.nsw.gov.au/archives/magazine/galleries/tilly-devine-and-the-razor-gang-wars#expand3 (accessed 5 May 2022).
29 Judith Allen, "Leigh, Kathleen Mary (Kate) (1881–1964)," *Australian Dictionary of Biography*, National Centre of Biography, Australian National University, https://adb.anu.edu.au/biography/leigh-kathleen-mary-kate-7164/text12375 (accessed 5 May 2022).
30 Stephen Garton, "'Feed Him to the Sharks': The Graeme Thorne Kidnapping," *Australian Cultural History* 12 (1993), 34.
31 "Teenage gangs ruin Mt Coot-tha park" *Sunday Mail* (Brisbane), August 22, 1954, 6.
32 "The Bikies," *Tharunka* (Sydney), July 1, 1967, 5.
33 Duncan McNab, *Outlaw Bikers in Australia: The Real Story*, Sydney: Macmillan, 2013, 7.
34 David Biles, "Serious Crime Rates," David Biles, ed. *Crime and Justice in Australia*, Melbourne: Sun Books, 1977.
35 Peter N. Grabosky, *Sydney in Ferment, Crime, Dissent and Official Reaction, 1788–1973*, Canberra: ANU Press, 1977, 147.
36 "The Bikies," *Tharunka* (Sydney), July 1, 1967, 5.
37 Mark Lauchs, Andy Bain and Peter Bell, *Outlaw Motorcycle Gangs: A Theoretical Perspective,* Palgrave Macmillan, 2015.
38 McNab, *Outlaw Bikers in Australia*, 46.
39 There are references to the Hell's Angels in Sydney, Perth and Melbourne in the press from 1970 although some sources say they were not established in Australia until 1973. ("Police seek bikies over attack," *Canberra Times*, 25 November 1970, 3; Stephen Monterosso, "From Bikers to Savvy Criminals. Outlaw Motorcycle Gangs in Australia: Implications for Legislators and Law Enforcement," *Crime, Law and Social Change* 69 (2018): 683.)
40 Grabosky, *Sydney in Ferment*, 147.
41 "Jail terms suspended," *Canberra Times*, March 30, 1974, 14.
42 Monterosso, "From bikers to savvy criminals," 684. For a first-hand account from a police commander, see Ron Stephenson, *Milperra: The Road to Justice*, Sydney: New Holland, 2004.
43 Christopher Dowling, Dominic Boland, Anthony Morgan, Julianne Webster, Yi-Ning Chiu and Roger Lowe, "The Changing Culture of Outlaw Motorcycle Gangs in Australia," *Trends and Issues in Crime and Criminal Justice*, 615 (February 2021), 1–16.
44 Mark Lauchs and Zoe Staines, "An Analysis of Outlaw Motorcycle Gang Crime: Are Bikers Organised criminals?", *Global Crime* 20, no. 2 (2019): 70–1.
45 For characteristic examples, see: Bill Beatty, "They Wore Photos on Their Feet," *Sydney Morning Herald, 17* January 1953, 9; "Death of the Larrikin," *Argus* (Melbourne), 8 June 1950, 2; "Melbourne 'Pushes': Larrikinism a Lost Art," *Sunday Times* (Perth), 10 April 1910, 1. For an extended discussion of the exaggerations and fabrications in these accounts, see: Melissa Bellanta, *Larrikins: A History*, Brisbane: University of Queensland Press, 2012, 57–63.

46 For example, Ambrose Pratt, "'Push' Larrikinism in Australia," *Blackwood's Magazine* 170 (July 1901): 27–40; and Manning Clark, *Manning Clark's History of Australia,* abridged by Michael Cathcart, Melbourne: Melbourne University Press, 1993, 360.
47 Bellanta, *Larrikins,* 57–105.
48 Bellanta, *Larrikins,* 6–7.
49 Simon Sleight and Jasper Heeks, "Urbanisation: Youth Gangs and Street Cultures," in James Marten, ed. *The Oxford Handbook of the History of Youth Culture*, Oxford: Oxford University Press, 2021.
50 Bellanta, *Larrikins,* 78–79, 43.
51 Bellanta, *Larrikins,* 127–54.
52 *Argus,* June 10, 1901, 6 (White Rose Football Club); see also Bellanta, *Larrikins,* 132.
53 David Hickie, *Chow Hayes, Gunman*, Sydney: Angus and Robertson, 1990, 14, 23, 79; see also Bellanta, *Larrikins,* 150.

11 Innocent Criminals

This chapter focuses on the death of a baby which occurred in one of the most lightly populated areas of Australia but gained international notoriety. It started as a tragedy, became understood as a crime and then segued into a different type of offence: one of the most infamous miscarriages of justice in Australian history.[1] The case of Azaria Chamberlain's disappearance and assumed murder had many of the features identified in Chapter 9 as likely to create extraordinary interest in a crime. The fever pitch of the attention and speculation completely diverted people away from the tragic loss which triggered the subsequent events. The glamorising of the assumed crime desensitised people to the plight of victims, with terrible effects on the Chamberlains and their family.

As we come to the end of our investigation of the history of Australian crime, this case of the prosecution and wrongful conviction of Lindy and Michael Chamberlain, people who had not committed any crime, also seeks to destabilise some of the assumptions we have been working with about guilt and innocence. It raises the possibility, indeed the likelihood, that other people we have studied as criminals were also instead victims of false claims, mistaken identity or biases with the criminal justice system.

The Chamberlain case provides an early example of what was assumed to be a crime and the people associated with it being commodified or made into a product.[2] This is commonplace in the twenty-first century, but the badges, posters, t-shirts and tea towels bearing images, cartoons, bumper stickers and slogans related to the Chamberlain case were a first for Australia and were followed by many books, television series, and endless newspaper and magazine articles. The case was also remarkable for attracting interest outside of the country, most notably through the 1988 film *Evil Angels* released as *A Cry in the Dark* in North America. It was an Australian-made film, directed by Fred Schepisi and starred one of the leading American actors of the period, Meryl Streep, who won best actress at the 1989 Cannes Film Festival for her performance. Just as the film *The Story of the Kelly Gang* tends to be used as if it were actual footage of Ned Kelly, *Evil Angels* now stands in for the original events. Items from the film have been taken into the collection of the National Museum of Australia, along with artefacts from the Chamberlain

DOI: 10.4324/9781003273561-12

family, including several items of Azaria and Lindy's clothing and their yellow 1977 LX Holden Torana V8 hatchback, which played a key role in the unfolding events.[3]

One element the film portrays well is the high level of interest in the case at the time, with scenes set in homes, businesses and restaurants around the country with people debating the facts of the case and giving their strongly held, but often poorly based, opinions about it. The popularity of the film is one of the signs of the ongoing interest in the Chamberlain case. The line delivered by Streep "The dingo's got my baby" has been reused in other popular culture productions from the *Simpsons* to *Seinfeld.* When made, 8 years after Azaria's disappearance, the film was somewhat controversial because it portrayed the events as a miscarriage of justice when many Australians were still persuaded that the Chamberlains were guilty.

Even without these fictional portrayals, because it occurred in the more recent past, there is a huge amount of surviving evidence about this case, including documents, images, film and audio generated at the time and accounts produced by those involved since then, led by Lindy Chamberlain herself. The news of the disappearance of Azaria Chamberlain came to public attention on 18 August 1980. In the first radio reports, listeners were already being guided to consider a dingo taking a baby from a tent as shocking and bizarre, even though it was reported that six people had been treated for dingo bites in the previous 2 months at Ayer's Rock, and that another child was known to have been killed by dogs in the Northern Territory.[4] The difficulty of finding the baby, or her remains, in the scrub or at the undulating foot of the Rock was acknowledged. Details that were included from the beginning and became significant in the reception of the case were the Chamberlain's Seventh-day Adventist religion and the name they had given their daughter, Azaria.

The Azaria Chamberlain Case

Before we start to analyse the significance of the Chamberlain case, we need to know what happened, allowing us to separate the sequence of events from the stories that were told about them. In August 1980, the Chamberlain family went on a camping holiday to Uluru in Australia's Northern Territory, taking advantage of Michael's posting as a Seventh Day Adventist pastor in Mount Isa, NSW to see some of the continent's red centre. The Territory was the most lightly populated political division in the country with 120,000 residents in 1.4 million square kilometres and had only gained self-government in 1978. The red sandstone monolith which drew the Chamberlains was then generally known as Ayer's Rock, before it was returned to custodianship of its traditional owners, the A<u>n</u>angu people, in 1985.

Seventh-day Adventism was a small but well-established Christian religion in Australia, having been brought to the continent in the late 1800s from the United States.[5] The name refers to keeping the seventh day, Saturday, as the sabbath or holy day. Seventh-day Adventism is a Bible based faith which regards the body as a temple and so most members are vegetarian and avoid the use of stimulants including coffee, cigarettes and alcohol. They are best known in Australia for their food brand Sanitarium, which makes the nation's bestselling breakfast cereal, Weetbix. The Adventists also run very successful private hospitals.

The Chamberlain family of parents, two young boys and a 9-week-old baby girl drove to Uluru in their 1977 Torana and set up their tent in the camping ground. The Chamberlains engaged in the usual activities of the time, visiting caves and climbing the rock, a controversial practice which was stopped in 2019. Along with other campers, they noticed that dingos were hanging around, looking for bits of food they could grab and run away with, pulling clothes off drying lines and nipping at children.[6] As happened later at Fraser Island, these wild animals had become habituated to the presence of tourists and were not afraid to approach them. Two children had been attacked by dingos at Uluru in the days before the Chamberlains' arrival.

On their second evening, Lindy put Azaria and one of the boys to sleep in the family tent and then returned to the shared cooking area. When the campers gathered there heard a cry, she went back to the tent, where she saw a dingo running off into the scrub surrounding the campground. She realised that Azaria was gone and called for help. Michael and other campers tried to follow the dingo but in the dark it was impossible.

The park rangers and police were summoned, and more organised tracking attempted, with up to 300 people involved. Blood was found in the tent, dingo tracks nearby and drag marks, including a hollowed-out spot with what could have been drops of blood. It was a week before any other concrete evidence was found. This was some of the clothing Azaria had been wearing; the jumpsuit (onesie) stained with blood was found by a tourist on the far side of the Rock, four kilometres from the campground. Being pressured by the media, the Chamberlains made a statement saying that that Azaria's disappearance and presumed death was God's will, in keeping with their beliefs. They sadly returned to Mount Isa.

A coronial inquest was held in December 1980 and heard the Chamberlains' evidence of seeing a dingo, hearing its growl and then finding paw prints and drag marks. The media heavily covered the proceedings and when the findings were broadcast live on television in February 1981 in an attempt to quash the rumours about the Chamberlains that were already circulating, it drew the greatest number of viewers since the moon landing in 1969.[7] The coroner concluded that Azaria had been attacked by a dingo but that a human being had disposed of the body. He said "the death of this baby in an area where previous attacks causing bodily injury had occurred, was too high a price, and a totally unnecessary price, to pay in the cause of conservation" of the dingo as a non-endangered species.[8] In his view, a dingo had taken Azaria, dingos were a dangerous carnivore and they needed to be culled to protect visitors.

The Northern Territory police were not satisfied with this outcome and continued their investigations. Items the Chamberlains had had with them at Uluru were confiscated as were other possessions from their permanent home in the Seventh-day Adventist centre of Coorangbong near Lake Macquarie in New South Wales. The outcome of the first inquest was officially suppressed by the Northern Territory Supreme Court and a fresh inquest ordered. Starting in December 1981, it heard from a world expert in forensic pathology that there was a bloody handprint on the jumpsuit, and that holes in it had the appearance of having been cut with a knife or scissors.[9] Another British forensic biologist was asked to examine the car. She found a spray of a substance which was identified as having the characteristic profile of foetal blood, the blood of a very young child, like Azaria.[10] In the testing process, the samples were destroyed so there was no capacity for the defence to scrutinise them or to retest.

Aided by the forensic report, an alternative explanation for Azaria's disappearance was developed. That was, when Lindy left the cooking area, she had taken Azaria to the family car, held her down in the passenger side footwell and stabbed her to death with a pair of nail scissors, before placing her body in Michael's camera bag, burying it, digging it up, removing its clothing and then reburying it. In this version, Michael was not directly involved in the killing but had covered up for his wife. As Howe argued, "science was successfully paraded as the diviner of truth … [and] overwhelmed the direct or first-hand evidence of the people who were there."[11] The conclusion of a second inquest was that the Chamberlains should face trial for murder and accessory to murder.

At the trial, held in Darwin in September and October 1982, the media were present each day to report on what was said by whom and how the Chamberlains, especially Lindy who was pregnant, dressed, acted and reacted. After a 6-week hearing without a body, a motive or any eyewitnesses and relying heavily on forensic evidence, Lindy was found guilty of murder and given a life sentence with hard labour, while Michael was also found guilty as an accessory but given a suspended sentence so he could look after their two sons.[12] Lindy served time in Darwin's women's prison, while people worked on appeals and challenges to her conviction. Their daughter Kahlia was born after her first month in prison, in November 1982 and two days later Lindy was released on bail pending an appeal. An appeal was made to the Federal Court in February 1983 which was rejected in April, forcing Lindy to return to jail. A further appeal was made to the High Court in Canberra in 1984 and by a vote of 3:2 the conviction was again upheld.

While many people in Australian society were very quick to condemn and demonise Lindy, there were others who saw her conviction as a grave miscarriage of justice. One of her great supporters was Barry Boettcher, Foundation Professor in the Department of Biological Sciences at the University of Newcastle and a specialist in blood and forensic science. He worked with the Chamberlain's legal team from 1982 and helped to demonstrate that the forensic evidence should be re-examined. New investigations led to the purported foetal blood being correctly identified as a sound insulation compound sprayed onto car interiors. In 1984, 131,000 people signed a petition asking the governor general to have the case reopened and the following year, the book *Evil Angels* (the basis for the 1988 film) was published by barrister John Bryson, making a detailed and persuasive case for the innocence of the Chamberlains.

In February 1986, after Lindy had been in jail for 3 years, the knitted jacket (known as a matinee jacket) that Lindy had said Azaria was wearing at the time of her disappearance was found not far from where the jumpsuit had been discovered 6 years earlier. Underscoring the risks of the area, it was located during the search for a missing hiker whose body was found nearby where he had fallen from the rock. The Chamberlain family was notified only after the news appeared on television, and the NT's executive council quickly agreed to release Lindy on remission. Her conviction was not overturned but they chose to remit the rest of her sentence.

A long-term campaign of letter writing led to the establishment of a Royal Commission of Inquiry by the Northern Territory government which heard from 145 witnesses. The tens of thousands of letters sent directly to Lindy are now held in the National Library of Australia in Canberra. Although at the time it was often said that women were Lindy's harshest critics, 90% of the letters were written by women from all over the country, many identifying with her as mothers and expressing their sadness at her situation, their anger at her treatment and their admiration for her, as well as in some cases, remorse for earlier negative assumptions about her.[13] Some women saw Lindy's experience as a cautionary tale – that blaming her as a bad mother was backlash against the improving status of women in that period. The enquiry concluded the case was not sound and after yet another appeal, Lindy and Michael's convictions were quashed in 1988. It took another 5 years for the Chamberlains to receive compensation from the Australian government in the amount to $1.3 million and reimbursement for legal fees. In 1995, a third coroner's inquest was conducted. It returned an open verdict, saying there was not enough evidence of either murder or dingo attack to make a positive finding. Only in 2012, 32 years after the saga had started, did a fourth inquest conclude that a dingo was to blame, what had been dismissed by one of the earlier prosecutors as "a calculated, fanciful lie."

The story continued to evolve outside of these legal processes. New theories continued to come forward and any related event is used to retell the tale once again. When their first coroner, Denis Barritt died in 1997, his obituary was headed "Coroner who found the dingo did it." When a dingo killed a child on Fraser Island in 2001, the Chamberlain case was recalled; and in 2004 a man claimed that he had shot the dingo that killed Azaria and saw her body. In 2017, Michael Chamberlain passed away and the yellow Torana that he had driven to Uluru was put on display at his memorial service. The Chamberlain case is long and complex and although ultimately it was found that no crime was committed, it offers much for historians of crime to unpack about how assumptions are made about guilt and innocence.

Aftermath and Analysis

Considering there were no witnesses, no body and no confession, why were people so willing to condemn Lindy and to a lesser extent Michael for the awful crime of the premeditated murder of their baby girl? This is particularly perplexing because it was never thought of as an act of postnatal depression, despair or desperation like concealment of birth cases or murders of abusive husbands in the nineteenth century. It was portrayed as a crime which had been planned and coolly carried out, for no apparent gain, placing Lindy in the category of a monstrous mother and Michael as an ineffectual man willing to do her bidding.

There is a whole suite of reasons which contributed to the enormous interest in the case and the overall conclusion that there was something suspicious about the Chamberlains and their explanation that a dingo had taken Azaria. People delighted in applying their own incomplete knowledge through what seemed to them to be a logical analysis and ended up at a completely wrong conclusion. Not all of these factors overtly appeared in the charges against the Chamberlains or the court proceedings, but they provide the backdrop to the case, and influenced the opinions of the police, court officials and jurors who were the important decision makers.

For some, first issue was the name "Azaria." It was considered odd in a country of conventional, generally Anglo-derived names. People made up their own definitions of what it meant and the one with the most traction was "sacrifice in the desert." When it became known that Lindy had a sewn a black dress for the baby (now held by the National Museum of Australia), that Michael kept a small coffin in his garage, and that they belonged to religion other than Catholic or the usual protestant denominations, the puzzle solvers concluded that there was a plan to kill Azaria in a ritualistic way. The couple's acceptance of the death of Azaria created resentment amongst members of the public, who expected more denial, even hysterics, at first blaming their Seventh-day Adventist religion's belief in divine intervention and then concluding it meant the Chamberlains had killed their daughter.[14] One theory was that with Adventists' focus on bodily health, the couple could not accept a child who was imperfect, so Azaria needed to be disposed of because she had a disability (she did not). The more accurate explanations, that her name meant gift of god and came from a baby name book, the dress was a party frock in a flamenco style and the coffin was used in anti-smoking education workshops, were disregarded.

The attribution of Azaria's disappearance to the action of a dingo was received by most as unlikely, many as worthy of ridicule and some as evidence of Lindy's evil nature – trying to shift the blame for her own terrible crime to an innocent animal.[15] Australians had been brought up to believe that there were no warm-blooded predators in Australia and only the cold-blooded creatures posed a risk: spiders, snakes, sharks, jellyfish and crocodiles. Most people imagined dingoes as like the dogs they knew as pets, and drawing on their own experience concluded that a wild dog could not commit such an act of betrayal and would not even be physically capable of carrying or dragging a baby, or of opening its jaws far enough to grab and hold the infant's head.

Dingoes were also by reputation cowardly, and it was not believed that one would have willingly been in the camping area or come so close to the tents. People were so sure that a dingo could not have taken Azaria and so disturbed by this possibility that it was the aspect which was most defused by humour. Appalling jokes circulated, ridiculing the idea that "the dingo did it." One was: What would have changed the course of History? A dingo in Bethlehem. Amongst the letters written to Lindy were many from country people who attested to seeing dingoes attacking and killing young livestock and to the measures taken to protect young children from them including placing them in raised vehicles at night rather than in tents on the ground.[16] In later trials, experts on dingo behaviour were called and evidence presented to show that dingoes lived in close proximity to Indigenous peoples and lost their natural timidity when exposed to other groups as well. The biologists used dingo skulls and doll's heads to show that dingoes were physically capable of holding and dragging an infant. More stories of dingo attacks on children came out and more occurred, especially on Fraser Island in Queensland. It was revealed that the Head Ranger at Uluru had been considering a dingo cull before Azaria's disappearance. In spite of all of this scepticism, this was an extraordinary instance of animal agency, in which the act of a dingo had grave repercussions, causing harm to a family, a huge investment of resources in a series of legal actions and deep divisions in Australian society.[17]

As the mother of the victim, Lindy came in for particular scrutiny.[18] Under this surveillance, many concluded that her demeanour was not right. Instead of collapsing in an emotional heap like Graeme Thorne's mother, she was composed and even angry as false allegations and false evidence were used against her. She was outspoken, pragmatic, and to some people, hard. She was not mourning in a way they deemed appropriate. Under cross-examination, she was sharp and difficult. People read this coolness as guilt or self-promotion rather than her individual coping method, stemming from her personality and her faith. When it became clear during the first trial that she was pregnant, she was again condemned, for seeking to replace the baby she had killed, or making a play for sympathy. In the worst interpretations, she was viewed as an anti-mother or a witch who was pure evil.[19] The case allowed people to voice opinions about the proper roles of mothers at a time when traditional gender roles had been challenged by second-wave feminists for more than a decade.

The location at Uluru gave the case a particular charge. The Rock was regarded as a kind of mythical place which at this time was increasingly viewed as a spiritual centre of Australia. Australians have always vacillated between seeing themselves as people of the city or the bush, of the beach or the interior plains, but in the 1980s, with a rising appreciation of Indigenous cultures and the approaching Bicentenary, the red centre was gaining in significance. This gave events an exotic appeal.

It was also an uncertain place in terms of the visible presence of Aboriginal people and their culture. The loss of Azaria in this place echoed settler colonist anxieties about the child lost in the bush, unable to survive its harshness and hidden perils. It raised questions about how Aboriginal and non-Aboriginal Australians would live together in a place where the traditional owners and their beliefs retained authority. There was questioning of the possible implication of the traditional owners in Azaria's disappearance, despite their active involvement in the search, during which trackers located footprints, drag marks and furrows made by the dingo. Rumours circulated that it had been a camp dog that took Azaria, and that locals had hidden her remains.

Adopting a different position, many visitors believed that behaviour considered disrespectful by the A<u>n</u>angu including climbing the Rock and taking away sand or stones would lead to spiritual revenge.[20] In either case, Lindy was irresponsible in exposing her infant to such a place, showing herself to be uncaring and a bad mother.[21] Further, the setting in the Northern Territory had implications for how the case was dealt with. The police and justice systems lacked some of the maturity of other jurisdictions more used to dealing with complicated matters. Eager to protect their growing tourist industry, the Northern Territory government wanted to quash the idea that dingos were dangerous and had a motive for finding the Chamberlains guilty and the dingo innocent.

As with other popularised cases, the lack of closure was an important factor. Although the matinee jacket which Lindy said Azaria had been wearing was eventually found, her body has never been recovered. This led to a line of argument that said she had not actually died, but rather been kidnapped or found and raised by Indigenous people, creating space for even more speculation.

All of these aspects of the case tended to make people assume the Chamberlains were guilty, and this was also the dominant view in the media. In his book about the case, *Evil Angels*, John Bryson asserts that the vast majority of the media assumed the Chamberlains were guilty.[22] *As Michelle Arrow argues in the essay accompanying this chapter, this put an inflection on everything which was reported, guiding readers, viewers and listeners to reach similar conclusions.* Ambitious journalists, wanting to be the one to find the next piece in the puzzle, made the case into a sort of soap opera, with a narrative arc which people could follow day by day. Supporters of the Chamberlains were conscious of this imbalance and set up a Chamberlain

Information Service which produced 15 issues of an *Azaria Newsletter* to try to put an alternative view into circulation.[23] The Chamberlains themselves retained an agent to manage their media appearances when Lindy was released from jail in 1986.

All of these elements gave the Azaria Chamberlain case a very high level of interest and the public a strong sense of who the offenders were. The only problem was that there was no crime committed. The dingo did do it and it was only the wild flights of the human imagination, powered by stereotypes, biased assumptions, vested interests and flawed logic which made possible the belief that the Chamberlains had murdered their daughter. Through this process, what was a very personal and domestic trauma for one family was appropriated as public property. People felt that they had every right to know, gossip, theorise and expound on the fine details of the case and the guilt or innocence of the Chamberlains, while the family had no right to privacy at all, compounding their trauma and leading to the breakdown of the marriage and Lindy moving away from Australia for many years. Since her return, Lindy has worked hard to try to make people understand how harmful this obsession with crime can be, how journalists compete with one another for the front page story, how the opinions of future jurors can be influenced by information leaked by the police, how religious prejudice operates and the effects of a comprehensive invasion of privacy, asking that people pay more attention to facts, popular or not, and less to suppositions and opinions.[24] She set up a website where she can tell the story in her own way. It opens with these words:

> This is the story of a little girl who lived, and breathed, and loved, and was loved. She was part of me. She grew within my body and when she died, part of me died, and nothing will ever alter that fact. This is her story, and mine.
>
> Lindy Chamberlain-Creighton

Closing Thoughts on an Australian Underworld

I chose the Chamberlain case deliberately as the final "crime" in this book to encourage reflection on the other cases treated here. How many of them also involved people who were not guilty but were convenient targets for society and the forces of justice to hold to account for specific crimes? As historians, we need to keep an open mind and critically assess the evidence from the past, reflecting on how race, class, gender, religion, ethnicity and poverty might have operated in channelling people into crime because other options were closed to them, or because they were criminalised by society. As an educated, middle class, white woman, Lindy Chamberlain was of a type who rarely ended up being seen as criminal. That was part of the shocking appeal in her case. How many more people were assumed to be guilty because they did fall easily into the familiar categories, they did look the part, and had to serve their full sentences without anyone writing letters on their behalf or raising money for an appeal?

Another category of innocent criminals is those who offended against laws in place during their lifetimes which have subsequently been changed. We can see these in the many convicts who committed status offences, such as being absent from a Sunday church service, which would not have been punished if they were not serving convicts. Through the nineteenth century, actions were made criminal which had previously been permitted and in many cases are again acceptable. Looking at the *NSW Police Gazette* for just one day in February 1882, we see fines levied on William Somers for bathing in the ocean at Manly during daylight hours, on several young women for loitering on the footway near Circular Quay and a man for driving a cab across a city intersection at more than a walking pace.[25] For these offences, they all faced financial penalties, or imprisonment if they could not pay, and had their names, ages and descriptions published in the *Gazette*. Should they be considered as part of the history of crime in Australia for actions which would now be unremarkable? Actually, yes, because people must be placed in the context of their own times. They knew they were breaking the law and so must be considered as offenders. But they are hardly the stuff of underworlds.

Looking at the end of the period we treated, a wave of decriminalisation was occurring as social values changed through the 1960s and 1970s, bringing pressure for old laws to be set aside. One was the ban on off-track betting, which was addressed by establishing government-run Totalisation Agency Boards (TABs). Feminists called for the decriminalisation of abortion, to give women the right to choose whether they would continue a pregnancy or not. Abortion was made available but not decriminalised for several more decades, starting with Western Australia in 1998. Decriminalising homosexual activity was called for by gay activists from the early 1970s and supported by those who agreed that the state should not interfere with relations between consenting adults. It was achieved first in South Australia, so often a leader in progressive reform in the country, in 1975 and not until 1997 in Tasmania. The government of Tasmania has since apologised to those convicted under its laws and gave them the right to have their criminal records expunged, reversing their criminalisation.[26] Should they be considered part of Australia's criminal history?

The key group in Australia which contains many innocent criminals is Aboriginal and Torres Strait Island peoples. Colonisation, poverty, cultural disruption and prejudice have all contributed to high rates of conviction and imprisonment. Looking at the issue historically, it is clear that the dispossession of Aboriginal people disrupted (but did not displace) their own systems of Law and left them at the mercy of a foreign law that many did not understand. While that law purported to be colour blind, both it and those who enforced and administered it were guided by racist assumptions and an underlying desire to be rid of what they constructed as the Aboriginal problem. Criminalisation was not just an individual matter but a tool of the ongoing colonial project which resulted in Aboriginal people going from societies which had no need of prisons to amongst the most incarcerated people on earth in just over two centuries. A Royal Commission into Black Deaths in Custody brought attention to the issue in 1991 but had little impact on incarceration rates or deaths. The criminalising of Aboriginal people remains an issue requiring attention at all levels and will not be resolved without genuine reconciliation.

In fact, very few of the people encountered in this book could be considered part of a criminal underworld, although their passing associations with crime might make it seem as though they were. If pressed, arguments could be made that Ned Kelly, Kate Leigh and the Razor Gangs, the 'Ndrangheta, Jim Smith and Patrick Brady in the Shark Arm case and the outlaw motorcycle clubs were underworld figures. But even so, career criminals like these are responsible for only a limited component of the history of crime in Australia. Relinquishing the idea of an Australian underworld in no way diminishes the importance of crime in our history. Crimes which were an unusual occurrence in a person's life, whether caused by passion, greed or fear, as quick responses to opportunity or long delayed acts of desperation, and the responses to them, are rich sources for historians seeking to understand the societies in which they occurred.

Suggested Readings

Craik, Jennifer. "The Azaria Chamberlain Case and Questions of Infanticide." *Australian Journal of Cultural Studies* 4, no. 2 (1987): 123–51.

Howe, Adrian. *Lindy Chamberlain Revisited: A 25th Anniversary Retrospective*. Sydney: Southwood Press, 2005.

Sanders, Noel. "Azaria Chamberlain and Popular Culture." Graeme Turner, ed. *Nation, Culture, Text: Australian Cultural and Media Studies*. London: Routledge, 1993.

Staines, Deborah, Michelle Arrow and Katherine Biber, eds. *The Chamberlain Case: Nation, Law, Memory*. Melbourne: Australian Scholarly Publishing, 2009.

Wood, Briar. "The Trials of Motherhood: The Case of Azaria and Lindy Chamberlain." *Moving Targets: Women, Murder and Representation*. Berkeley: University of California Press, 1994.

ESSAY: THE MEDIA VERSUS LINDY CHAMBERLAIN

Michelle Arrow

A couple of years ago I was invited to do an interview about the Chamberlain case for a true crime podcast. I declined, because the disappearance of Azaria Chamberlain was not a "true crime" but Australia's most notorious miscarriage of justice. This framing remains common: *Evil Angels*, John Bryson's book about the case, is still found in the "true crime" section of Australian book shops.[27] Yet the crime at the heart of the Chamberlain case was the persecution of the Chamberlains themselves: any attempt to understand this must contend with the media's treatment of the case.

The Chamberlain's wrongful conviction was largely attributed to the prosecution's reliance on flawed forensic science.[28] Yet it is clear that the miscarriage of justice was also facilitated by the media, creating a deeply prejudicial atmosphere around the Chamberlains. As activist Norman Young noted, "well before either the coronial inquests or the trial the Chamberlains were found guilty in the higher court of public opinion."[29] This "court" was a mediated public sphere, comprised of newspaper headlines, talkback radio, press photographs and television news, reporting the story of the Chamberlains with a frenzied intensity.

The mass media were crucial to constructing the Chamberlain case as a "public" event.[30] While media interest in the case was muted immediately after Azaria's disappearance, the Chamberlains quickly attracted press attention for their religiosity (which sparked bizarre rumours about Azaria having been sacrificed) and their willingness to speak publicly about their loss.[31] The media's coverage was disproportionate: the findings of the first coronial inquest were the first to be televised live, watched by millions.[32] Journalists stoked public prejudices: many did not believe that a dingo could take a baby, fuelling suspicion about Azaria's possible murder. Many reporters were overly credulous about the forensic evidence, and a number of them worked with police to advance the prosecution agenda.[33] The media quickly commodified the case: Chamberlain stories sold huge numbers of newspapers and magazines and there was intense bidding for leads.[34] After Lindy was released from prison in 1986, media interest intensified, and the Chamberlains hired celebrity agent Harry M. Miller to manage their media appearances. The significant fees he secured for interviews were a landmark example of chequebook journalism in Australia.[35] Each subsequent development in the case generated national and international media coverage.

Perhaps most pernicious was the ways that the male-dominated news media appraised Lindy Chamberlain through a gendered, sexist lens.[36] Lindy's attractive appearance and outspoken directness transgressed conventions of both femininity and motherhood. Kerryn Goldsworthy suggested that women, in particular "were convinced of her guilt chiefly on the grounds of what they saw as her flaunting [...] her tanned shoulders and her large wardrobe. Their logic was that a woman interested in looking attractive at such a time must be a bad woman and everyone knows that a bad woman cannot be a good mother."[37] During her trial, when she was heavily pregnant and not speaking to the media, Lindy's stony stoicism was perceived as "hardness." She remained a divisive figure long after her release from prison.

The media's manipulative treatment of Lindy Chamberlain was not always visible to the general public at the time, though it has been subsequently examined by Bryson's *Evil Angels*, the 1988 film of the same name, and the 2004 mini-series *Through My Eyes*.[38] Most recently, the 2021 documentary *Lindy Chamberlain: The True Story* scrutinised the media's treatment of the Chamberlains. One particular incident is instructive. Not long after Azaria died, Lindy was interviewed by a television journalist who showed her a photo of her daughter's bloodied jumpsuit. He asked her: why are Azaria's clothes relatively intact if she was taken by a dingo? Lindy responded:

> If you've ever seen a dingo eat, there'd be no difficulty at all. Because if you watch them eat the carcass of a cow, or something like that, they don't eat the skin. They use their feet like hands and pull back the skin as they go, and they'll just peel it like an orange.

This response became notorious, and highly prejudicial. Yet when the full recording later emerged during the Morling Royal Commission, it was apparent that Lindy had burst into tears on takes one and two. The infamous answer was captured on the seventh take.[39]

We don't know who made the decision to use the seventh take, rather than the second one. But it is clear that these kinds of choices had a devastating effect on the Chamberlain family. The slow accretion of moments like this, which nurtured community prejudice about Lindy as a "cold" mother and likely murderer, played a crucial role in this tragic case. It is also likely that similar decisions continue to be made in Australian newsrooms every day, with similarly devastating effects. The Chamberlains suffered enormously because they did not always follow the narrow social scripts afforded to grieving parents or "good" mothers. Sadly, this is a lesson that both journalists and the public need to learn and relearn, over and over again.

PRIMARY SOURCE: AZARIA CHAMBERLAIN'S MATINÉE JACKET, 1980

This knitted matinée jacket became a key piece of evidence through its absence. Lindy Chamberlain stated that Azaria had been wearing a jacket over her jumpsuit when she was taken by the dingo, but when only the jumpsuit and nappy were found, prosecutors were able to cast doubt over other aspects of her testimony. The state of the bloodied and bitten jumpsuit played a central role in the forensic case against the Chamberlains. When the matinée jacket was found 6 years later, it also had a powerful impact, leading to Lindy's release from jail and ultimately, advancing the long process of persuading the public and the courts of the Chamberlains' innocence. This photograph of the delicate but soiled and torn jacket captures the transformation which occurs when ordinary items become evidence of crime.[40] It is now held by the National Museum of Australia along with the labelled envelopes and evidence bag in which it was placed during the Royal Commission of Inquiry into Chamberlain Convictions (1987).[41]

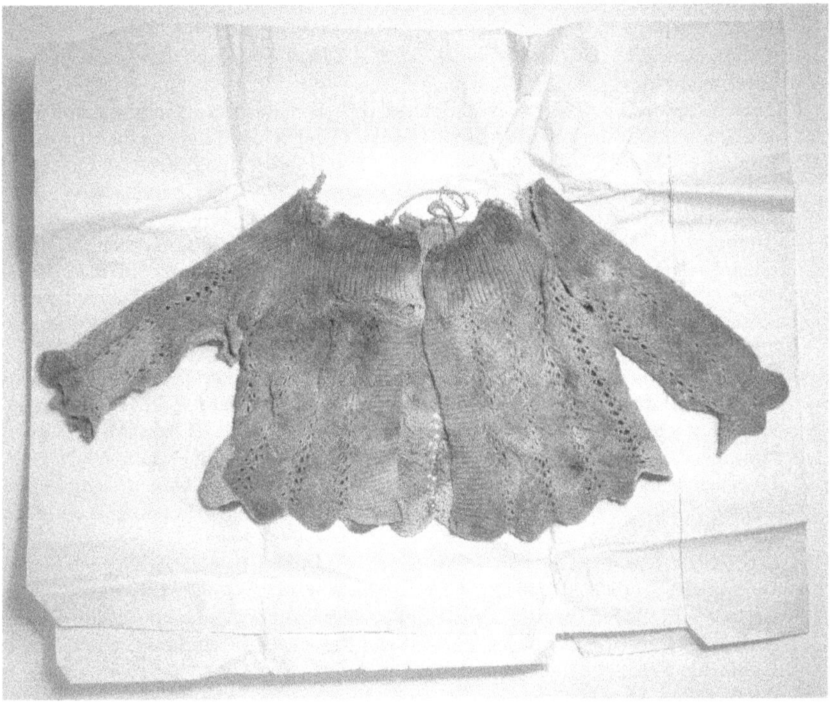

Figure 11.1 Knitted matinée jacket worn by Azaria Chamberlain on the night of her disappearance, 17 August 1980.

Source: National Museum of Australia. Lindy Chamberlain-Creighton collection no. 5, MA23131426. Used with the kind permission of the Chamberlain family.

Notes

1 Adrian Howe, *Lindy Chamberlain Revisited: A 25th Anniversary Retrospective*, Sydney: Southwood Press, 2005, 1.
2 This is explored by Belinda Middleweek in "Deviant Divas: Lindy Chamberlain and Schapelle Corby and the Case for a New Category of Celebrity for Criminally Implicated Women," *Crime Media Culture* 13, no. 1 (2017): 85–105.
3 Yellow 1977 LX Holden Torana V8 hatchback, Dr Michael Chamberlain Collection, National Museum of Australia, Object number, 2013.0068.0004 E.
4 A radio news report of the event broadcast on 18 August 1980 is available at Lindy Chamberlain-Creighton, Recordings, https://lindychamberlain.com/recordings/ (accessed June 2, 2022).
5 Alwyn P. Salom, ed. *The Seventh-day Adventist Church in Australia*. Melbourne: Christian Research Association, 2002.
6 Judith West, interviewed by Glen Williams, "I was there," *Sunday Life!* (date unknown), 35; and The Trial Transcript in Crown v Lindy and Michael Chamberlain ("The Dingo Trial"): Selected Excerpts, Famous Trials, https://www.famous-trials.com/dingo/462-transcript (accessed 16 September 2022)
7 Noel Sanders, "Azaria Chamberlain and Popular Culture," Graeme Turner, ed. *Nation, Culture, Text: Australian Cultural and Media Studies*, London: Routledge, 1993, 88.
8 Quoted by Jennifer Craik in "The Azaria Chamberlain Case and Questions of Infanticide," *Australian Journal of Cultural Studies* 4, no. 2 (1987): 137.
9 Briar Wood, "The Trials of Motherhood: The Case of Azaria and Lindy Chamberlain," *Moving Targets: Women, Murder and Representation*, Berkeley: University of California Press, 1994, 65.
10 Craik, "The Azaria Chamberlain Case," 139–40.
11 Howe, *The Chamberlain Case Revisited*, 273.
12 Wood, "The Trials of Motherhood," 67.
13 Howe, *Lindy Chamberlain Revisited*, Ch. 1 "Marginalised Voices: The Silent Majority."
14 Craik, "The Azaria Chamberlain Case and Questions of Infanticide," 132.
15 Julie Marcus, "Prisoner of Discourse: The Dingo, the Dog and the Baby" [1989], Adrian Howe, ed. *Lindy Chamberlain Revisited: A Twenty-Five Anniversary Retrospective*, Sydney: LHR Press, 2005, 203.
16 Howe, *Lindy Chamberlain Revisited*, 86–91.
17 Wood, "The Trials of Motherhood," 93.
18 This is explored by Wood in "The Trials of Motherhood."
19 Dianne Johnson, "From Fairy to Witch: Imagery and Myth in the Azaria Case," *Australian Journal of Cultural Studies* 2, no. 2 (1984).
20 Anne Barker, Tourists return rocks stolen from Uluru, 20 April 2004, https://www.abc.net.au/worldtoday/content/2004/s1091138.htm (accessed 7 January 2022).
21 Marcus, "Prisoner of Discourse," 205.
22 John Bryson, *Evil Angels* [1985], Melbourne: Penguin, 1988.
23 Middleweek, "Deviant Divas," 92.
24 Lindy Chamberlain-Creighton, "Reflections: A Real Kick in the Guts," Deborah Staines, Michelle Arrow and Katherine Biber, eds. *The Chamberlain Case: Nation, Law, Memory*, Melbourne: Australian Scholarly Publishing, 2009, 213–17.
25 "Offences Not Otherwise Described," *New South Wales Police Gazette and Weekly Record of Crime* 6 (8 February 1882), 50.
26 "Homosexual convictions to be expunged by Tasmanian Government," ABC Premium News, Sydney, 17 December 2015.
27 Bryson's book was categorised as "true crime" by the online bookseller Booktopia as recently as January 2022. John Bryson, *Evil Angels Melbourne: Viking*, 1985.

28 Katherine Biber, "Evidence in the Museum: Curating a Miscarriage of Justice," *Theoretical Criminology* 22, no. 4 (2018): 506.
29 Norman H. Young, "Against the Odds: The Fight to Free Lindy Chamberlain," Staines et al., eds. *The Chamberlain Case: Nation, Law, Memory*, Melbourne: Australian Scholarly Publishing, 2009, 172.
30 Deborah Staines, "A Legal Trauma, A Public Trauma: Lindy Chamberlain and the Chamberlain Case," in Staines et al., *The Chamberlain Case*, 200.
31 Fay Anderson, "'Photographing Lindy': Australian Press Photography and the Chamberlain Case, 1980–2012," *Media International Australia* 162, no. 1 (2017): 12.
32 Belinda Middleweek, "Defiant Divas: Lindy Chamberlain and Schapelle Corby and the Case for a New Category of Celebrity for Criminally Implicated Women," *Crime, Media, Culture* 13, no. 1 (2017): 91.
33 John Bryson, "Against the Tactician," in Staines et al., *The Chamberlain Case*, 271–283.
34 Middleweek, "Defiant Divas," 91–2.
35 Emily Watkins, "Australia's Most Memorable Cases of Chequebook Journalism," *Crikey* 29 May 2018, https://www.crikey.com.au/2018/05/29/australias-most-memorable-cases-of-chequebook-journalism (accessed 20 January 2022).
36 Anderson, "Photographing Lindy," 10.
37 Kerryn Goldsworthy, "Martyr to her Sex," in Staines et al., *The Chamberlain Case*, 37.
38 Michelle Arrow, "'I Can Only Go on the Evidence of My Own Eyes': Witnessing the Chamberlain Case on Film and Television," in Staines et al., *The Chamberlain Case*, 240–252.
39 Mark Joffe, *Lindy Chamberlain: The True Story*, Sydney: Easy Tiger Productions, 2020.
40 For more consideration of this process, listen to the History Lab, Season 1, Episode 1: Lindy Chamberlain and the afterlife of evidence, 30 May 2018, https://historylab.net/s1ep1-lindy-chamberlain/ (accessed 7 June 2022).
41 Report of the Commissioner the Hon. Mr. Justice T.R. Morling, Royal Commission of Inquiry into Chamberlain Convictions, Canberra: Government Printer, 1987. https://nla.gov.au/nla.obj-2085028529/view?partId=nla.obj-2086182377 (accessed 24 June 2022).

12 Researching the History of Crime in Australia

Having reached the final chapter in this book, and referred to its endnotes as you went, you will have some sense of the types of sources that underpin it. In our research, the authors of the essays and I drew upon a wide range of sources both from the time when the crimes occurred and from other scholars who have examined those crimes in the years that followed. This chapter will offer guidance for how you can conduct your own research into the history of crime in Australia.

I have illustrated this chapter with the example of researching the disappearance of the Beaumont children in Adelaide on Australia Day, 1966.[1] Although the case has never been resolved, the assumption is that, while on a visit to the city's Glenelg Beach, the three children, Jane, Arnna and Grant, aged 9, 7 and 4, were abducted and murdered. Extensive police investigations found witnesses who had seen the children at a park and a cake shop in Glenelg and reported that they had been seen in the company of a tall blonde-haired young man.[2] Nothing further of any substance could be discovered although investigations extended across the country, included bringing in a Dutch clairvoyant, and continue up to the present day.[3] Their parents' willingness to allow the children to travel independently from their home in Somerton Park to the beach by bus was not unusual at the time, but their disappearance led to criticism that they should have been more carefully supervised as well as concern that what had been a safe and orderly city had become dangerous. These fears spread from parents to children, from Adelaide to other cities and other beaches.[4] In investigating the development of Adelaide's sinister (and false) reputation as strongly linked with violent crime, Matthew W. Rofe identifies the disappearance of the Beaumont children as the second in a series of 6 criminal episodes including abduction, rape and murder in and around Adelaide which left at least 26 people dead, 6 of them children, between 1958 and 1999.[5] A $1,000,000 reward is still on offer by the Government of South Australia for information and assistance that leads to a conviction for the suspected murders of the Beaumont children, or the recovery of their remains.[6]

DOI: 10.4324/9781003273561-13

Choosing a Topic

The first step in any research project is to decide what the general topic of the research will be, guided by your reason for undertaking the research. Are you interested in crime in a particular geographical area or timeframe? In a specific crime or criminal, or a type of crime more generally? In how crime reflects or informs other issues in Australian history? If you are writing an honours thesis, undertaking background research for a novel, developing an episode for a podcast, looking for content for a walking tour or just curious about past crime, you will have a lot of freedom to decide on what you want to investigate. If you are preparing an assignment for an undergraduate course and have to address a set question, some of these decisions will already have been made for you, but you will still have the opportunity to decide on exactly what approach you will take to your chosen question.

The Beaumont Children Project

My constraints in choosing a sample research topic were that it should be a crime not yet discussed in this book but fit within the broad timeframe of Australian crime up to 1980. In addition, choosing a crime which occurred in South Australia enabled me to extend a treatment which has focused on the country's southeast and choosing a crime I knew little about allowed me to expand my knowledge of Australian crime. It was also one about which I was curious and wanted to know more. Having an underlying interest in your research topic is always important, as it makes the work personally as well as academically rewarding.

Secondary Research

As with all history research, once you have decided on the topic, the next step is to see what others have already written about it. This type of research is called secondary research (even though I suggest that you do it first!). It is secondary in the sense that the sources are at one remove from the events being researched. The secondary sources of interest to you are those produced by historians and other closely aligned scholars, including criminologists, sociologists, geographers, legal scholars and archaeologists. Secondary sources provide you with the background you need to see your specific case in context. Without them, it is easy to think that your case is wonderfully unique and terribly interesting, based only on its individual characteristics. With secondary sources, you can start to see what you are investigating as part of a larger whole. By building up a good understanding of other related or similar cases, you can make judgments about what was really special about yours, or indeed, what made it typical or representative. In addition, you may find that someone else has already undertaken exactly the same study you planned to do. Our overall understanding of history only advances if each person adds to what is known and understood, rather than just repeating what others have already found.

Your initial instinct to start researching might be to enter some keywords into a search engine and see what turns up. However, since the internet caters to a very broad and diverse audience, the types of accounts of crime you will find there vary greatly in quality. Unless they have been through of process of external checking, we do not know on what they are based or how accurate they are. Even more authoritative sites, such as the web pages of public museums and libraries, usually offer only a short overview of a topic for a general readership which gives little indication of the sources used to inform the account. They are very useful as a starting point, but further research needs to be done.

That deeper research is best undertaken using specialist search tools provided by school and university libraries, the various Australian state libraries and the National Library of Australia. These include their own catalogues and the databases to which they provide access, such as Informit (for material published in Australia) and Historical Abstracts (for works of history published internationally). Where limits can be put in place, search for both books and shorter works like refereed journal articles and chapters, but exclude non-scholarly sources like newspaper and magazine articles. While newspaper reporting of crimes, investigations and prosecutions *as they occur* is of interest as primary sources, journalists are not historians and their writing about past events should not be used as a foundation for scholarly history. A simple way to remove sources which do not follow scholarly protocols is limiting your search to peer-reviewed material.

Unless the case you are interested in is very well known, you might not find anything specifically treating it. In that case, broaden your focus to the same type of crime in the period and to more general histories of the era. When doing so, ensure that the sources you locate treat crime in Australia. Although baby farming in Britain or kidnapping in the United States might have some relevance for the same crimes in Australia, they took place within different societies and different legal systems and can only be used as points of comparison. Where there are many sources related to your topic, give preference to those published more recently but do not dismiss older sources if they take a perspective that newer work does not cover.

When you have decided on the secondary sources which look to be suitable as the foundation for your history, it is time to start reading them critically. This does not mean looking to find fault with them, but actively engaging with them as you read. The following questions can be helpful to keep in mind:

- Who is the author? What authority do they have to write about this topic? You should be able to find the author online and see their qualifications and other publications, giving you a sense of whether they have developed expertise in this field (and often turning up other useful sources they have written).

- What type of source is it? Who is the intended audience?
- When was it written? Was it published by a reputable outlet like a university press or a scholarly journal?
- What is the main argument? What does the author say about the topic and how do they present their interpretation of it?
- On what sources is the book or article based? Are assertions backed up with evidence?

Active reading of secondary sources will give you confidence that you understand what is already known about the topic and how people have approached it. As you become more familiar with the topic, you should also start to develop your own research questions that will enable you to take a fresh approach and add to what is known. You might think that as a beginning historian, it is beyond your capacity to shed new light on a well-treated topic. However, everyone brings their own individual perspective and evidence unavailable when earlier research was done might now be accessible to you. While making an entirely original contribution is only required at the doctoral degree level, originality and insight are rewarded at every level of historical endeavour. You might just pick up on something that no one else had yet considered.

The Beaumont Children Project

For my project on the Beaumont children, I started the secondary research with my own university's online library catalogue. Since this is one of the popularised cases which has never been resolved, much has been written about it. Using the search term "Beaumont children" (enclosed in quotation marks so only that exact phrase was captured) quickly brought up almost 1500 results. Fortunately, I could easily limit my search by excluding all newspaper articles. This reduced the list to just 30 books, book chapters and journal articles. I went through these sources and discarded those that only make passing reference to the case, are sensationalised or true crime accounts, or from other fields, such as studies of fictional works about missing children. This created a manageable set of sources on this crime which I saved in a Word folder created for this project. Look back to the endnotes for the section of this chapter where I introduced the case to see some of these sources. Broadening the focus, I also looked for and read histories of Adelaide in the 1960s and other instances of child disappearance and abduction which took place at that time.

From this secondary research, I was able to develop a more precise topic and research questions. Scholars studying the disappearance of the Beaumont children argue that, like the Thorne kidnapping, it was understood at the time as signalling a loss of innocence in Australian society particularly as it seems to have involved abduction. Other scholars have already investigated how this impacted ideas about "stranger danger" and increasing concern to limit children's freedom of movement within their communities. I wondered about a longer history of abduction in South Australia and whether there really was something new occurring.

These thoughts sent me back to the databases with a new focus on abduction. This is the nature of research. It is what is called an iterative process. As you read and develop better understandings, further, more refined questions develop which need to be pursued to reach further insights. This is one of many reasons why plenty of time needs to be allocated for research projects. Those done at the last minute will not allow for this extended research and often end up being superficial and unoriginal because they do not take into account what is already known on a topic.

Primary Research

Once you have a good grasp of the relevant secondary literature and have refined your research topic, it is time to get into that fascinating primary material. Primary refers to evidence that was generated at or near the time when the events occurred. For historians of crime, the most reliable forms of primary evidence are those created in the process of committing or responding to the crime: a ransom note, a court transcript, a murder weapon. The next in rank, and much more common, are those which report on what happened. This could be an eyewitness account, a crime scene photograph or a police record. Notice that primary evidence is much broader than just written sources, although they will likely tend to predominate. Historians of crime also draw upon photographs, view material objects and even walk through landscapes (including cityscapes) to help them understand the crimes they are studying.

Perhaps the most accessible form of primary evidence for researching the history of crime in Australia is the Trove database hosted by the National Library of Australia. Relevant categories include newspapers and government gazettes; images, maps and artefacts; and diaries, letters and archives. Newspapers offer the greatest amount of coverage with crime included in almost every issue. In the nineteenth century, accounts of court proceedings even for minor cases were often very detailed, providing easily access to information about crimes and offenders. In terms of reporting crime as news, historians need to be mindful of the biases that infuse journalistic accounts of crime, as has been explored in this book with regard to the popular crimes and Lindy Chamberlain. Like other sources, newspapers must be read critically and with an understanding of their editorial policies, ownership and audiences. Government gazettes are a very valuable resources for the crime historian as they were designed to report the activities of government including changes to the legal system and contain reports on specific crimes as well as crime statistics.

Not everything can be found via Trove. For reasons of copyright, most newspapers do not appear in Trove after 1954 and there can be a gap until the mid-1980s when other online databases like Access Australia (Newsbank) commence coverage. Ask your librarian about access to any databases which might fill in this period. There are other primary sources held in institutional (universities, businesses, churches), local, state and national libraries, archives and museums. A good place to start your research into these sources is the online computer catalogue of the state archives (or public records office) of the colony or state in which the crime you are researching took place. Some of these archives, libraries and museums field many queries about the history of crime and have developed guides to the crime-related records in their collections. These include the Guide to Crime at NSW State Archives; the Justice, Crime and Law research topic guide at the Public Record Office Victoria which directs users to criminal trial briefs, capital files, inquests and prison registers; and the Queensland State Archives information on courts, which includes guides to murder records and criminal depositions. Libraries Tasmania makes available online Lower Court records up to 1900, Supreme Court records 1874–1928 and registers of Crown Law Criminal Cases 1853–1858.

Once you have located the primary sources, as for secondary sources, you need to be thinking critically as you read, view or listen to them.

- Who created the document, image, object or (for oral history) recording?
- When and where was it created?
- What type or form is it (e.g. newspaper, memoir)?
- Why was it created (for what purpose)?
- Who was the intended audience? How would its original audience have understood it?
- What can we learn from this source? Go beyond just the information it contains to consider the language, what it reveals about the author's attitudes and experience, what it suggests about the expectations of the intended audience?
- Is the source supported or contradicted by other sources you have consulted, either primary or secondary? How can you account for this? Does it relate to authorship or audience, for example?

Until recently, historians had to organise our own encounters with primary sources individually and they took place in the quiet of a library or archives reading room. The revolution of digitisation of records has transformed access to primary sources but also how they can be used. Large projects have set up freely available databases which enable new types of analysis to be undertaken. *Michael Kilmister discusses some of these crime-related digital archives in his essay, offering advice on their strengths and drawing attention to some limitations.*

Locating and reading, viewing or listening to primary evidence is the most exciting part of researching the history of crime, and it can be quite addictive. You might need to set yourself some limits on how much time you will spend on this, and this will depend on the scale of the project you are undertaking.

The Beaumont Children Project

For my project on the Beaumont children, I thought about what I wanted from the primary sources. Because the events of the case are already well known, I did not need to try to follow them through the newspapers. What I did want to know was about how novel this case was, assuming it began as an abduction of the children and ended in their murder. For an overview of abduction in South Australia, I used the Prosecution Project database, which showed that there had been 25 abduction cases prosecuted in the state between 1847 and 1942. Knowing about the response to the Graeme Thorne kidnapping with its novel attempt to secure a ransom, I wondered what made these abductions different and less shocking to contemporaries.

By looking at newspaper coverage of the cases using the Trove newspaper database, I found that most of these related to young women and girls willingly leaving home with older men without their parents' permission. In 1929, for example, 15-year-old Lena Clark was taken out of the state by Allan Bickerton Brindley and it was her parents who sought to have him prosecuted.[7] The charge in most of the cases was abduction of a female under 18 (or 16) years of age with intent to have carnal knowledge. Abduction was also the charge in a 1942 case in which Mary Ann McGuffie took her own daughter from her parents-in-law who had legal custody of the girl.[8] These early findings suggest that abduction was not a new crime in South Australia in 1966, but that the disappearance of the Beaumont children was not like these past offences, where the victim and perpetrator were known to one another. Abduction of young children who were unknown to the offender was a departure.

This sent me back to do more research, to see whether there were earlier instances prosecuted not as abduction, but as child stealing, rape or murder. Finding a case in 1953, in which a 4-year-old boy was lured away by a 29-year-old man while on an early evening walk to a neighbourhood fish shop with another child of the same age suggest this was the case.[9] The charges laid were child stealing and indecent assault. Of course, one case is not a sufficient basis for an argument, so the iterative process of research, into both primary and secondary sources, continues.

Putting It All Together

Having familiarised yourself with the topic and its context through secondary research and developed an in-depth knowledge through primary research, it is time to think about how you will write (or talk) about the topic. You might want to tell the story of the crime from start to finish. This is known as a narrative history and is the form that will hold the greatest appeal to a broad audience. If you are writing for a university course, this narrative history will need to be present in your work, but it will not be enough to meet the requirements of your assignment. To do that you will need to analyse your findings and draw out the larger insights they inform. Your course convenor will provide you with a guide to preparing your assignment according to disciplinary conventions.

The history of crime in Australia is a growing field with an increasing audience. I hope that the suggestions for undertaking research made here will make readers feel confident about how to embark on researching their own contribution to it. History can be imagined as like a jigsaw puzzle, with each individual project being a single piece. Each foray into crime history fills in one small element of the overall picture but it only makes a useful contribution if it connects with the pieces all around it. When designing your projects, ensure that they do not stand apart from the big picture, but link in with what others have already investigated, whether to challenge or to further strengthen current understandings.

ESSAY: USING DIGITAL ARCHIVES OF CRIMES AND CRIMINALS

Michael Kilmister

Digitised archives have radically changed the way we investigate criminal pasts. The swift expansion of digitally available court records, newspapers and other archival material related to law and crime – and digital tools for handling and interpreting that data – enables different research questions and offers new ways of answering those questions. This essay will encourage you to explore this emerging research frontier. The emphasis here will be on freely accessible digital repositories and resources created by government agencies like museums and libraries, and by grant-funded research teams, rather than pay-to-use services. While digitisation is opening up exciting research possibilities, there are potential pitfalls.

Sources on the history of crime in Australia have been the focus of several digitisation initiatives, at least in part due to the ubiquity of criminal activity and its copious documentation by legal agencies in both Australia and the United Kingdom. The penal origins of most Australasian colonies have meant that relevant criminal justice records were generated beyond their borders; for the modern student of crime history, digitisation has dramatically improved access to these geographically dispersed archives.[10] The *Old Bailey Online* and *Digital Panopticon* are projects that have transported the records of the metropole to the periphery.[11] The former is an open-access searchable database of almost 200,000 criminal trials held at London's central criminal court; the latter amalgamates 50 datasets relating to the lives of 90,000 convicts sentenced to transportation at the Old Bailey. Apart from expediting research, the bridging of overlapping datasets represented by these two international projects enables innovative kinds of historical inquiry, including data mining and distant reading techniques to identify word and topic frequency patterns in texts like court proceedings or convict records.[12]

While large-scale digitisation can reveal powerful insights into groups of offenders across time and place,[13] they can equally be used to construct a narrative of an individual offender's journey through the judicial system.[14] Digitised databases can also aid in the investigation of a variety of topic areas outside crime history, including gender and social histories. Indeed, *Founders and Survivors*, a database that traces the lives of Tasmanian convicts and their families, is one project that researchers are using to construct a picture of topics like intergenerational health and mortality.[15]

Another Australian-centric project in this space is the *Prosecution Project*.[16] Its creators have digitised 150 years of criminal trials from courts around the nation, enabling comparative and longitudinal investigations of the prosecution process and outcomes down to variables such as place of offence and sex of offender.[17] The *Prosecution Project* – like the *Digital Panopticon* – can also visualise search results in diagrams and charts. Other digital archives have melded document databases with mapping tools to create spatial visualisations. *Convict Landscapes*, for example, has harvested location data from convict records to distribute across an interactive map of Port Arthur 1830–1877, showing where and when offences were committed and who did the offending.[18] These kinds of visual tools contextualise documents, enhance comparative analyses and invite research questions that interrogate the geography of crime.[19]

While digitisation has made research more convenient, making meaning out of potentially tens of thousands of documents unearthed in searches and harnessing them to answer a research question might appear an intimidating prospect. Recognising this, archives usually publish user-friendly guides to get you started or to contextualise the datasets. For example, *Old Bailey Online* provides historical background of the court and its proceedings, suggestions for further reading, and help on search methodologies, while NSW State Archives and Records has a webinar library for navigating their collections.[20] Large and complex datasets also create a demand for the research community to become involved with curation and documentation. Teams behind digital projects often advertise for volunteers to transcribe data, and others rely on their userbase to correct errors and tag documents to make them findable. As research technologies become increasingly sophisticated or applied, becoming familiar working with digital data – including engaging with its advantages and problems – will only benefit you and the discipline.[21]

The depth and breadth of online archives and associated research tools will inspire, but they are not without their shortcomings. The projects discussed here omit data or have limits based on their curation, meaning our analyses will be incomplete if we rely on just one resource alone. As scholars closest to these projects have suggested, the crime records of regions, centres, and time periods not captured by high-profile repositories like *Old Bailey Online* are at risk of being neglected.[22] We can avoid pitfalls by always taking the time to critically analyse findings from the digital data in the light of the scholarly literature, and being careful to frame research questions as problems that can be solved by more than one tool or method. By remaining open to exploring all sources of archival material, we might stumble upon undigitised materials or ask new questions of existing data, which can, in turn, act as a springboard for new digital collections or research that will inspire future crime historians.

Notes

1 Two of several true crime accounts of this case are Alan Whiticker, *Searching for the Beaumont Children: Australia's Most Famous Unsolved Mystery*, Milton, Qld.: John Wiley & Sons, 2006; and Alan Whiticker and Stuart Mullins, *The Satin Man: Uncovering the Mystery of the Missing Beaumont Children*, Sydney: New Holland, 2013.

2 Beth Spencer, "Who's Watching the Children? The Beaumont Case Revisited," *Southerly* 61, no. 2 (2001): 138.

3 Victoria Berezowski, Xanthé Mallett, Justin Ellis and Ian Moffat, "Using Ground Penetrating Radar and Resistivity Methods to Locate Unmarked Graves: A Review," *Remote Sensing* 13, no. 2880 (2021): 17.

4 Elizabeth Ellison, "Badland Beach: The Australian Beach as a Site of Cultural Remembering," *International Journal of Media and Cultural Politics*, 12, no. 1 (2016): 122.

5 Matthew W. Rofe, "The City of Corpses? Contested urban identity and the stigma of crime in Adelaide, South Australia," *Landscape Research*, 41, no. 8 (2016), Table 1.

6 Beaumont Children, Crimestoppers, https://crimestopperssa.com.au/case/beaumont-children/ (accessed 4 June 2022).

7 "Pleads Guilty to Abduction," *Truth*, 20 October 1929, 1.

8 "Supreme," *Advertiser* (Adelaide), 30 January 1942, 12.

9 "Child-stealing in City Alleged," *News* (Adelaide), 21 February 1953, 1.

10 Barry Godfrey, et al., "Crime, Penal Transportation, and Digital Methodologies," *Journal of World History* 32, no. 2 (2021): 243.

11 See: Tim Hitchcock, Robert Shoemaker, Clive Emsley, Sharon Howard and Jamie McLaughlin, et al., *The Old Bailey Proceedings Online, 1674–1913* (accessed 29 January 2022), https://www.oldbaileyonline.org, version 8.0; and *The Digital Panopticon: Tracing London Convicts in Britain and Australia, 1780–1925*, https://www.digitalpanopticon.org (accessed 29 January 2022).

12 Anne Helmreich, Tim Hitchcok and William J. Turkel, "Rethinking Inventories in the Digital Age: The Case of the Old Bailey," *Journal of Art Historiography* 11 (2014): 1–25.

13 For example: Robert Shoemaker and Richard Ward, "Understanding the Criminal: Record-Keeping, Statistics and the Early History of Criminology in England," *British Journal of Criminology* 57, no. 6 (2017): 1442–461.

14 Richard Ward, and Lucy Williams, "Initial Views from the 'Digital Panopticon': Reconstructing Penal Outcomes in the 1790s," *Law and History Review* 34, no. 4 (2016): 894.

15 James Bradley, et al., "Research Note: The Founders and Survivors Project," *The History of the Family* 15, no. 4 (2010): 467–77, http://foundersandsurvivors.org/ (accessed 29 January 2022); *Founders and Survivors: Australian Life Courses in Historical Context 1803–1920*, https://foundersandsurvivors.com/ (accessed 1 February 2022).

16 See: Mark Finnane, et al. *The Prosecution Project Database*, https://prosecutionproject.griffith.edu.au/prosecutions, version 1, 17 July 2016 (accessed 29 January 2022).

17 Mark Finnane and Alana Piper, "The Prosecution Project: Understanding the Changing Criminal Trial through Digital Tools," *Law and History Review* 34, no. 4 (2016): 873–91.

18 See: Richard Tuffin, et al., "Convict Labour Landscapes, Port Arthur 1830–1877," *Convict Labour Landscapes*, https://www.convictlandscapes.com.au/portarthur/ (accessed 1 February 2022).

19 Godfrey, et al., "Crime," 251–255.

20 See: NSW State Archives and Records, "Webinars," https://www.records.nsw.gov.au/archives/webinars (accessed 1 February 2022).
21 Godfrey, et al., "Crime," 257.
22 *Ibid.*, 256; Sharon Howard, "Bloody Code: Reflecting on a Decade of the Old Bailey Online and the Digital Futures of Our Criminal Past," *Law, Crime and History* 5, no. 1 (2015): 13.

Index